Bloom's Major Literary Characters

King Arthur

George F. Babbitt

Elizabeth Bennet

Leopold Bloom

Sir John Falstaff

Jay Gatsby

Hamlet

Raskolnikov and Svidrigailov

Bloom's Major Literary Characters

Leopold Bloom

Edited and with an introduction by
Harold Bloom
Sterling Professor of the Humanities
Yale University

CHELSEA HOUSE
PUBLISHERS
A Haights Cross Communications Company

Philadelphia

©2004 by Chelsea House Publishers, a subsidiary of
Haights Cross Communications.

A Haights Cross Communications ⚓ Company

Introduction © 2004 by Harold Bloom.

Printed and bound in the United States of America.

10 9 8 7 6 5 4 3 2 1

Library of Congress Cataloging-in-Publication Data applied for.

ISBN 0-7910-7668-7 HC
      0-7910-7978-3 PB

Contributing editor: Eileen O'Halloran

Cover design by Keith Trego

Cover: © Hulton/Archive by Getty Images Inc.

Layout by EJB Publishing Services

Chelsea House Publishers
1974 Sproul Road, Suite 400
Broomall, PA 19008-0914

www.chelseahouse.com

Contents

HAROLD BLOOM

The Analysis of Character

"Character," according to our dictionaries, still has as a primary meaning a graphic symbol, such as a letter of the alphabet. This meaning reflects the word's apparent origin in the ancient Greek character, a sharp stylus. *Charactēr* also meant the mark of the stylus' incisions. Recent fashions in literary criticism have reduced "character" in literature to a matter of marks upon a page. But our word "character" also has a very different meaning, matching that of the ancient Greek *ēthos*, "habitual way of life." Shall we say then that literary character is an imitation of human character, or is it just a grouping of marks? The issue is between a critic like Dr. Samuel Johnson, for whom words were as much like people as like things, and a critic like the late Roland Barthes, who told us that "the fact can only exist linguistically, as a term of discourse." Who is closer to our experience of reading literature, Johnson or Barthes? What difference does it make, if we side with one critic rather than the other?

Barthes is famous, like Foucault and other recent French theorists, for having added to Nietzsche's proclamation of the death of God a subsidiary demise, that of the literary author. If there are no authors, then there are no fictional personages, presumably because literature does not refer to a world outside language. Words indeed necessarily refer to other words in the first place, but the impact of words ultimately is drawn from a universe of fact. Stories, poems, and plays are recognizable as such because they are human utterances within traditions of utterances, and traditions, by achieving authority, become a kind of fact, or at least the sense of a fact. Our sense that

vii

literary characters, within the context of a fictive cosmos, indeed are fictional personages is also a kind of fact. The meaning and value of every character in a successful work of literary representation depend upon our ideas of persons in the factual reality of our lives.

Literary character is always an invention, and inventions generally are indebted to prior inventions. Shakespeare is the inventor of literary character as we know it; he reformed the universal human expectations for the verbal imitation of personality, and the reformation appears now to be permanent and uncannily inevitable. Remarkable as the Bible and Homer are at representing personages, their characters are relatively unchanging. They age within their stories, but their habitual modes of being do not develop. Jacob and Achilles unfold before us, but without metamorphoses. Lear and Macbeth, Hamlet and Othello severely modify themselves not only by their actions, but by their utterances, and most of all through *overhearing themselves*, whether they speak to themselves or to others. Pondering what they themselves have said, they will to change, and actually do change, sometimes extravagantly yet always persuasively. Or else they suffer change, without willing it, but in reaction not so much to their language as to their relation to that language.

I do not think it useful to say that Shakespeare successfully imitated elements in our characters. Rather, it could be argued that he compelled aspects of character to appear that previously were concealed, or not available to representation. This is not to say that Shakespeare is God, but to remind us that language is not God either. The mimesis of character in Shakespeare's dramas now seems to us normative, and indeed became the accepted mode almost immediately, as Ben Jonson shrewdly and somewhat grudgingly implied. And yet, Shakespearean representation has surprisingly little in common with the imitation of reality in Jonson or in Christopher Marlowe. The origins of Shakespeare's originality in the portrayal of men and women are to be found in the *Canterbury Tales* of Geoffrey Chaucer, insofar as they can be located anywhere before Shakespeare himself, Chaucer's savage and superb Pardoner overhears his own tale-telling, as well as his mocking rehearsal of his own spiel, and through this overhearing he is emboldened to forget himself, and enthusiastically urges all his fellow-pilgrims to come forward to be fleeced by him. His self-awareness, and apocalyptically rancid sense of spiritual fall, are preludes to the even grander abysses of the perverted will in Iago and in Edmund. What might be called the character trait of a negative charisma may be Chaucer's invention, but came to its perfection in Shakespearean mimesis.

The analysis of character is as much Shakespeare's invention as the representation of character is, since Iago and Edmund are adepts at analyzing both themselves and their victims. Hamlet, whose overwhelming charisma has many negative components, is certainly the most comprehensive of all literary characters, and so necessarily prophesies the labyrinthine complexities of the will in Iago and Edmund. Charisma, according to Max Weber, its first codifier, is primarily a natural endowment, and implies a primordial and idiosyncratic power over nature, and so finally over death. Hamlet's uncanniness is at its most suggestive in the scene of his long dying, where the audience, through the mediation of Horatio, itself is compelled to meditate upon suicide, if only because outliving the prince of Denmark scarcely seems an option.

Shakespearean representation has usurped not only our sense of literary character, but our sense of ourselves as characters, with Hamlet playing the part of the largest of these usurpations. Insofar as we have an idea of human disinterestedness, we tend to derive it from the Hamlet of Act V, whose quietism has about it a ghostly authority. Oscar Wilde, in his profound and profoundly witty dialogue, "The Decay of Lying," expressed a permanent insight when he insisted that art shaped every era, far more than any age formed art. Life imitates art, we imitate Shakespeare, because without Shakespeare we would perish for lack of images. Wilde's grandest audacity demystifies Shakespearean mimesis with a Shakespearean vivaciousness: "This unfortunate aphorism about art holding the mirror up to Nature is deliberately said by Hamlet in order to convince the bystanders of his absolute insanity in all art-matters." Of *Hamlet*'s influence upon the ages Wilde remarked that: "The world has grown sad because a puppet was once melancholy." "Puppet" is Wilde's own deconstruction, a brilliant reminder that Shakespeare's artistry of illusion has so mastered reality as to have changed reality, evidently forever.

The analysis of character, as a critical pursuit, seems to me as much a Shakespearean invention as literary character was, since much of what we know about how to analyze character necessarily follows Shakespearean procedures. His hero-villains, from Richard III through Iago, Edmund, and Macbeth, are shrewd and endless questers into their own self-motivations. If we could bear to see Hamlet, in his unwearied negations, as another hero-villain, then we would judge him the supreme analyst of the darker recalcitrances in the selfhood. Freud followed the pre-Socratic Empedocles, in arguing that character is fate, a frightening doctrine that maintains the fear that there are no accidents, that overdetermination rules us all of our lives. Hamlet assumes the same, yet adds to this argument the terrible passivity he manifests in Act V. Throughout Shakespeare's tragedies, the most interesting personages seem doom-eager, reminding us again that a Shakespearean reading of Freud would be more illuminating than a Freudian exegesis of Shakespeare. We learn more when we discover Hamlet in the Freudian Death Drive, than when we read *Beyond the Pleasure Principle* into *Hamlet.*

In Shakespearean comedy, character achieves its true literary apotheosis, which is the representation of the inner freedom that can be created by great wit alone. Rosalind and Falstaff, perhaps alone among Shakespeare's personages, match Hamlet in wit, though hardly in the metaphysics of consciousness. Whether in the comic or the modern mode, Shakespeare has set the standard of measurement in the balance between character and passion.

In Shakespeare the self is more dramatized than theatricalized, which is why a Shakespearean reading of Freud works out so well. Character-formation after the passing of the Oedipal stage takes the place of fetishistic fragmentings of the self. Critics who now call literary character into question, and who proclaim also the death of the author, invariably also regard all notions, literary and human, of a stable character as being mere reductions of deeper pre-Oedipal desires. It becomes clear that the fortunes of literary character rise and fall with the prestige of normative conceptions of the ego. Shakespeare's Iago, who wars against being, may be the first deconstructionist of the self, with his proclamation of "I am not what I am." This constitutes the necessary prologue to any view that would regard a fixed ego as a virtual abnormality. But deconstructions of the self are no more modern than Modernism is. Like literary modernism, the decentered ego came out of the Hellenistic culture of ancient Alexandria. The Gnostic heretics believed that the psyche, like the body, was a fallen entity, mechanically fashioned by the Demiurge or false creator. They held however that each of us possessed also a spark or pneuma, which was a fragment of the original Abyss or true, alien God. The soul or psyche within every one of us was thus at war with the self or pneuma, and only that sparklike self could be saved.

Shakespeare, following after Chaucer in this respect, was the first and remains still the greatest master of representing character both as a stable soul and a wavering self. There is a substance that endures in Shakespeare's figures, and there is also a quicksilver rendition of the unsettling sparks. Racine and Tolstoy, Balzac and Dickens, follow in Shakespeare's wake by giving us some sense of pre-Oedipal sparks or drives, and considerably more sense of post-Oedipal character and personality, stabilizations or sublimations of the fetish-seeking drives. Critics like Leo Bersani and René Girard argue eloquently against our taking this mimesis as the only proper work of literature. I would suggest that strong fictions of the self, from the

Bible through Samuel Beckett, necessarily participate in both modes, the sublimation of desire, and the persistence of a primordial desire. The mystery of Hamlet or of Lear is intimately invested in the tangled mixture of the two modes of representation.

Psychic mobility is proposed by Bersani as the ideal to which deconstructions of the literary self may yet guide us. The ideal has its pathos, but the realities of literary representation seem to me very different, perhaps destructively so. When a novelist like D. H. Lawrence sought to reduce his characters to Eros and the Death Drive, he still had to persuade us of his authority at mimesis by lavishing upon the figures of *The Rainbow* and *Women in Love* all of the vivid stigmata of normative personality. Birkin and Ursula may represent antithetical and uncanny drives, but they develop and change as characters pondering their own pronouncements and reactions to self and others. The cost of a non-Shakespearean representation is enormous. Pynchon, in *The Crying of Lot 49* and *Gravity's Rainbow*, evades the burden of the normative by resorting to something like Christopher Marlowe's art of caricature in *The Jew of Malta*. Marlowe's Barabas is a marvelous rhetorician, yet he is a cartoon alongside the troublingly equivocal Shylock. Pynchon's personages are deliberate cartoons also, as flat as comic strips. Marlowe's achievement, and Pynchon's, are beyond dispute, yet they are like the prelude and the postlude to Shakespearean reality. They do not wish to engage with our hunger for the empirical world and so they enter the problematic cosmos of literary fantasy.

No writer, not even Shakespeare or Proust, alters the available stock that we agree to call reality, but Shakespeare, more than any other, does show us how much of reality we could encounter if only we retained adequate desire. The strong literary representation of character is already an analysis of character, and is part of the healing work of a literary culture, which implicitly seeks to cure violence through a normative mimesis of ego, *as if it were stable*, whether in actuality it is or is not. I do not believe that this is a social quest taken on by literary culture, but rather that we confront here the aesthetic essence of what makes a culture *literary*, rather than metaphysical or ethical or religious. A culture becomes literary when its conceptual modes have failed it, which means when religion, philosophy, and science have begun to lose their authority. If they cannot heal violence, then literature attempts to do so, which may be only a turning inside out of the critical arguments of Girard and Bersani.

I conclude by offering a particular instance or special case as a paradigm for the healing enterprise that is at once the representation and the analysis of literary character. Let us call it the aesthetics of being outraged, or rather of successfully representing the state of being outraged. W. C. Fields was one modern master of such representation, and Nathanael West was another, as was Faulkner before him. Here also the greatest master remains Shakespeare, whose Macbeth, himself a bloody outrage, yet retains our imaginative sympathy precisely because he grows increasingly outraged as he experiences the equivocation of the fiend that lies like truth. The double-natured promises and the prophecies of the weird sisters finally induce in Macbeth an apocalyptic version of the stage actor's anxiety at missing cues, the horror of a phantasmagoric stage fright of missing one's time, of always reacting too late. Macbeth, a veritable monster of solipsistic inwardness but no intellectual, counters his dilemma by fresh murders, that prolong him in time yet provoke him only to a perpetually freshened sense of being outraged, as all his expectations become still worse confounded. We are moved by Macbeth, however estrangedly, because his terrible inwardness is a paradigm for our own solipsism, but also because none of us can resist a strong and successful representation of the human in a state of being outraged.

The ultimate outrage is the necessity of dying, an outrage concealed in a multitude of masks, including the tyrannical ambitions of Macbeth. I suspect that our outrage at being outraged is the most difficult of all our affects for us to represent to ourselves, which is why we are so inclined to imaginative sympathy for a character who strongly conveys that affect to us. The Shrike of West's *Miss Lonelyhearts* or Faulkner's Joe Christmas of *Light in August* are crucial modern instances, but such figures can be located in many other works, since the ability to represent this extreme emotion is one of the tests that strong writers are driven to set for themselves.

However a reader seeks to reduce literary character to a question of marks on a page, she will come at last to the impasse constituted by the thought of death, her death, and before that to all the stations of being outraged that memorialize her own drive towards death. In reading, she quests for evidences that are strong representations, whether of her desire or her despair. Such questings constitute the necessary basis for the analysis of literary character, an enterprise that always will survive every vagary of critical fashion.

Editor's Note

My Introduction contemplates the intricate relations between Poldy, William Shakespeare, James Joyce, and God.

David Hayman juxtaposes Poldy with Stephen, while Joyce's great biographer, Richard Ellmann, invokes Flaubert's Emma Bovary as foil.

Hugh Kenner, dean of antiquarian High Modernists, takes an early, rather negative view of Mr. Bloom (he amended it later), after which Fritz Senn also undervalues the sublime Poldy, as somehow being inarticulate.

Poldy fares little better in the feminist version of Suzette A. Henke, for whom he has regressed to the pleasures of "pre-Oedipal, oceanic union."

At least the new Bloomusalem is admitted as a benign Utopian fantasy by Vincent J. Cheng, after which however Marilyn Reizbaum discovers in Poldy an element of Jewish self-hatred that I myself am totally unable to discern.

Peter Francis Mackey, somewhat refreshingly, gives us a Bloom who can dream and hope, while Karen R. Lawrence, with feminist fierceness, surveys the fetishes in Poldy's pockets.

Amiably apocalyptic, Zack Bowen celebrates Poldy's settling down for slumber upon Molly's superb rump, after which Andrew Gibson concludes this volume with the best of its essays, a wise celebration of Leopold Bloom as inside outsider, endowed by James Joyce with "sanity, openness, moderation, and psychological resilience."

HAROLD BLOOM

Introduction

It is an odd sensation to begin writing an introduction to a volume of Joyce criticism on June 16, particularly if one's name is Bloom. Poldy is, as Joyce intended, the most *complete* figure in modern fiction, if not indeed in all of Western fiction, and so it is appropriate that he have a saint's day in the literary calendar: Bloomsday. He is, thankfully, no saint, but a mild gentle sinner; in short, a good man. So good a man is he that even the critic Hugh Kenner, who in his earlier commentary saw Poldy as an instance of modern depravity, an Eliotic Jew as it were, in 1980 could call Joyce's hero "fit to live in Ireland without malice, without violence, without hate." How many are fit to live, in fact or fiction in Ireland or America, without malice, without violence, and without hate? Kenner, no sentimentalist, now finds Poldy what the reader must find: a better person than oneself.

Richard Ellmann, Joyce's biographer, shrewdly says of Poldy that "he is not afraid that he will compromise his selfhood." Currently fashionable criticism, calling itself "Post-Structuralist Joyce," oddly assimilates Joyce to Barthes, Lacan, Derrida; producing a Poldy without a self, another floating signifier. But Joyce's Poldy, as Ellmann insists, is heroic and imaginative; his mimetic force allies him to the Wife of Bath, Falstaff and Sancho Panza, and like them his presence is overwhelming. Joyce's precursors were Dante and Shakespeare, and Poldy has a comprehensiveness and immediacy worthy of his ancestry. It is good to remember that, after Dante and Shakespeare, Joyce cared most for Wordsworth and Shelley among poets. Wordsworth's heroic naturalism and Shelley's visionary skepticism find their way into Poldy also.

How Jewish is Poldy? Here I must dissent a touch from Ellmann, who

1

says that when Poldy confronts the Citizen, he states an ethical view "more Christian than Judaic." Poldy has been unbelieving Jew, Protestant and Catholic, but his ethical affirmations are normative Jewish, as Joyce seems to have known better than Ellmann does. When Poldy gazes upon existence, he finds it good. The commonplace needs no hallowing for Poldy. Frank Budgen, taking the hint from Joyce, emphasizes how much older Poldy seems than all the other inhabitants of Joyce's visionary Dublin. We do not think of Poldy as being thirty-eight, prematurely middle-aged, but rather as living in what the Hebrew Bible called *olam*: time without boundaries. Presumably, that is partly why Joyce chose to make his Ulysses Jewish rather than Greek. Unlike a modern Greek, Poldy is in surprising continuity with a lineage of which he has little overt knowledge. How different would the book have been if Joyce had centered on a Greek living in Dublin? The aura of exile would not be there. Joyce the Dubliner in exile, tasting his own stoic version of a Dantesque bitterness, found in Poldy as wandering Jew what now seems his inevitable surrogate. Poldy, not Stephen, is Joyce's true image.

Yet Poldy is certainly more like Homer's Ulysses than like the Yahwist's Jacob. We see Poldy surviving the Cyclops, but not wrestling with one among the Elohim in order to win a name for himself. Truly Jewgreek, Poldy has forsworn the Covenant, even if he cannot escape from having been chosen. Joyce, too, has abandoned the Church, but cannot escape the intellectual discipline of the Jesuits. Poldy's sense of election is a little more mysterious, or perhaps it is Joyce's sense of his hero's election that is the true mystery of the book. At the end of the Cyclops episode, Joyce evidently felt the necessity of distracting himself from Poldy, if only because literary irony fails when confronted by the heroic pathos of a creation that defies even Joyce's control.

> —Are you talking about the new Jerusalem? says the citizen.
> —I'm talking about injustice, says Bloom.
> —Right, says John Wyse. Stand up to it then with a force like men.

But that is of course not Poldy's way. No interpolated sarcasm, however dramatically wrought, is able to modify the dignity of Poldy's rejoinder:

> —But it's no use, says he. Force, hatred, history, all that. That's not life for men and women, insult and hatred. And everybody knows that it's the very opposite of that that is really life.
> —What, says Alf.
> —Love, says Bloom. I mean the opposite of hatred.

Twelve delirious pages of hyperbole and phantasmagoria follow, detailing the forced exit of the noble Poldy from the pub, and ending in a grand send-up indeed:

> When, lo, there came about them all a great brightness and they beheld the chariot wherein He stood ascend to heaven. And they beheld Him in the chariot, clothed upon in the glory of the brightness, having raiment as of sun, fair as the moon and terrible that for awe they durst not look upon Him. And there came a voice out of heaven, calling: *Elijah! Elijah!* And he answered with a main cry: *Abba! Adonai!* And they beheld Him even Him, ben Bloom Elijah, amid clouds of angels ascend to the glory of the brightness at an angle of forty-five degrees over Donohoe's in Little Green Street like a shot off a shovel.

It is all in the juxtaposition of "ben Bloom Elijah" and "like a shot off a shovel," at once a majestic deflation and complex apotropaic gesture on Joyce's own part. Like Falstaff and Sancho Panza, Poldy runs off with the book, and Joyce's strenuous ironies, dwarfing the wit of nearly all other authors, essentially are so many reaction-formations against his love for (and identity with) his extraordinary hero. Homer's Ulysses may be as complete as Poldy, but you wouldn't want to be in one boat with him (you would drown, he would survive). Poldy would comfort you in every sorrow, even as he empathizes so movingly with the pangs of women in childbirth.

Joyce was not Flaubert, who at once was Madame Bovary and yet was wholly detached from her, at least in aesthetic stance. But how do you maintain a fixed stance toward Poldy? Falstaff is the monarch of wit, and Sancho Panza the Pope of innocent cunning. Poldy's strength, as Joyce evidently intended, is in his completeness. "The complete man" is necessarily a trope, but for what? On one side, for range of affect, like Tennyson's Ulysses, Poldy is a part of all that he has met. His curiosity, his susceptibility, his compassion, his potential interest—these are infinite. On another side, for cognitive activity, Poldy, unlike Stephen, is certainly not brilliant, and yet he has a never resting mind, as Ulysses must have. He can be said to have a Shakespearean mind, though he resembles no one in Shakespeare (a comparison of Poldy and Shylock is intrusive). Poldy is neither Hamlet nor Falstaff, but perhaps he is in Shakespeare, or Shakespeare reborn as James Joyce, even as Stephen is the younger Dante reincarnated as Joyce. We can think of Poldy as Horatio to Stephen's Hamlet, since Horatio represents us, the audience, and we represent Shakespeare. Poldy is our representative, and it is Joyce's greatest triumph that increasingly we represent him, as we always have and will represent Shakespeare.

Post-Structuralist Joyce never wearies of reminding us that Poldy is a trope, but it is truer to say that we are tropes for Poldy, who as a supermimesis of essential nature is beyond us. I may never recover from a walk through a German park with a dear friend who is the most distinguished of post-structuralists. When I remarked to him, in my innocent cunning, that Poldy was the most loveable person in Western fiction I provoked him to the annoyed response that Poldy was not a person, but only language, and that Joyce, unlike myself, knew this very well. Joyce knew very well that Poldy was more than a person, but only in the sense that Poldy was a humane and humanized God, a God who had become truly a bereft father, anguishing for his lost Rudy. Poldy is not a person only if God is not a person, and the God of Jews, for all his transcendental sublimities, is also very much a person and a personality, as benefits his immanent sublimities. Surely the uniqueness of Yahweh is the complete God, even as Poldy is a complete man, and God, after all, like Poldy is Jewish.

II

French post-structuralism is of course only a belated modernism, since everything from abroad is absorbed so slowly in xenophobic Paris. French Hegel, French Freud, French Joyce are all after the event, as it were, just as French romanticism was a rather delayed phenomenon. French Joyce is about as close to the text of *Ulysses* and *Finnegans Wake* as Lacan is to the text of *Three Essays on the Theory of Sexuality* or Derrida to Hegel and Heidegger. Nor should they be, since cultural belatedness or Alexandrianism demands the remedy of misprision, or creative misreading. To say that "meaning" keeps its distance from Poldy is both to forget that Poldy is the Messiah (though which Messiah is not clear) and that one name (Kabbalistic) for Yahweh is "language." The difference between Joyce and French Joyce is that Joyce tropes God as language, which is to say that Joyce, heroic naturalist, was not a Gnostic and Lacan was (perhaps unknowingly).

As a knowing Gnostic, I lament the loss of Joycean heroic naturalism and of Poldy's natural heroism. Let them deconstruct Don Quixote; the results will be as sorrowful. Literary criticism is a mode which teaches us not to read Poldy as Sancho Panza and Stephen as Don, but more amiably take us back to Cervantes, to read Sancho as Poldy. By a Borgesian blessing in the art of mistaken attribution, we then will learn to read not only *Hamlet* and the *Inferno* as written by Joyce, but *Don Quixote* as well, with the divine Sancho as an Irish Jew!

Joyce necessarily is closer to Shakespeare than to Cervantes, and Joyce's obsession with *Hamlet* is crucial in *Ulysses*. His famous reading of Hamlet, as expounded by Stephen, can be regarded as a subtle coming-to-terms with Shakespeare as his most imposing literary father in the English language. Ellmann, certainly the most reliable of Joyce scholars, insisted that Joyce "exhibits none of that anxiety of influence which has been attributed to modern writers ... If Joyce had any anxiety, it was over not incorporating influences enough." This matter is perhaps more dialectical than Ellmann realized. Not Dante, but Shakespeare is Joyce's Virgil, as Ellmann also notes, and just as Dante's poetic voice matures even as Virgil fades out of the *Commedia*, so Shakespeare had to fade out of *Ulysses* even as Joyce's voice matured.

In Stephen's theory, Shakespeare is the dead king, rather than the young Hamlet, who becomes the type of the Romantic artist, Stephen himself. Shakespeare, like the ghost, has been betrayed, except that Anne Hathaway went Gertrude one better, and cuckolded the Bard with both his brothers. This sexual defeat has been intensified by Shakespeare's loss of the dark lady of the sonnets, and to his best friend, a kind of third brother. Shakespeare's revenge is to resurrect his own dead son, Hamnet, who enters the play as prince Hamlet, with the purpose of vindicating his father's honor. Such a resurrected son appears to be free of the Oedipal ambivalences, and in Joyce's view does not lust after Gertrude or feel any jealousy, however, repressed, for the dead father. So Stephen and Poldy, as two aspects of Shakespeare/Joyce, during the "Circe" episode gaze into a mirror and behold a transformed Shakespeare, beardless and frozen-faced ("rigid in facial paralysis"). I do not interpret this either as the view that Poldy and Stephen "amount only to a paralytic travesty of a Shakespeare" (W.M. Schutte) or that "Joyce warns us that he is working with near-identities, not perfect ones" (Ellmann). Rather, I take it as a sign of influence-anxiety, as the precursor Shakespeare mocking the ephebe Joyce: "Be like me, but you presume in attempting to be too much like me. You are merely a beardless version, rigid in facial paralysis, lacking my potency and my ease of countenance."

The obscene Buck Mulligan, Joyce's Black beast weakly misreads *Hamlet* as masturbation and Poldy as a pederast. Joyce himself, through Stephen, strongly misreads *Hamlet* as the cuckold's revenge, a play presumably likelier to have been written by Poldy than by Stephen. In a stronger misreading still, I would suggest that Joyce rewrites *Hamlet* so as to destroy the element in the play that most menaces him, which is the very different, uncannily disinterested Hamlet of Act V. Stephen quotes the subtle Sabellian heresy that the father was Himself His Own Son. But what we may call the even subtler Shakespearean heresy (which is also Freudian) holds rather that the Son was Himself His Own Father. This is the Hamlet of Act V, who refers to his dead father only once, and then only as the king. Joyce's Hamlet has on Oedipus complex. Shakespeare's Hamlet may have had one, but it passes away in the interval between Acts IV and V.

Stephen as the Prince does not convince me; Poldy as the ghost of the dead king, and so as Shakespeare/Joyce, is rather more troublesome. One wishes the ghost could be exorcised, leaving us with the fine trinity of Shakespeare/Poldy/Joyce, with Poldy as the transitional figure reconciling forerunner and latecomer, a sort of Messiah perhaps. Shakespeare is the original Testament or old aesthetic Law, while Joyce is belated Testament or new aesthetic dispensation. Poldy is the inner-Testamentary figure, apocryphal and apocalyptic, and yet overwhelmingly a representation of life in the here and now. Joyce went on to write *Finnegans Wake*, the only legitimate rival to Proust's vast novel in western literature of our time. More than difficulties, both real and imaginary, of the *Wake* have kept Joyce's common readers centered upon *Ulysses*. Earwicker is a giant hieroglyph; Poldy is a person, complete and loving, self-reliant, larger and more evocative even than his book.

DAVID HAYMAN

Dublin, June 16, 1904 and
Two Characters and a City-Scape

The Wandering Bloom

If, from the point of view of Joyce's readers, Stephen is prolonging an already established curve, his equal-opposite comes to us fresh and strange through that grand opening sentence of "Calypso": "Mr Leopold Bloom ate with relish the inner organs of beasts and fowls" (55). He is the very substance of the Old Testament smoke-eating "Jehovah, collector of prepuces" (201) though somewhat softened by the passage of the centuries. Bloom's day is a complete life: past, present, and probable future. Joyce builds him gradually through the memories and reactions of others as well as through his own memories and sensations, delightful as they are trivial, served warm with a seasoning of life and laced with laughter. Putting the facts together, we find that he is thirty-eight years old, the son of a Hungarian Jewish immigrant who changed his name from Virag and married an Irish woman. His recollection of Virag's suicide, combined with a sense of having abandoned or lost the traditions of his fathers, reflects in a lighter vein Stephen's distress over his mother's death and his gnawing "agenbite of inwit." He has married Molly Tweedy, the daughter of an Irish Sergeant Major stationed on Gibraltar and a Spanish Jewess of questionable morals. They have had a daughter, Milly, fifteen, now a photographer's assistant in the market town of Mullingar, and a son, Rudolph, named after his grandfather, but dead at eleven days, eleven years ago.

From Ulysses: *The Mechanics of Meaning*. ©1970 by The University of Wisconsin Press.

Intelligent, but untrained and only moderately gifted, Bloom is not a good provider. Having been a peddler of trinkets, a traveler for blotting paper, a clerk in a slaughter house, and, in hard times, a salesman for the "Royal Hungarian Lottery," he now makes a meager living canvassing for ads for the *Weekly Freeman*.[11] As Madame Marion Tweedy, Molly helps support the family with her singing and is currently planning a tour with Blazes Boylan as her manager. Since the death of their son, which was traumatic for both of them, Bloom and Molly have had no normal sexual relations. Molly seems to have gone her own way. She is now beginning what appears to be her first affair with the "Worst man in Dublin" (92), as Bloom calls Boylan. Recently, instead of renewing normal relations, Bloom has advertised for a mistress. Under the pseudonym Henry Flower, he is now corresponding with a lovelorn typist, who signs herself Martha Clifford. He is, however, thoroughly monogamous. Molly was and is his great romance: the seduction on the Hill of Howth, like Shakespeare's seduction in a rye field, remains the sensual event of his life.

A diffident and abstemious man in convivial and bibulous Dublin, Bloom has many acquaintances but few friends. Though he may be a Mason[12] and hence may partake of a secular mysticism (see, by way of contrast, Stephen's esoteric preoccupations), he makes little of that association and less of his prior commitments to Protestantism and Catholicism, to say nothing of the Judaism into which he was born but apparently not initiated. Moderate in everything, except perhaps his secret lusts, he enters *Ulysses* as a thoroughly eclectic and vaguely sympathetic man in a city full of quirky individuals, a man who sips cautiously the cup of life, taking care not to swallow too many bubbles. Altogether, he is a worthy successor to the numerous nineteenth-century antiheroes and especially to Charles Bovary, whose miseries and joys are scamped in Flaubert's account of the philandering Emma.

Bloom's day begins with an 8 a.m. breakfast at 7 Eccles Street ("Calypso"), a very ordinary Dublin address and the former home of Joyce's friend Byrne, the "Cranly" of the Portrait. While Molly lies upstairs in old man Cohen's jingling bed which her husband believes that Tweedy brought back from Gibraltar, Bloom buys a breakfast kidney at the Jewish pork butcher's, serves her tea, and gets the mail which contains, along with a letter to him from Milly, a note to Molly from Boylan, who is coming to see her at 4:00 in the afternoon. This note and this knowledge keep Bloom away from home till 2 a.m. Unlike Stephen, who must decide whether or not to return to Mulligan and the tower, Bloom must decide when to return to Molly. After breakfast, he goes to the garden privy, where he reads and then wipes himself with a prize story in *Titbits*, an emblem of his literary ambitions. Like

Stephen, but for this day only, Bloom is in mourning and keyless. Having changed his suit so that he can attend the funeral of little Paddy Dignam of the red nose, he inadvertently leaves his keys in Molly's room.

"Lotus Eaters" finds Bloom at 10 o'clock in another part of town on his way to the baths. His actions and reactions reflect the coming euphoria. As Henry Flower, he picks up and eventually reads a teasing letter with a flower enclosure from Martha Clifford. He tells the cadger, M'Coy, about his wife's tour and promises to sign him in at the funeral. He buys some soap for his bath and orders some lotion for Molly and inadvertently gives Bantam Lyons a tip on the horse Throwaway in the Gold Cup race. Finally, to kill time, he drops in to watch a mass with cool and comic objectivity.

At 11 o'clock ("Hades"), he joins the funeral party and crosses town to Glasnevin cemetery in a carriage with Simon Dedalus, Martin Cunningham, and John Power, for whom he is clearly an outsider. During the ride he sees Stephen on his way to the beach and points him out to a barely civil Simon, who turns the youth into an object of Bloom's fatherly concern. After the cemetery he tells one of Molly's rejected admirers, the pompous John Henry Menton, that he has a dint in his hat, only to be rudely ignored. This action parallels not only the behavior of Ajax' ghost toward Ulysses but also the gracious thankyou Bloom received years earlier when he picked up Parnell's hat.

Bloom turns up next at the drafty *Freeman* office ("Aeolus"), where he is negotiating the terms and layout for an ad for the House of Keyes. We see him only briefly and share few of his thoughts and words in this chapter, which is dominated by the journalistic grubs. Rushing back and forth, suffering minor indignities, and winning minor concessions from busy pressmen and the cantankerous editor, he is curtly rebuffed when he interrupts the pub-pilgrimage to ask for one final favor. All in all he cuts a figure of comic competence in a world of empty words and sham concerns: "Time someone thought about (easing the pains of childbirth)," thinks the ever-considerate canvasser reacting against the rhetoric, "instead of gassing about the what was it the pensive bosom of the silver effulgence. Flapdoodle to feed fools on" (161).[13]

In "Lestrygonians," between 1 and 2 p.m., Bloom's thoughts turn on food and disgust as he searches for a suitable place to eat. Rejecting Burton's Restaurant where the masticating horde turns his stomach, he settles on Davy Byrne's pub. There he finds a flea-bitten admirer in Nosey Flynn. Earlier he has met a former flame, Josie Powell Breen, married now to the dotty Denis, whose behavior gives us a foretaste of Bloom's moon-madness in "Circe." Unlike those who grudgingly applaud Stephen, Bloom's admirers are a curious lot, whose admiration springs from ignorance rather than understanding and whose presence and praise is an embarrassment to him and to us. After his snack, Bloom wanders toward the National Library, a keyless man in quest of copy for the Keyes ad. On his way he helps a blind stripling across the street, a gesture that foreshadows his meeting with the weak-eyed Stephen. Finally he dodges into the museum opposite the library to avoid meeting Boylan: "Straw hat in sunlight. Tan shoes. Turnedup trousers. It is. It is" (183).

During the Shakespeare argument in "Scylla and Charybdis," where Stephen sketches a Bloomlike bard, Bloom is part of the background. Only Mulligan, who has just seen him in the museum investigating the hinder parts of a Venus, notes his presence. Bloom's great moment comes when he sails out of the library between Buck and Stephen in an innocent parody of the mythical escape. We see him briefly in "Wandering Rocks" renting pornography for Molly. Neither he nor Stephen is included in the catalogue of watchers at the end of this chapter.

Shortly before 4 p.m. ("Sirens"), he drops in at the Ormond Hotel bar during a wary and curiously sensual pursuit of Boylan, whose visit to Molly shames and subconsciously pleases him. Sad and lonely, his head filled with thoughts of Molly, he lunches on liver and cider in the company of Stephen's uncle Richie Goulding and stealthily writes a note to Martha. For much of this time Bloom is orchestrated into the musical texture of "Sirens," where the foreground is occupied by flirtatious barmaids to whose charms he is generally deaf but into whose orbit are drawn brilliant performers (siren singers) like Simon Dedalus and Ben Dollard, the unfrocked priest Father Cowley, the sly cadging Lenehan, and of course dashing Blazes Boylan, who quickly departs in his hired cab but whose jingling progress we follow to his goal. True to his word in the *Exiles* notes, Joyce has made the seducer an insipid if flashy fancyman, a powerful but unworthy rival, as Molly's reactions in "Penelope" indicate. Boylan, the carefree conqueror, represents the world of trivial business deals, sporting life, pub talk, and casual alliances. He is appropriately seen in transit and conveniently dismissed to remain a presence only in the minds of other characters and a reproach to Bloom.

It is 5 o'clock ("Cyclops") when Bloom, keeping an appointment to help settle the affairs of Dignam's widow, stations himself in front of Barney Kiernan's pub. Here the focus is on the assorted drinkers gathered around a broken down "patriot" who calls himself "citizen" and glories in his and Ireland's past. Much against his wishes, Bloom is dragged into the group which knows him as a freemason and a Jew and suspects him of having won on Throwaway, a twenty-to-one bet at the Ascot Races (325). His failure to buy anything for the thirsty cadgers (or accept anything but a "knock-me-down cigar") combines with his oppressive reasonableness in this den of unreason or false reasoning to provoke an anti-Semitic eruption. Bloom's last gesture is a gallant defense of the Jews, among whom he numbers the son of an apostate (Mendelssohn), apostates (Marx and Spinoza), a gentile (Mercadante), and of course Jesus Christ. It prompts the irate and drunken citizen-cyclops to throw a biscuit tin in the direction of the departing cab in a scene that foreshadows Stephen's street brawl in "Circe."

For all the minutiae in *Ulysses*, and despite the completeness of Bloom's characterization, mercifully, much is left to our imaginations. We share his thoughtstream for only a handful of the day's hours and in relatively few chapters. Though he defecates and urinates before us, he shaves, dresses, and bathes offstage. We accompany him neither to Keyes's shop where he conducts business nor to Mrs. Dignam's house where he discusses insurance. Though the missing details may be tucked into his revery, there is little room for redundancy in a book where every gesture bears on character and theme. Mulligan's shaving, dressing, and bathing must suffice for Bloom as well. It is fitting then that, after two blank hours, Bloom appears on Sandymount Strand at 8 p.m. ("Nausikaa"). There he watches the flirtatious behavior of Gerty MacDowell, a coy virgin in her early twenties, nourished on lady's periodical literature. During Gerty's deliberately but archly seductive leg-swinging performance, Bloom is silent, the distant stranger of her sentimental dream. His own performance is reflected through her monologue by a sugary shock of pleasure and shame. In the second half of the chapter we shift our field and see the departing Gerty through Bloom's objective eyes as he straightens out his clothes and contemplates but rejects the idea of repeating the experience. The masturbation during the fireworks display for the Mirus Bazaar, a sunset ceremony (that follows the celebration of the Virgin in a neighboring church!), partially explains his abstinence in "Circe."

Having dozed off briefly on the beach, but still unwilling to risk an encounter with Boylan, Bloom goes to the Holles Street hospital ("Oxen of the Sun") to enquire about Mina Purefoy, who is still in childbirth. Dixon, the young intern who once dressed a bee sting for him, draws him into the anteroom. He sits there, uncomfortably abstemious, among the clever young sports, and there he sees the young student (Bannon) who is Milly's first boyfriend. Among the barflies at Kiernan's he was out of place but intellectually superior. Here, the unwitting or good-natured butt of witticisms and the victim of Mulligan's veiled hostility, he is in beyond his intellectual depth. Concerned over Stephen's drunken condition, he follows him to Burke's pub and then to nighttown.

What actually occurs to him in "Circe" is simple but muzzy for the reader who must attend not only to events but to illusions. Joyce involves us from the start in the hallucinated context, generating through his stage directions a dream landscape out of the banal materials of nether Dublin. Furthermore, he plunges us into not one but two overwrought psyches artfully interrelated. Yet, we can generally distinguish between the conscious and the subconscious events. Bloom's subvocal hallucinations, which never contribute to the action, begin when he first recognizes his "Brain-fogfag." They accelerate during a series of comic, imaginary encounters with his father, with Molly, with Josie Breen, and finally with two members of the watch. Out of this last encounter is generated the first major sequence, Bloom's farcical trial for shame (457). All of this occurs as the confused canvasser chases after Stephen and Lynch, whom he lost when he dodged into a shop. The sound of "church music" draws him to Bella Cohen's house, where he is propositioned by Zoe, whose request for a cigarette prompts him to begin a lecture that quickly turns him on again. This second and more extravagant hallucination gives Bloom a chance to play the benefactor of mankind and to suffer martyrdom at the hands of the inquisition. Clearly an extension of his pronouncement on brotherly love in "Cyclops," it concludes with a litany of Bloom's adventures sung by the "Daughters of Erin" as Bloom is burned "mute, shrunken, carbonized:"

> Kidney of Bloom, pray for us.
> Flower of the Bath, pray for us.
> Mentor of Menton, pray for us.
> Canvasser for the Freeman, pray for us.
> Charitable Mason, pray for us.
> Wandering Soap, pray for us.
> Sweets of Sin, pray for us.
> Music without Words, pray for us.
> Reprover of the Citizen, pray for us.
> Friend of all Frillies, pray for us.
> Midwive Most Merciful, pray for us.
> Potato Preservative against Plague and Pestilence,
>   pray for us. (498–99)

A few moments later Bloom enters the brothel where he finds Stephen by the pianola. He continues to hallucinate mildly until the appearance of the whoremistress, whom he imagines in the shape of a masterful Bello and to whom he joyfully submits in the wildest and most degrading of his visions, being turned in his imagination into something approximating one of Circe's pigs. The grotesque, absurd, and obscene sequence concludes with the sound of a snapping trouser button after a mawkish interlude with Bloom's muse, the calendar-art nymph on his bedroom wall. Virtually restored and saved from the depths of himself, Bloom has a final relatively mild hallucination, participating in Boylan's seduction of Molly as an exaggerated version of that comic byword, the complacent husband. The whole experience, though it dominates the chapter, has taken relatively little time, but it has steeled Bloom for what is to come: the encounter with Stephen and his return to Molly's bed. Having capitulated to impulses that crippled him, he is free to resume a role that is both dominant in him and appropriate.

As Bloom emerges from his last hallucination, Lynch makes the equation that signals a transfer of our attention to Stephen, pointing to the mirror in which both are joined in the likeness of Shakespeare under the antlered hatrack (567).[14] Stephen, who begins by raving incoherently, spewing out the garbled contents of the day's thoughts, finally breaks into his drunken dance and begins hallucinating aloud. Having previously taken Stephen's money in safe keeping (seconding in this the advice of old Deasy, his precursor, and inverting the behavior of the pawnbroker Dodd, his dark reflection), a masterful Bloom pays the damages after the attack on the lampshade and runs out into the street. He arrives too late to prevent the fight, but still manages to fend off the police while Stephen lies in a drunken stupor. It is at this point that the symbolic link between the two men is confirmed by Bloom's vision of Rudy as an eleven-year-old Pre-Raphaelite dream child with a "mauve" face, a ghastly-sweet emanation hovering over the prostrate poet. The moment is worthy of the Dublin Christmas Pantomime, but the reader may be moved as well as amused and shocked.[15]

Concerned and eager to help, anxious to make contact with the youth he has identified with his son, Bloom escorts the sodden bard to the nearby cabman's shelter for undrinkable coffee and an inedible bun. Thanks to the presence of a returning sailor who spins improbable traveler's tales, conversation is difficult if not impossible. Still, for the first time this day, Bloom is in command of the fate of another whom he respects, and, though tired, he is more than usually alert and talkative. Stephen, by contrast, distracted and bored, speaks rarely and at cross purposes with Bloom. Seizing on the fact that his protégé claims to have eaten nothing for over a day (656), Bloom decides to offer him a bed for the night and brave Molly's wrath. As they walk home together, Stephen warms to a discussion of music and begins singing, inspiring the practical-minded Bloom to outline the advantages of a musical career. During the song, the older man completes the transition to fatherhood by echoing in milder and muddier terms Simon Dedalus' opinion of Mulligan's influence:

... he purposed (Bloom did), without anyway prying into his
private affairs on the *fools step in where angels* principle advising
him to sever his connections with a certain budding practitioner,
who, he noticed, was prone to disparage, and even, ... with some
hilarious pretext, ... deprecate him.... (664–65)

In response to this, a horse mires and Stephen maunders about "usurpers."

At 7 Eccles Street ("Ithaca"), Bloom shows Stephen into the kitchen,
makes two cups of cocoa, lacing Stephen's generously with Molly's breakfast
cream, a further sign of new-won independence. Their conversation turns on
their common backgrounds, their differences, and the similarities that
underlie them (see the delightful equation of the Jewish and Irish traditions
[688].) It is only after Stephen has sung his anti-Semitic ballad that the
"secret infidel" Bloom offers him a bed and accepts his refusal. After
Stephen's departure through the gate, unlocked by an "aruginated male key,"
Bloom must face the facts he has been avoiding. This he does in the fashion
of a returned wanderer, taking inventory first of his worldly situation,
inspecting (?) documents that relate his past, observing the evidence of
another's usurpation, and deciding what is to be done about it (nothing).
Brushing the remains of Boylan's picnic from his bed, he kisses Molly's rump,
gives her a slightly modified account of his day, and lies down head to her
feet to sleep, a wary, much-traveled Sinbad. He has asked her to "get his
breakfast in bed with a couple of eggs" (738) and mentioned a possible future
association with Stephen. Joyce's "Gea-Tellus," the great mother to whose
womb Bloom returns, then begins the musings out of which, for all his
failings, the returned traveler emerges her man, the one to whom she has
once said, "Yes." (...)

Two Characters and a City-Scape

Stephen/Bloom: Opposite Equivalents

If, under Joyce's microscope, Bloom personifies everyman as outsider, his
position is not unmotivated. Incapable of servicing Molly, and essentially
estranged from his daughter as love object, too self-deprecating and
insufficiently imaginative to "succeed" but too abstemious and industrious to
fail totally, too obviously alien and cosmopolitan to be accepted by the Irish
provincials and too Irish not to be concerned, he is doomed to a perpetual
search for the center, which for him means balance. Seen from another angle,
in a society peopled by eccentrics, the outrageously moderate Bloom must
seem peculiar. Unlike Stephen, the rebel who consciously courts rejection,

Bloom must tread warily in the face of rejection. He tempts no gods, risks no thunderous retribution, accepts his lot, and returns good for evil. Though the memory of his father's suicide darkens his day and he contacts madness through Mr. Breen, he risks neither. His main concern is to hang on to the social norm, to confirm his position as father, husband, citizen, in a world that repulses his advances on all fronts. He is out of phase with his society and antiheroic in his adjustment, but he is without pride or cynicism or pretense. Gross pragmatism, while occasionally a source of wisdom, more often leads him clownishly to overvalue trifles that Stephen just as absurdly ignores. His treatment of the cake of soap, the flower, the card, his preoccupation with numbers, food, manners, and facts tend to make Bloom himself an object among objects and prepare us for his eventual reduction to a catalogue of particulars in "Ithaca."

We watch through the daylight hours Bloom's growing preoccupation with a little knot of closely-related and virtually universal concerns, which, during the evening hours, he faces on an instinctual level. But if on this day the meaning of the key to his house is made manifest to him, his worries make few visible ripples on the calm surface. Faced with Molly's infidelity and possible desertion, Milly's coming of age, and his failure to produce a son, haunted by the memory of his father and his own lack of a tradition in tradition-bound Ireland, he finds relief in exceptional social and mental activity. Individually, given their history and Bloom's disposition, none of these concerns is particularly grave. Coalescing under the heading "function," they demand some sort of resolution, for they constitute the everyman's reason for being. But given his peculiar relationship to Molly and the world, Bloom can do nothing about them. In the end, action takes the form of passive resignation or adjustment, the acceptance of the inevitable as inevitable. Bloom has come as close as he can to self-discovery and to the restoration of his manhood. In the process he has incriminated and cleansed each of us of a variety of lusts and anguishes.

Though we find ourselves agreeing with Bloom's judgments, identifying with his foibles, understanding his errors, siding with him against adversaries, and preferring him over his peers, we are never allowed to forget his comic identity, to lose perspective or distance. His frustrations, conflicts, aspirations, inadequacies, fears, and joys are always comic on a relative scale, just as his actions are often rendered funny by the reactions of others to them. When, among the outhouse fumes, he pictures himself a writer of pulp fiction and then wipes himself with his model's story; when, busily researching the Keyes advertisement, he mixes with the learned in the library; when, intent on seeing a woman's silk-stockinged calf, he is frustrated by a passing tram; when, against the citizen's monumental chauvinism and terrible envy, he preaches fair play and Christian love to the gentiles in Barney Kiernan's pub; when, in short, he pursues an infinitude of unworthy ends and brushes off innumerable slights and injuries, he plays the endearing fool in our eyes.

Perhaps the secret of Bloom's success lies in the fact that many of the shocks he deals to our sensibility are shocks of recognition light enough for us to endure and that the blows he receives bruise but do not break his spirit. Our introduction to the sensual man, coming as it does after our initiation into Stephen's perturbed and rarefied intellect is more like a warm bath than a cold shower. It may take a while for us to recognize ourselves in the kidney-eater who sees the cat's "lithe black form," and "the gloss of her sleek hide" and then pointedly notes "the white button under the butt of her tail." But after the metaphor-ridden thoughtstream of Stephen, Bloom's commonsense cat's-eye view of himself as a giant is endearing: "Wonder what I look like to her. Height of a tower? No, she can jump me" (55). Muffing an opportunity to assert his superiority, he has reduced himself to human size and proclaimed his vulnerability. Never straining for the right word, the precise thought, Bloom coasts along seeing only what is there and telling himself, never others, what he sees (as opposed to what he thinks). By contrast, Joyce has made Stephen uncharitable and unapproachable, though admirable—the consummate ironist.

Unlike the traditional butt of comic or farcical laughter, Bloom has been turned into a surrogate perceiver and reactor for the unwary reader. In this he is very different too from the traditional first person narrator or even the modern unreliable narrator, both of whom set out to win our applause. To the extent that he comes to us through his stream of consciousness, he comes as one unaware of our presence and unprepared to make a play for sympathy. (It is appropriate that when Bloom makes a public bid for sympathy in "Cyclops," "Oxen of the Sun," or "Eumaeus," his companions respond negatively.) Perhaps Joyce has succeeded in making him seem a "good" man, for the expression in unguarded moments of his true and valid motives combined with his generous spirit, his freedom from cant, and his sharply focussed humorous view of life endear him to us as the habits of a canting Conmee and a crass Kernan in "Wandering Rocks" do not. Repeatedly, we share his unexpressed pain and distress and experience without sentimentality what relief is possible for him. We may even feel for him, what he cannot feel for himself, a painful embarrassment over his pleasures and tastes or a vague sadness over his failure to see his weakness vis-à-vis Stephen or to appreciate his strength in relation to Molly. Beyond all of this is our sense that Bloom is bigger than life, that he has been deliberately overdrawn as a monster of normality. The result is comedy, yes, but a comedy generously sprinkled with pathos which, like so much that is modern, turns back on the reader almost as much as it does on the weak, blind, foolish, or stunted protagonist.

The fact that we know more about Bloom as a sentient human being than we do about any other literary hero does not set him apart. Quite the contrary, it underlines his role as the unexceptional man, *l'homme moyen sensuel* in Montaigne's famous phrase, a figure who experiences but does not capitulate to exceptional desires, who takes life as it comes, who expresses to himself what he prudently leaves unsaid, and who represses what he fears to admit or face, a man who is neither brave nor cowardly. But every man is in some way separate from the crowd and Bloom is doubly distinguished, being not only a potential cuckold but a Jew in Dublin. A norm for the world—the city man—he is nevertheless a fringe figure and an outsider in his own city if not in his own eyes. Joyce makes good use of this condition, which gives Bloom enough distance from his fellows to make him a perfect commentator on their foibles but leaves him Irish enough and mature enough to show understanding and sympathy. Like Stephen's Shakespeare, he is more than just another husband in what the unmarried John Eglinton calls a "French triangle," just as he is more than that cliché of Jewish humor, the Jew who takes it from all comers—a cultural Pierrot. For one thing he is an accomplice in his fate as well as a victim, for another he has not given up hope or resorted to acts of comic desperation. He is also one who suffers for his indecision, a trait he shares with Stephen, but, unlike Stephen and like the majority of men, he is not sufficiently aware of himself to understand the nature of the decisions he could make or to question the psychological motivation for his errors.

Using Kierkegaard's categories, Arnold Goldman[1] has perceptively defined Stephen in terms of his attitude as the "ironic" man and Bloom as the "comic" man. An example might help clarify this distinction. Bloom with humorous pathos accepts the death of a casual friend, saying "Poor Dignam," and with distanced anguish says "Poor Papa" about his father, old and alone, deserted in the West of Ireland and sad enough to take a poisonous overdose of medicine. Stephen, haunted too by his personal ghost, is clearly incapable of saying with genuine or distanced sympathy "poor mother," and instead is forced to avenge her death on his own spirit while defending himself against the charge of matricide like a Fury-ridden Orestes. The one man in his weakness recognizes the world in which he has no power, the other in his strength sees the world as within himself, and himself as responsible. Neither position is completely adequate, but Stephen's is intolerable if not tragic while Bloom's is simply undistinguished. Accordingly, still certain of his potential but emasculated by the ghost of his own inadequacy and feeling cheated of his spiritual patrimony, Stephen wanders about "reading the book of himself." Despair and guilt have left him almost as unsure of his artistic vocation as he once was of his priestly one. However, if Bloom's assurance is the product of ignorance and limited capacities, Stephen's confusion is the confusion of brilliance and too much knowledge. Discontented with and frustrated by the ideals toward which his art and learning point, but unable to accept the world, which could save him, he has turned to the Devil and become Mulligan's man. During his day he walks painfully in the Buck's cast-off boots, testing the alternatives which his talents leave open to him: teaching, journalism, scholarship, singing, living by his wits. Since he sees only desolation in his future and unpaid debts in his past, he is incapable of accepting or rejecting these temptations. It is his best qualities, his honesty and pride, that make him a bitter brooder and an ascetic rather than a carefree hedonist like Mulligan or an amoral sponge like Lynch. As a result, he is what the Buck calls an "impossible person" (9) whose cynicism and irony are a negative faith which alone saves him from maudlin despair. The grotesque mock-heroic climax of "Circe" seems inevitable. The appropriate ironic response to a reasoned failure to take a stand is mindless action. He must be reduced and freed of his rational self so that he can make the gestures of rejection that will symbolically recapitulate the conclusion of the Portrait, obliterate what followed that false start, and restore him to youth and sanity. It matters and it does not matter that these gestures are no more than drunken maunderings, a pantomime of action, that he himself is unconsciously wearing at that moment the mask not of the artist-hero but of the pathetic clown, and that he neither breaks the light of the world nor holds his own in an argument against force. (Christ after all faced a similar failure and Hamlet achieved his goal only by inadvertence.) The climax of "Circe" approximates a tragic denouement, a moment of truth, a purging that should be followed at least in the mind of the reader by a theophany or elevation, suggested both by Bloom's vision of Rudy and by their shaky rapport in "Eumaeus" and "Ithaca," and confirmed in "Penelope." But Joyce's tragedy is in a minor key, jocular tragedy not to be taken *too* lightly, and what Stephen needs is not the father Mulligan says he seeks or the motherly woman he misses, but self assurance, a sense of humor, and objectivity, qualities possessed by Bloom in good measure.

Bloom and Stephen, by nature and/or nurture exiles and opposites, are emotional father and son, but each needs the other in himself far more than in the flesh. It is with the younger Bloom, revitalized by her meditations on Stephen, that Molly may resume her relations. It is with his own mature self engaged by the world that Stephen may hopefully identify. Through concern for himself (a self he has habitually neglected), Bloom has obliged Molly to reconsider her rejection of him. After his experiment with sound in "Proteus," Stephen opens his eyes to find the world "there all the time without" him but then immediately translates the temporal into the eternal, adding "and ever shall be, world without end" (37). What Stephen needs is an awareness of the here and now. On the pragmatic level, though exile is a permanent and necessary condition for Stephen as artist and Bloom as Jew in Ireland, each can modify his adjustment. Bloom can live within the society into which he was born; accommodating himself to a split worldview and facing up to past failures, he may even resume an ambiguous marital arrangement in a position of strength. Stephen can either decide to exist in a Dublin all of whose many facets are personally repugnant and obnoxious to his still distant goals as artist or he can reject his guilt and allegiances along with offers of an easier life and, with his eyes open this time, make an unromantic second flight. Both must adjust in terms of Ireland (and Dublin), which becomes a middle term, a comitragic country that produces heroes and betrayers in equal numbers and a superabundance of dreamers and clowns.

NOTES

11. For a full account of their addresses and his jobs, see Molly's monologue (*Ulysses*, p. 772).

12. Bloom's Masonic connections, which function as a parallel for Athena's protection of Ulysses, might help explain the edge he seems to have on the other Jews in the book. But we may question the existence of these connections.

13. The reference to Dan Dawson's speech, which gets short shrift ever from the journalists.

14. Implicit in this image is the view that it would take a combination of two natures to make a Shakespeare for our times. But since we move quickly from an identity of opposites to a father-son relationship, it is worth noting the role played by Shakespeare in the view of Stephen as Bloom's spiritual son. By a sort of metempsychosis ("O, rocks! ... Tell us in plain words," Molly-Calypso says [64].), Joyce links Shakespeare, who last an eleven-year-old son, Hamnet, to Bloom, whose son, dead at eleven days, would now be almost eleven, to Stephen, who is now twenty-two but who met Bloom eleven years ago.

15. For a fuller treatment of the farcical component of this chapter and the book as a whole, see my "Forms of Folly in Joyce: A Study of Clowning in *Ulysses*" (in ELH 43 [June 1967]: 260–83). Both Hugh Kenner and Marilyn French have written extensive and original studies of this chapter. (See "Circe" in Clive Hart and David Hayman, eds., *James Joyce's "Ulysses": Critical Essays* [Berkeley; University of California Press, 1974], pp. 341–62; *The Book as World: James Joyce's "Ulysses"* [Cambridge: Harvard University Press, 1967], pp. 185–206.)

(...)

1 Arnold Goldman, *The Joyce Paradox: Form and Freedom in His Fiction* (Evanston, Ill.: Northwestern University Press, 1966). Though I would question Joyce's use of Kierkegaard as a source, this view is helpful in distinguishing between Stephen's and Bloom's modes.

RICHARD ELLMANN

Bloom Unbound

In the *Cyclops* episode, the tampering with the surface of events is effected by means of a pair of narrators. The episode must have been difficult to write—how compose anything beyond the *Sirens*?—but Joyce manages to bring it off. Probably this episode profits from the famous scene in *Madame Bovary* where Emma and Rodolphe exchange tender sentiments about love while the judges of the cattle fair call out the prizes for pigs. Flaubert grants nature a straightforwardness against the false sentimentality of Emma and Rodolphe. Joyce in the *Cyclops* episode disproves sentimentality and swinishness both. He had already worked with inflation and deflation in the *Aeolus* episode, where Stephen's parable undercut Dublin's oratory. But that was a benign deflation; there is another kind of deflation, a malign one, which is inspired by meanness rather than by honesty. One of the two narrators of *Cyclops*—the one who carries the burden of the narrative—is a man of this kind, a man never named, but privately identified by Joyce with Thersites, the meanest-spirited man in the Greek host at Troy. It is Thersites who declares in Shakespeare's *Troilus and Cressida*, 'Lechery, lechery; still, wars and lechery.' His is a savage temperament, bent upon reduction. Joyce makes his Thersites a collector of bad and doubtful debts, an occupation which opens to him the worst secrets about everybody. That there might be a better side is inadmissible. A sponger and backbiter, he has no better side

From *Ulysses on the Liffey*. ©1984 by Faber and Faber.

himself. He expresses more patently than Mulligan or Boylan the spirit of denial; sexless himself, he happily denies sexuality (as well as decency) to others. Much of what he claims to know is false, as his evident relish in every malicious tidbit implies. What he sees he sees vividly, but he has a blind eye.

Joyce lets Thersites lead off: 'I was just passing the time of day with old Troy of the D.M.P. at the corner of Arbour hill there and be damned but a bloody sweep came along and he near drove his gear into my eye.' Here, as Gilbert indicates, is the first of the multitudinous references to putting out eyes which punctuate this episode, and allude to Odysseus' blinding of the Cyclops with a sharpened stick. But what is equally pointed is Thersites' obsequiousness towards the D.M.P., the Dublin Metropolitan Police. He is a coward before authority, frightened by any breach of the law, and Joyce reminds us of this at the end by having Thersites say that the Citizen, had he succeeded in hitting Bloom with the biscuit tin, would have been lagged for assault and battery and Joe Hynes for aiding and abetting him. Thersites pretends to be an outlaw, but no one minds more sheepishly than he the tables of the law.

As counterpart to Thersites Joyce establishes a second narrator, whose interruptions are sometimes a bit dull. They are not for that reason less necessary. Thersites initiates, the other narrator seconds in a different mode. What Thersites puts baldly, the second narrator figleaves over. Joyce speaks of the technique of this episode as gigantism, no doubt thinking of the size of the Cyclops, but it is actually a give and take between belittlement and magnification. Thersites is all bile, his counterpart all oil. One is myopic, the other hypermetropic. Thersites can take fairly innocent acts and make them out to be vile, his counterpart takes vile acts and makes them part of a frothy blancmange. In the Linati schema, Joyce indicates that Galatea plays a part in this episode, and it must be she, out of Handel's *Acis and Galatea*, who is wooed by Polyphemus the Cyclops but is unyielding there, as here, to his point of view. She trips while he lumbers. Perhaps also, since Joyce identifies the first narrator with Thersites, he has another narrator in mind, of an opposite disposition. His identity may be surmised: he strongly resembles Dr Pangloss, in that he glosses over what Thersites regards as the worst of all possible worlds and makes of it the best. In this triad of chapters where the presence of Hume begins to be felt, he is joined by another eighteenth-century philosopher, 'that moderate man Voltaire'.

Besides the Cyclopeans Thersites and Pangloss, whose different eyefuls make double vision the dialectic of the episode, another Cyclopean, the Citizen, is introduced. The Citizen reflects the intensities of the first two in that, as a chauvinist, everything Irish is good, everything un-Irish is vile. Yet Joyce notes that the Cyclopeans were not only inimical to foreigners, but also unfriendly to each other. The Citizen is flagwaver and xenophobe, but he is also sponger and braggart, and, as Thersites attests, is not so Irish as he pretends, since he has broken the patriotic code by buying up the holding of an evicted tenant.

Joyce was delighted with the theme of the *Cyclops*. One-eyeism required the two one-eyed narrators and the one-eyed Citizen. In one way or another all the characters except Bloom are monocular. But Joyce was also pleased that Odysseus, asked his name by the Cyclops, replied '*Outis*' (a pun on his real name) or 'No one', as if disdaining any identity; then, to compensate, when he and his men are almost safe away from the wrathful, blinded Cyclops, the hero cried out to him his full name, including its other half, Zeus (in Joyce's etymology). With this hint of his enemy's whereabouts and true identity, the Cyclops threw the rock which almost cut short these epical adventures. Joyce could easily see that in the *Cyclops* episode he must have Bloom, nominally a Christian, avow himself to be a Jew, and do so at the expense of prudence. He must also have Thersites know that Bloom's father had changed his name by deedpoll from Virag to Bloom.

To emphasize his theme Joyce frolics a good deal with namelessness and with names, with identity and mistaken identity. Among the details with which he thickens the major elements, little Alf Bergan imagines he has seen Paddy Dignam—or, as Doran half misnames him, Willy Dignam—still alive. The Citizen is never named, and Bloom in large stretches of the chapter, especially beginning and end, is referred to without being named. A dark horse has won the race, and Bloom is called 'a bloody dark horse himself'. The Citizen, because of his purchase of the evicted tenant's holding, is only half the man he seems. Bloom is temporarily blinded in not knowing what has stirred up the Citizen and the rest against him. But there is in fact a steady attack upon Bloom from all directions: he is not Bloom but Virag; he is not a man; he takes to his bed at times like a menstruant woman; he is no Irishman but what Thersites calls a Jerusalem cuckoo; he is no patriot, the Citizen insists; he is no husband, being a cuckold; no father (his child must be a bastard); worst of all, from Thersites' point of view, he is no treater. These are all aspects of Odysseus as *outis*, attempts to make him embody no-ness.

As a result of the hostility to Jews which Thersites manifests from the first page of his narrative, and of Bloom's assertion of himself in argument, as well as of the resentment at Bloom's supposed winnings on the race, he is placed in physical danger for the first time in the day. The Citizen's physical attack with the biscuit tin is the culmination of a series of lesser attacks. In *Scylla and Charybdis*, Shakespeare suffered the indignities of love; here in the *Cyclops*, Bloom must suffer the indignities of hatred. Thersites cannot abide

Bloom or anything about him, his appearance, his speech, his vocabulary, his fund of information, his refusal to drink, his generosity to the widow Dignam. Joyce presents Bloom here as his worst enemy sees him. Not that Thersites is altogether disrespectful; as Joyce indicated to Frank Budgen, there is a sneaking admiration for Bloom's conversance with all subjects. Thersites is himself almost tonguetied, his only remarks to the company being about drink.

Yet it is here that Bloom must show himself to be, on a minuscule stage, a true hero. Joyce was alive to the danger of falling into a little propaganda, in the way that he thought Tolstoy's 'Master and Man' had done. Up to now Bloom has confronted hostile forces chiefly in his mind. Now he must meet them directly. He must be allowed to state an ethical view which is superior to that of the people around him. It is more Christian than Judaic, more Platonic than Aristotelian: Joyce selected what he needed. But it must not be sentimental. Bloom has said that Ireland is his nation, but he adds, 'And I belong to a race too ... that is hated and persecuted. Also now. This very moment. This very instant.' The Citizen accuses him of Zionist daydreams, 'Are you talking about the new Jerusalem?' 'I'm talking about injustice', Bloom replies. John Wyse Power advises, 'Stand up to it then with force like men.' This rebuke leads Bloom to his culmination, 'But it's no use.... Force, hatred, history, all that. That's not life for men and women, insult and hatred. And everybody knows that it's the very opposite of that that is really life.' 'What?' asks Alf Bergan. 'Love ... I mean the opposite of hatred. I must go now.' To urge men to love, and then to speak of his own departure, connects Bloom for a moment to Christ. More naturalistically, with this position Bloom shows himself to be a two-eyed man; he counters directly the various exponents of single vision, the Citizen's chauvinism, Thersites' hatred, Pangloss's illusion.

In the Linati schema Joyce indicates that the cast of characters in this episode includes another interloper, Prometheus. Prometheus is a stranger addition to the cast than Galatea. It is likely that Joyce has in mind not the Prometheus of Aeschylus but of Shelley, whom he ranked (along with Shakespeare and Wordsworth) as one of the three great poets in English. Shelley's Prometheus is unbound when he retracts his curse against Jehovah, 'I wish no living thing to suffer pain'. He abjures as Bloom does the use of force, and Demogorgon is thereby enabled to announce as Bloom does the reign of love, which 'folds over the world its healing wings'.

> To defy Power, which seems omnipotent;
> To love, and bear....
> This, like thy glory, Titan, is to be

Good, great and joyous, beautiful and free;
This is alone Life, Joy, Empire, and Victory.

It is love which saves from what Blake called 'Single vision and Newton's sleep', and imparts true vision, perspective.

Perspective is itself parodied at the end of the episode when its two historians, Thersites and Pangloss, each having stared from his one eye in magnificent disregard of the other, combine their dictions with a sudden click: 'And they beheld Him even Him, ben Bloom Elijah, amid clouds of angels ascend to the glory of the brightness at an angle of fortyfive degrees over Donohoe's in Little Green Street like a shot off a shovel.' In terms of the book's argument, this apotheosis flouts space just as the *Sirens* episode flouted time and its musical articulation. 'Am I walking into eternity along Sandymount strand?' Stephen asks in *Proteus*, and Bloom is propelled towards eternity now. Since the apotheosis is a comic one, it at once exalts Bloom and recalls him to purely human proportions.

Bloom's upholding of love against 'force, hatred, history, all that', dovetails with Stephen's earlier statement that 'history is a nightmare from which I am trying to awake'. To both of them history presents itself as monolithic and glowering, the encrustations of time ready to encompass the present and future. The Citizen meets the ferocity of history with an equal ferocity. Bloom meets it with a certain kindness, a certain humour (not touched on by Shelley's Demogorgon), a certain refusal to be taken in. Against the false dialectic of Thersites and Pangloss—the impulse to wrinkle and the impulse to smooth over, to belittle and to bloat, Bloom asserts a monistic decency. His defence of love, more Christian than the Christians', rouses the Cyclops's anger, but more, it awakens the whole book towards its fourth level of meaning, the anagogic one, in which 'Love's bitter mystery' is to triumph. Stephen's theory of art has prescribed for it the act of love, but it is Bloom who must disclose what love is.

HUGH KENNER

The Hidden Hero

His advent has been heralded by Mr Deasy, who alleges of dying England
that Jews are in all the highest places, including finance and the press, eating
up (it is their way) the nation's vital strength (2.348). These propositions
prove to fit Leopold Bloom with inadvertent accuracy. As to high places, he
lives on Eccles Street, to which all roads lead upward; its north-western end
is the highest place within the 1904 municipal boundaries of Dublin. As for
finance and the press, he is employed by the *Freeman's Journal*, moreover on
its money-making rather than its editorial side, though as ad-man he makes
futile efforts to affect the content of the news columns, where he tries to
plant 'puffs' for his clients. And, as for eating up the nation's vital strength,
we know from the *Portrait* (203) that Ireland is 'the old sow that eats her
farrow', and we shall shortly be watching Bloom consume a pork kidney.
Since Mr Deasy had also said that there were no Jews in Ireland, Bloom has
somehow escaped his gaze, as he also escaped that of *Thom's*, where 7 Eccles
Street in 1904 is listed as vacant.

The census of 1901 places 2048 Jews in Dublin.[1] Since its criterion was
religious affiliation, this count, too, would not have included Bloom, who
was never circumcised (13.979), was baptised a Protestant in consequence of
his father's apostasy, and moved still farther from the tents of Judah when he
underwent Catholic baptism in October 1888 prior to his marriage with

From *Ulysses*, Revised Edition. ©1987 by Allen & Unwin, Ltd.

Marion Tweedy (17.542). And whether Jewry would at any time have acknowledged him is doubtful: Jewish affiliation is traced through the mother, and Leopold's mother Ellen Higgins Bloom had herself an Irish mother, Fanny Hegarty (17.537). So he undergoes the disadvantages of a Jewish name and appearance unsupported by any claim to solidarity with an interwoven community. (That may be why he has taken up Freemasonry.) He lived among Jews as a boy, on and around Clanbrassil Street on the south side of the river, but at 38 he looks back on his Jewish friends—Owen Goldberg, J. Citron, Philip Moisel, Julius Mastiansky, others—as belonging to his remote past. The same seems true of all his friendships now, though like any Dubliner he has much acquaintance. He is rather frequently disregarded and snubbed, though with no special malice. The Irish can be great overlookers of non-Celts.

Since the publication of *Ulysses* in 1922 Bloom has been further victimised by cliché. He gets called 'the little man', though at 5 feet 9-1/2 inches (17.86) he exceeds, as Ulysses should, the average Dublin height.[2] Nor is he anonymous of feature; 'he was very handsome', Molly recalls (18.208) of their courting days, and 'splendid set of teeth he had made me hungry to look at them' (18.307). He is quietly witty, too, and when not preoccupied as on Bloomsday by intolerable worry he can be what Dublin much prizes, a man ready of tongue (12.893). Least of all is he what he is easily taken for, the forgotten man with no economic niche, weaver of a fiscal rope of sand. At a time when, as Sean O'Faolin tells us in *Vive Moi!*, a Cork policeman maintained a family on a pound a week, Bloom has five guineas' income immediately foreseeable (8.1060) plus cash in the bank worth six months of Stephen's wages and, moreover, could buy and sell most of the people he deals with on Bloomsday did he care to liquidate insurance and securities that total nearly £1500 (17.1855). Ireland, he affirms, is his country (12.1431), but he is not so Irish as to drink his modest income up.

Stature, relative wealth, an exalted dwelling-place, handsome features, polysemous wit, a famously beautiful wife: Bloom may be said, albeit misleadingly, to possess these salient attributes of his prototype the Homeric chieftain. Not that we receive any encouragement to think of him in that way. The essential facts come inconspicuously and late: Bloom's height, for instance, when the long book has not many more pages to run and the hero (engaged, it is true, like Ulysses, in 'a stratagem') is climbing over an area railing. Next, the datum is repeated in a demeaning context, as if it were an advertisement for a stray tog:

£5 reward, lost, stolen or strayed from his residence 7 Eccles street, missing gent about 40, answering to the name of Bloom,

> Leopold (Poldy), height 5 ft 9-1/2 inches, full build, olive complexion, may have since grown a beard, when last seen was wearing a black suit. (17.2001)

Penelope of Ithaca composed no such notice, and £5 under-values the absent hero whose worth the Phaeacians valued at thirteen bars of gold, as many cloaks and tunics, a sword of silver and bronze and ivory, a gold intaglio wine-cup, other treasures (*Odyssey* VIII, 392–431). No, *Ulysses* will let us suppose in the first Bloom pages that a commonplace man is getting breakfast for his wife, and will proceed to modify this impression of ordinariness so imperceptibly we may need to combine exceptional attention with various outside knowledges, as of the elevation of Eccles Street, the size of Irishmen, the worth of a turn-of-the-century pound sterling, to perceive anything out of the way at all. Joyce is as cunning as his mythical hero, whose normal strategy was to withhold his identity.

Mulligan, we have noticed, is all outside; the book does not grant him a hint of inner life. Stephen by the end of 'Proteus' has become virtually all inside, the great bright world subsumed into his phrasemaking. Bloom at first is a balance; we move in and out, in and out, the 'out', however, closely in touch with the 'in', prompting, controlling.

> — Milk for the pussens, he said.
> — Mrkgnao! the cat cried.
> They call them stupid. They understand what we say better than we understand them. She understands all she wants to. Vindictive too. Cruel. Her nature. Curious mice never squeal. Seem to like it. Wonder what I look like to her. Height of a tower? No, she can jump me.
> — Afraid of the chickens she is, he said mockingly. Afraid of the chook-chooks. I never saw such a stupid pussens as the pussens.
> — Mrkrgnao! the cat said loudly. (4.24)

Though on a later reading we may think we glimpse Molly, *femme fatale*, behind 'she', and Bloom's masochism in the unsquealing mouse, still at first reading none of this is arcane the way Stephen's thoughts tend to be arcane, woven if not of wind then of insubstantialities, fine words, swift perverse associations, the mind enamoured of its own prestidigitation.

The way of Stephen's mind is something new in fiction, one reason completing *A Portrait of the Artist as a Young Man* cost Joyce ten years of trouble though he had written most of *Dubliners* in fourteen months. Achieved with such toil, the short novel's *style indirect libre* can perform with seeming ease and in the same movement both narrative and something more elusive than 'characterisation', the portrayal of one unique sensibility's individuating rhythm. To characterise, since Theophrastus, has been to classify, to offer the typical: Volpone is the Fox, Scrooge is the Miser, the Pardoner is the Avaricious Hypocrite. Though to enliven and individuate a type was Shakespeare's miraculous gift, still the type is there, discernible: Falstaff the Fat Roisterer, Hamlet the Melancholic. But Stephen Dedalus: is he the Artist? That is not satisfactory, nor is the Sensitive Youth, nor the Tortured Apostate. He is difficult to speak of because he seems so delicately individuated by style that we, not the author, must impose the categories with which discussion proceeds. And in the first three episodes of *Ulysses* that style undergoes prodigious leaps of development. The dazzling 'Proteus', with its crystalline inventions—'The new air greeted him, harping in wild nerves, wind of wild air of seeds of brightness' (3.266)—hardly a sentence resembling anything English has known before, a lucid, edged, energised particularity, in keeping company with the new century's most inventive new poetry nearly persuades us that fiction as we have known it is obsolescent, that new domains of sensibility, not character, lie open, that 'prose-poem', even, may connote something shapely.

Whereupon:

> Mr Leopold Bloom ate with relish the inner organs of beasts and fowls. He liked thick giblet soup, nutty gizzards, a stuffed roast heart, liverslices fried with crustcrumbs, fried hencod's roes. Most of all he liked grilled mutton kidneys which gave to his palate a fine tang of faintly scented urine. (4.1–5)

Though neither Smollett nor Dickens any more than Henry James would have written down that last word, we seem back in their domain. Is Mr Bloom a caricature? Have we perhaps a parody of dead-end naturalism, as the deadly documentation proceeds—'His hand took his hat from the peg over his initialled heavy overcoat and his lost property office secondhand waterproof' (4.66)? He exists, does Mr Bloom, comfortably in fiction's familiar world of nouns, all those *things* jostled by their attributes, all cerebration either an expository flight or a fly's crawl over the obvious.

And we seem to be being told everything, held as were early cinema audiences by the novel fascinations of watching the perfectly commonplace take its course in an unfamiliar medium. A writer who can get down a cat's word accurately—'Mrkrgnao!'—or make us *see* a mere tea-kettle on the fire—'It sat there, dull and squat, its spout stuck out'—is compelling us to read what we had never thought to read with attention, an account of a man.

getting through his own front door (a dozen lines of text!) on his way to purchase a mere breakfast kidney. ('Illiterate, underbred,' thought Virginia Woolf.[3]) We seem to follow him to the butcher's and back home step by step. Our attention lulled by so much urban specificity, we may not notice him getting back into the house, and a few pages later Joyce raps the desk for a lesson. Bloom on his way to the privy is made to reflect:

> Where is my hat, by the way? Must have put it back on the peg.
> Or hanging up on the floor. Funny I don't remember that. (4.485)

Novelists normally don't know where characters' hats are. The heady experience of frequenting a novelist who does know may encourage us to turn back, expecting to find out more about Bloom than Bloom knows himself. If we do, this is what we find

> Quick warm sunlight came running from Berkeley Road, swiftly, in slim sandals, along the brightening footpath. Runs, she runs to meet me, a girl with gold hair on the wind.
> Two letters and a card lay on the hallfloor. He stooped and gathered them. Mrs Marion Bloom. His quickened heart slowed at once. Bold hand. Mrs Marion.
> — Poldy!
> Entering the bedroom he halfclosed his eyes and walked through warm yellow twilight towards her tousled head. (4.240)

So there has been a skip in the narrative. We never did see Bloom pass through that door, nor take his hat off and dispose of it.

As to why we do not see him; entering the door, what we see is in general what he is conscious of, and he does not bestow attention on passing back in, the way he did on how to leave it unlocked when he went *out*. Also he has had a bad scare ('Grey horror seared his flesh') and has no mind for the mechanics of entry; all he wants is 'to smell the gentle smoke of tea,[4] fume of the pan, sizzling butter. Be near her ample bedwarmed flesh. Yes, yes.' What scared him was a premonition of death. In grey air under a covered sun, suddenly a member of 'the oldest people' wandering from 'captivity to captivity', he had felt 'age crusting him with a salt cloak' and had had to remind himself that he was alive (4.232).

As to the hat: when he entered his 'quickened heart' was slowed by another unpleasant jolt: the envelope addressed 'Mrs Marion' in a 'bold hand'. Not only is 'Mrs Marion' a presumption that there is no Mr Leopold worth considering, but also the 'bold hand' is recognisably Boylan's, and we are having our first experience with the principle that any irruption of Boylan into his perceptual field has the effect of suspending Bloom's faculties. That is why he is not aware of what he did with his hat, and his 'Funny I don't remember that' affirms that we have here a silence of a special kind, a hiatus of perception, not an elision to speed the story up.

So the cry, 'Poldy!', breaks in upon a blankness for which the book has no notation to offer, and the next thing Bloom knows he is in the bedroom, approaching her 'ample bedwarmed flesh', walking through 'warm yellow twilight', warm as the sunlight that greeted him in the street, yellow as the sunlight's gold hair on the wind.

This sequence of narrative skips is something to examine, and the effect of 'Where is my hat by the way' is to nudge us back to examine it. 'Calypso', the first Bloom episode, abounds in little skips of that sort, hiatuses, narrative silences. There is much that the Blooms do not say to each other, much also that the book does not offer to say to us. Pondering such instances, we may learn how largely *Ulysses* is a book of silences despite its din of specifying, and may notice how eloquent is the Blooms' rhetoric of avoidance and also the author's. Some of the most moving things the book has to say are things never said.

Consider, for instance, that we are not present at an affair of some moment, the day's leavetaking. Bloom will be gone all day, and this is unusual; his job is undemanding and he is (Molly testifies) normally underfoot

> he ought to chuck that Freeman with the paltry few shillings he knocks out of it and go into an office or something where hed get regular pay or a bank where they could put him up on a throne to count the money all the day of course he prefers plottering about the house so you cant stir with him any side whats your programme today. (18.503)

Knowing that the writer of the 'bold hand' will be coming by, knowing what this portends, it would be callow and un-Bloomlike to just slip out the front door. Having left the jakes, he did go back up to take leave of her, he must have. And he would have meant to retrieve his latchkey, too, from the trousers in the bedroom wardrobe, though given the emotional import of the scene it is not surprising that he in fact forgot it again, and is some time remembering that he forgot.

The text has details to sustain our sense of the probable. Joyce clearly did think out such a scene, and very pointedly did not write it: a scene during which Bloom learns, what was not explicit earlier, that Boylan is coming at four, and Bloom says that he will not be home early, will dine out and perhaps go to the Gaiety. 'At four she said', we learn early in 'Sirens' (11.188), and she didn't say that in our hearing any time in 'Calypso'. True, there were other things she didn't say in our hearing, notably 'Met him pike hoses', and if that were all we had to go on we might suppose she specified 'at four' during one of those little narrative skips. But no, we'd best assume she said it at the second meeting, the one with the cards, the one Bloom remembers while he talks with McCoy perhaps half an hour afterward. 'Who's getting it up?' asks McCoy, preternaturally tactless, and Bloom thinks

> Mrs Marion Bloom. Not up yet. Queen was in her bedroom eating bread and. No book. Blackened court cards laid along her thigh by sevens. Dark lady and fair man. Letter. Cat furry black ball. Torn strip of envelope.
> *Love's.*
> *Old.*
> *Sweet.*
> *Song.*
> *Comes lo-ove's old....* (5.154)

Not up yet. ('Who's getting it up?' Not up *yet*.) The cat is on her bed, the cat we saw starting upstairs as Bloom left for the privy (4.468).

This is the scene we are after, and lest we think he's remembering some earlier day, not today, we are apprised that the torn strip of Boylan's envelope is still in sight. And the cards are the cards Molly recalls in 'Penelope'—'yes wait yes hold on he was on the cards this morning when I laid out the deck union with a young stranger neither dark nor fair' (18.1313).[5] As for 'going to the Gaiety', 'I said I' is all Bloom imparts to himself in 'Hades' (6.185); Molly again is more explicit: 'he said Im dining out and going to the Gaiety' (18.81).

So they had that talk, and we hear of it in bits, and some of the bits are eighteen hours surfacing. It's by no means a trivial scene that we've failed to witness; they both know that when they meet again things will be irreversibly altered between them. Why, then, are we excluded from the bedroom of the Blooms during those last minutes together? If Joyce were the implacable realist we're sometimes told about, he would have forced us to watch.

But he is not; he is a connoisseur of performances. Social and psychic reality, for Joyce, are aspects of performance. In *Finnegans Wake* a very small troupe of players—perhaps six, plus supernumeraries—fills the air with hundreds of voices, congests the page with thousands of names. Speech for Joyce, as for men of the Renaissance, is the distinctively human act. Silence, a failure of role, is the stuff of drama (so Shakespeare, compared to Ibsen, is merely 'literature in dialogue'—*Critical Writings*, 39).

What a role is for any actor knows; it tells you what to say next. As such it is Joyce's equivalent for the formulas which by Milman Parry's hypothesis told Homer what to say next; Homer, like Bloom, like everyone, was improvising aloud and needed to run no risk of being left speechless. Joyce understood as early as *Dubliners* that it is not only the bard for whom speechlessness is a peril; it is anyone at all confronted by anyone else's expectations. Nothing creates more social awkwardness than the sudden simultaneous silence of everyone present, and roles can prevent this from ever happening.

If I am Boylan, man of the world, I say things like 'That'll do, game ball' and 'What's the damage?'—things like that (10.304, 325). If I am a stately buck, I say 'God, isn't he dreadful?' and 'The mockery of it' (1.51, 34). These two men of the future are great successes, thanks to their skill at imposing their roles on the situation. Boylan's very hand can speak with authority, as in the wordless riposte Molly recalls with disfavour: 'no thats no way for him has he no manners nor no refinement nor no nothing in his nature slapping us behind like that on my bottom' (18.1368). It was evidently eloquent at the time.

Failures of role are instructive. Mulligan's deserts him once, when Stephen casts back at him words it had once prompted, 'It's only Dedalus whose mother is beastly dead', and the Buck blushes as he says, 'Did I say that? Well, what harm in that?' (1.202) Boylan's deserted him when he learned the result of the Gold Cup and tore zip his tickets in a tantrum (18.423): less, one supposes, because he has lost £20 than because he feels made a fool of.

Stephen Dedalus apprises us that silence may *be* a role. A student of silence, exile and cunning, he sometimes talks nonsense, sometimes has nothing to say, is sometimes grossly offensive, and throughout the book is preparing to disappear. If other men say nothing when a role fails, he is preparing a role which shall consist in saying nothing.

And Bloom? Bloom has numerous roles, *Odysseus polyhistrion*, and does not know that one of them is Ulysses. Opposite the cat, his day's first interlocutor, he plays the kindly catkeeper, Leo pride of the ring. Opposite the Cyclops, he is an Eloquent Jew who could talk of a straw for an hour and talk steady (12.893). Opposite Molly, he is the unctuous lightbreakfastbringer, the pedagogue of Metempsychosis, the complaisant absentee, the man who won't be there, the—but this role is unscripted— incipient cuckold. What do you say to let your wife know that you know why Boylan is coming? No answer. And no scene.

Joyce writes nothing that is not already written. Like the Homer of Samuel Butler's imagination he does not like inventing, chiefly because he thinks human beings seldom invent, and the painful scene is unwritten because its silences will have outscreamed its speeches. A silence. What time is Boylan coming? At four. A silence. I shall be late. A silence. I think I shall dine out ('dine out', good God, 'dine out') and perhaps go to the Gaiety ('the Gaiety!'). This is not a normal morning. Normally their dialogue is scripted, as when Molly asks him the 'destination whither, the place where, the time at which, the duration for which, the object with which' (17.2296) in the case of temporary absences projected as well as effected. That has become *her* role, the intent shrew, and she has played it for nine months, ever since Milly's puberty. But we cannot imagine her having the immense coolness to run through that catechism this morning. So both are roleless, awkward, and we are shown no performance.

And we ought to observe how much silence pervades such of their conversation as we do hear. They are agreed to pretend that Blazes Boylan is coming to hear Molly sing. They agree to regard the projected concert tour—Molly with Boylan!—as a fund-raising project. They are agreed that Molly may put Boylan's letter not quite under the pillow, and that Leopold will see it, and that she will see him see it, and that neither will comment. They agree that 'Mrs Marion' will pass without remark. They are so much agreed on all this that they even agree to let the time of Boylan's arrival be unspecified—a casual drop-in merely—until (in that hidden interview) either Bloom asks for the time of the assignation or Molly volunteers it, on the shared understanding that Poldy must know how long to stay out of the house. Their conversation is guided by a set of agreements not to ask, not to comment.

'At four she said.' Though Boylan as it happens arrives late, 4 p.m. does mark a division in *Ulysses*, between the end of 'Wandering Rocks' and the start of 'Sirens'. This division is important enough to be signalled in several ways, not least by the advent of engulfing stylistic idiosyncrasies. Examining it on the plane of naturalistic action, we may say that it demarks two phases of Bloom's day. Up to 'Wandering Rocks' he is moving through a day's routine, benumbed by impending cuckoldry, whereas after 'Sirens' he is in free fall, routine and cuckoldry equally behind him, occupied chiefly with staying away from the house as long as he can, and evading the question how long that had better be. (He mustn't meet Boylan, and will prefer not to talk to Molly. When will she be asleep? 'Must be getting on for nine by the light. Go home.... No. Might be still up': 13.1212.)

But, until 4 p.m., benumbment. For eight hours Bloom goes through engrossing motions, busily curious, blocking off from his thoughts what ought to be the novel's principal topic, the Boylan–Molly liaison. From 'Calypso' to 'Wandering Rocks', *Ulysses* exemplifies a kind of fiction Ernest Hemingway is sometimes credited with inventing: the kind which foregrounds meticulously rendered detail which we may be misled into taking for the real theme. Such fiction can mislead. 'Big Two-Hearted River' was admired for years because it seemed to render with such immediacy a fisherman's absorption in his sport. That the theme of the whole story was what Nick Adams was not thinking of, was screening off from his mind by preoccupation with the little rituals of fishing, this was years in coming clear. *Ulysses*, similarly, was long regarded as an eccentrically detailed account of a man spending a Dublin day: 'the dailiest day possible', it was even called. Not at all. The man is virtually in shock.

In 'Lotos-Eaters' Bloom, embarked on his day, is adrift, erratic; he has nearly two hours to put in before the funeral, and there are welcome distractions: picking up his clandestine mail at the post-office box, idling in a church, buying soap, ordering Molly's lotion, indulging in a bath. The Boylan topic comes up once (raised by the unwelcome McCoy) and is at once suppressed; Dublin's lotos-anodynes are powerful in mid-morning.

In 'Hades' Blazes Boylan is actually sighted, saluting the cortège; Bloom instantly 'reviewed the nails of his left hand, then those of his right hand. The nails, yes' (6.200). He does not need to pursue this for long; in the rest of the episode death itself is an engulfing distraction. So, in the following episode, is business. Fussing with the absurd complications posed by Keyes' trivial ad—Can the crossed-keys design be obtained? Will 'puffs' be forthcoming? Can Keyes be persuaded to renew for a sufficient span?—he has room for but a single hasty thought of Eccles Street: 'I could go home still: tram: something I forgot' (7.230).

By 1 p.m. he has run out of distractions. There is nothing to do but walk and eat lunch, and the thought of Boylan assails him again and again.

—Will Boylan infect *Molly*? (8.102)
—How Boylan's fingers touched Molly's two Sundays past:

Touch. Fingers. Asking. Answer. Yes.
    Stop. Stop. If it was it was. Must. (8.591)

—Nosey Flynn's 'Isn't Blazes Boylan mixed up in it?'; whereupon

A warm shock of air heat of mustard hanched on Mr Bloom's heart. He raised his eyes and met the stare of a bilious clock. Two.

Pub clock five minutes fast. Time going on. Hands moving. Two.
Not yet. (8.789)

—How having lightly lunched he can dine at six: 'Six, six. Time will be
gone then. She...' (8.852).

—And, horrors, Boylan himself, walking straight toward him. 'Straw
hat in sunlight. Tan shoes. Turnedup trousers. It is. It is.' This crisis absorbs
fully 200 words. His breath is short; his heart troubles him; his hands search
pockets in a dumbshow of misdirection ('I am looking for that. Yes, that'). He
ducks out of sight into the museum gate (8.1168).

Ventral and sexual hungers, this episode implies, are intertwined. With
his mind on lunch Bloom at one moment lingers for half a page amid
memories of his idyllic time with *Molly*, sixteen years ago now, amid the
rhododendrons atop Howth (8.899), and at another moment is virtually
pursued by erotic fancies prompted by a window display (8.631). This
episode, 'Lestrygonians', and this one alone bears out what one might have
expected to be the premise of the book, that Bloom is a man driven by
Boylan's spectre. From no episode, indeed, is Boylan wholly absent, but
Joyce knew better than to let his menace grow dominant. A postcard he sent
his brother in 1907 from Rome illustrates amusingly the habit of mind that
served *Ulysses* so well. He has been to hear *Gotterdämmerung*, and 200 crisp
words convey the evening: the neighbour who smelt of garlic and got sleepy;
the man who said Wagner's music was splendid but intended only for
Germans; the horse which 'being unable to sing, evacuated'; the devotees
with scores; the people humming 'correctly and incorrectly the nine notes of
the funeral motive'; everything but the music, save for one phrase. A
malicious little masterpiece, the card situates us vividly at the performance,
yet permits Wagner's opera to be present only by indirection, between
sentences.[6] Wagner created that evening as Boylan creates the quality of
Bloom's day; Boylan, too, is absent from *Ulysses* most of the time.

And, so far as presence is conveyed by explicit textual attention, Bloom
eventually commences to be absent as well. In 'Scylla and Charybdis', where
he puts in time at the Library hunting down the design for Keyes' ad, we
barely see him, though we can trace his movements from little clues. And in
'Wandering Rocks' he is accorded one vignette out of nineteen.

Here he is immobile, savouring porn. At the midpoint of the hour
before the dreaded rendezvous, he is attending to his last errand for Molly,
who had asked for another book. So in this last of the 'naturalistic' episodes
we leave Bloom amid the circulation of indifferent Dubliners, devouring
what may pass for an account of what is on the threshold of occurring

Yes. This. Here. Try.
— *Her mouth glued on his in a luscious voluptuous kiss while his hands*
felt for the opulent curves inside her deshabille.
Yes. Take this. The end. (10.610)

Though Shakespeare, even when read with the aid of a glossary, has in the past shed little light on difficult problems (17.390), today the ancient technique of *sortes Virgilianae* ('he read where his finger opened') has disclosed a radiance in *Sweets of Sin*: a book in which the situation at home is mirrored. He has found what perhaps he did not know he was looking for, turning over the volumes at more than one bookseller's.

So Bloom's day until four; or, by Mr Clive Hart's precise calculations, until 3.18. We take leave of him absorbed in sexual fantasies, immobile amid indifferent mobilities, one citizen among dozens, among thousands, his private miseries translated into a few vulgar words in a book. 'Hands felt for the opulent.' His hands hold a block of bound paper labelled *Sweets of Sin*: a book within a book. He will shortly put down the inflated rental, a shilling, and take the drab pages with him into the next hours' aimlessness.

NOTES

1. Louis Hyman, *The Jews of Dublin* (Shannon, 1972), 60. This author's pertinacity was unflagging; he is notable for having run down Dlugascz, a Triestine Jew whom Joyce in one of his whimsical departures from verity installed in a porkbutcher's shop on Dublin's Dorset Street.

2. Lionel Trilling was the first to point this out (*Sincerity and Authenticity* (1972), 90). We can get at Dublin demographic norms obliquely. In Bloom's time, when most British infantrymen were Irish, the average recruit measured 5 feet 4-1/2 inches, and Dublin Municipal Policemen, with a minimum height of 5 feet 9 inches, looked like 'giants' to the general public.

3. Virginia Woolf, *A Writer's Diary* (New York, 1954), 49.

4. Ulysses on Calypso's isle was near death from longing to see but the smoke rising from his home: *Odyssey*, I, 57–9. Joyce's use of incidental Homeric phrases has never been studied.

5. Bloom's 'dark lady and fair man' goes by the look of the cards, where all Jacks have yellow hair; Molly's 'neither dark nor fair' must stem, like 'young stranger', from rules of interpretation.

6. *Letters*, II, 214.

FRITZ SENN

Bloom among the Orators:
The Why and the Wherefore
and All the Codology

Most of us take delight in the well-turned phrase. Eloquence is a virtue in many cultures, like the two that interest us here, the world of the Homeric epics and of Joyce's (but not only Joyce's) Dublin. *Ulysses*, in one of its many ways, brings the two together; the novel seems to assemble a more than average proportion of gifted speakers into its relatively narrow confines. These speakers find various pretexts to pass the time of day and night in loquacious company, and Joyce helps them in aligning a series of scenes in public houses or in publike constellations—a newspaper office, a library, a maternity hospital room, or a cabman's shelter, all of which can turn into the setting for a contest in verbal skills. *Ulysses* is full of talk and much of it may sound like talk for talk's sake. Don't let us forget that the one conspicuous narrative deviation on the first page of the novel, that metastatical word and name "Chrysostomos," re-Hellenizes "golden mouth" as a traditional figure of speech for men who had a way with words.[1]

No one is safe from the lure of the spoken word. Even as aloof a person as Stephen Dedalus is "wooed by grace of language" (140). Nor is he immune to the even greater temptation—in the Library episode—to display his own superior mastery of words and Shakespearean diction. Dubliners excel in talk and enjoy it; they are, moreover, competent judges of each other's performances. *Ulysses* contains many comments on the language of its

From *Joyce's Dislocutions: Essays on Reading as Translation*, edited by Jean Paul Riquelme. ©1984 by Fritz Senn and Jean Paul Riquelme.

protagonists. Even Molly Bloom, not Dublin's foremost intellectual, has been endowed with a shrewd sense for the wrong or pretentious note.

Skillful speakers, like tenors, are admired and successful. The performance itself can be more important than any information conveyed or idea presented. The glib talker, whatever his level, can usually make it through the day and at least get his drinks provided for. Lenehan is a case in point: "his adroitness and eloquence had always prevented his friends from forming any general policy against him," we learn in *Dubliners* (*D* 50) and find this comment confirmed in *Ulysses*, where he is still able to market a limited stock of witticisms, no matter how much the worse for wear, to his own best advantage. The stories in *Dubliners* highlight types who know how to turn a phrase and get on in the world, such as Gallaher in "A Little Cloud," with "his fearless accent" (*D* 70) and his memorable "sayings" (*D* 73). By 1904 he is still held out as a model for, of course; journalism. From all we know of Corley in "Two Gallants," he may not have much to say, but apparently he can say it with aplomb and it works well enough. Mrs Mooney, of "The Boarding House," is full of confidence; she has social opinion on her side and the right arguments, but also, we can assume, she will know how to reexpress them properly. Other characters remain tongue-tied and self-conscious. Thomas Malone Chandler only wishes "he could give expression to" his emotions (*D* 73), but clearly will never think up Byronic cadences; and no matter how he tries on rare occasions, he will never sound like a man of the world in a public bar. A man like Farrington, bulky and muscular, in "Counterparts" is miscast in a job that depends on copying words and sentences, and in a crisis he lacks the wit to cope with it verbally. When his tongue finds what he takes to be "a felicitous moment" (*D* 91)—and it looks like a fairly unique event—the words chosen actually precipitate his downfall and their first result is "an abject apology"; that is, the instant annulment of those words. Gabriel Conroy's superiority in "The Dead," such as it is, is also due to his command of words that suit the occasion. He can confect a speech, with allusions and quotations, and the speech is adequate (most likely he will be asked to speak again next year); his reputation is confirmed. Conversely, when he fails with words (as he thinks), he is disconcerted, afraid he may have "taken up the wrong tone." His accomplishment may be reinterpreted as "orating to vulgarians" (*D* 220), but, for all practical and public purposes, the power of words is an asset.

Among the hierarchies within *Dubliners* there is one that is rhetorical. This is seen best in the oratorical rivalry among the visitors of Mr Kernan, in "Grace," with the lower ranks vainly striving for attention and acknowledgment. The story appropriately begins with a defective tongue and culminates in the glib speech of a professional preacher with "resonant assurance."

Lily, the caretaker's daughter, is right: "The men that is now is only all palaver" (*D* 178). And it is largely palaver that men are judged by.

"winged speech"

The tale of the *Odyssey* can be interrupted in praise of the man who has a way with words, and this is often its hero. The preeminence of Odysseus in verbal as well as practical resourcefulness has led one classical critic—one of the few to be mentioned in *Ulysses*, and that in the chapter dealing with rhetorics—to claim that the initial epithet, *polytropos* (*Od.* 1.1), suggested the hero's ability to utilize "many tropes," that is the whole arsenal of rhetorical tricks.[2]

This semantic twist is doubtful enough, but the linguistic cunning of Odysseus needs little demonstration. It is established in his first speech, a skeptical reply to the nymph Calypso. The reply is introduced by the common formula "*epea pteroenta*," to alert the listener to the "winged words" that will follow. After them the nymph at once comments upon what he has said and how he has said it. "Thou that hast conceived and spoken such a word" is the stilted version of Butcher and Lang for the original

hoion de ton mython epephrasthes agoreusai (*Od.* 5.183),

which is, literally, something like: "Such a *mythos* (= word, saying, tale, fable) have you thought up to say aloud (publicly)." The point is that before the painful moment of parting, the goddess takes time out to remark upon the quality of the speech and to review it as a significantly clever example. We notice, by the way, that Joyce's Dubliners too have a penchant for evaluating words and speeches.

The first spoken words of Odysseus are sandwiched between "*epea pteroenta*" and "*hoion mython*," and even if Joyce never looked at the original, it is interesting that *epos* and *mythos*, both terms that primarily referred to the act of speaking, have come to stand for important concepts, important for Homer's art and for Western culture. *Ulysses* has helped to redefine their meaning.

Naturally the novel plaits a tag like "*epea pteroenta*" into its texture: "the winged speech of the seadivided Gael" (324). This phrase has become proverbial (Homer uses it more than a hundred times), almost the prototypical cliché, the kind of thing that Joyce tends to assimilate into his work both as one of the many literary comedowns, the timeworn and overused set pieces that have become unfit for any other than parodistic use, *and* in its (once) metaphorical aptness and precision. For "winged" sets words off from the more pedestrian duties that they normally perform. It signals occasions for them to soar above quotidian banalities.

As it happens, "winged" (or *pteroenta*, from *pteron*, feather) suggests that to parts of language can be attached what Joyce's first acknowledged patron saint in an emergency fixed onto himself. This is a procedure that, as we know, calls upon some ingenuity and has its inherent risks. The Daedalus myth, as built into *A Portrait* (where the image of a "winged form," *P* 169, is stimulated inter alia by the contemplation of the poise, balance, and rhythmic rise and fall of words, *P* 166–69, and where language itself, in accordance with myth-inspired ecstasy, begins to take off from the ground) and into *Ulysses*, implies both the success and the Icarian variant of failure. The hazardous plight of words engaged in ecstatic flight contributes much to the Joycean comedy of incongruities. There can be a rhetorical *hubris* too, an attempt by language to overreach, aim too high. For example, the speech by Dan Dawson, as reported in Aeolus, accumulates altitudes like "*serried mountain peaks*" and is in itself "*towering high on high*" (125), but there is one short step from "*overarching*" to "*overarsing*" (123).

"Most amusing expressions"

Ulysses begins on a raised platform, with a sustained showpiece and recital by the most accomplished orator and impersonator of them all, Buck Mulligan of the golden mouth and the inexhaustible (though perhaps, in the long run, slightly repetitious) repertoire. Never at a loss for the right word, he usurps many of Stephen's roles of priest and bard and also, at one turn, provides himself with wings. With "his hands at his sides like fins or wings ... fluttering his winglike hands" (19), he proclaims his ascension in a Daedalus-cum-Christ routine while doing an Icarian caper down toward the sea. From the start he links up with the classical tradition, uses familiar Homeric tags, and invents Homeric types of epithets. He generally finds a trope for every ploy. With his rapid changes of voice and act he is indeed, as a later parody has it, "mirth-provoking," and causes "considerable amusement" (307). One would naturally invite him to one's party, as George Moore does later in the day (and the exclusion of Stephen Dedalus, with his cryptic utterances and sullen asides, is understandable too). Mulligan is a worthy successor of Mahaffy and Oscar Wilde, a voluble quoter and himself eminently quotable. There is hardly a reader who would not remember the Buck's first words, spoken aloud, and ceremoniously. At least we remember that the Latin of the Mass is mockingly misappropriated.

The extroversatile Buck heralds Ulyssean techniques and a Homeric role that is to be played in a more modest key, and much more fumblingly, by Leopold Bloom, who has inherited some of the skepticism, much of the resilience, and most of the curiosity of Odysseus, as well as a number of minor traits but not, unfortunately, the verbal ingenuity. Bloom is not a gifted speaker. In a culture that values speech at times more than truth, he is denied eloquence. This is not to disagree with Richard Ellmann[3] and others who have emphasized Bloom's gift of expression or even his poetic diction. This diction, the remarkable crispness and spontaneity of his language, his certainly more than average wit, are confined to his unspoken thoughts. When lovable, adaptable, considerate, inquisitive Bloom opens his mouth and speaks aloud (what the Greeks called *agoreusai*, as in *Od.* 5.183), he may become a bit of a bore. At least that is how he strikes most of those who know him in Dublin (and the criteria applied throughout in this essay are, of course, mainly those of Bloom's fellow Dubliners and not some absolute standard of eloquence): Bloom knows it and is known for it. (You would not invite him to your party for the epigrammatic sparkle that he might provide.)

The brisk, supple commonsense of his many inner observations ("He boomed that workaday worker tack for all it was worth," 118, is a fair sample) rarely finds voice. With most of us Bloom shares the inhibitions that make us falter and grope for the clinching expression (which may be one of the reasons why it is so easy to empathize with him). He speaks as most of us do, haltingly. In the Aeolus chapter, which paradigmatically parades most rhetorical devices of the classical heritage, he comes out with a report like: "I spoke with Mr Keyes just now.... And he wants it if it's not too late I told councillor Nannetti from the *Kilkenny People*" (146). There is nothing wrong with that except some confusion and perhaps a certain lack of dramatic tension. This is how we conduct some of our daily conversation, but it is hardly the stuff that would make an irate, impatient, fidgety, and, moreover, thirsty, newspaperman hold his breath even if he were interested in the trivial business transaction. Mulligan would never speak like that.

Bloom's early morning classroom lecture about metempsychosis is faultless, and didactically sound, but it manifestly does not grip the attention of his audience of one. This is typical. Try asking readers of *Ulysses* if they remember what Bloom's first spoken words are, as they remember Mulligan's. Few of them do, and for good reason, for Bloom's opening line is singularly nonmemorable, a mere response to the cat's request (and significantly, Bloom tends to re-spond, re-ply, rather than initiate talk). What Bloom says is "O, there you are" (55).

The two openings of the novel contrast pointedly. Mulligan, from an elevated position, on top of an outstanding historical fortification, puts on an act, in a solemn voice, intoning, speaking up to "*Deus*," though frivolously. Bloom, in the most commonplace of all rooms, a kitchen, from below ground level, speaks, in the most ordinary fashion, down to an animal, but without condescension. The unspectacular words are sufficient for the rapport with the cat that is needed. Note, incidentally, that Bloom begins his day by saying "you," while Mulligan starts out with "I" ("*Introibo*") (3).

And, while on the subject of first words, we may observe that Stephen is first heard saying "Tell me" (4), which happens to coincide with the first words of the first line of the *Odyssey* in many translations.

With intimates like the cat or Molly or (for all we know) Milly, Bloom is still more at ease; with an old friend like Josie Breen he may even venture a flourish like "your lord and master:" (157). Toward others he is more reserved. Approaching Larry O'Rourke, he rehearses a little speech, which he then keeps for himself. He rarely tries to match the elocution of the Irishmen around him, but he admires them for their wit. Simon Dedalus is one of them: "Most amusing expressions that man finds. Hhhn: burst sidewise" (103). The Muse in general is reticent toward Bloom and does not inspire his expressions.

Surely a chapter like Circe gives evidence of Bloom's aspirations to be a great orator as well; he would enjoy swaying a large audience. In Eumaeus, with some of the inhibitions gone, his submerged eloquence finds a belated outlet but also, tragically, only a completely unresponsive audience. On the whole Bloom is aware of his limits and rarely exceeds them without provocation. Lenehan recalls an occasion when Bloom was holding forth on a favorite subject, astronomy, at some length, but it is obvious that the attention of most of his listeners was elsewhere, and Lenehan ultimately turns the event into the kind of lively story that Bloom could never bring off (233–35). Bloom is at his best as a silent observer and internal commentator. Ironically, his job connects him with the "modern art of advertising," which depends so much on the catchy phrase that Bloom can judge but not make up. The ideal "of magnetising efficacy to arrest involuntary attention, to interest, to convince, to decide" (683) remains an ideal.

Of course Bloom is not at all inarticulate, he is simply not particularly eloquent; his talk, not very exciting, is still more interesting than that of some others. Early in the day he runs into one of the least inspired speakers, Charles M'Coy, who treats him to an unwelcome, protracted report on his response to the news of Dignam's death. This textbook illustration of narrative tedium (which Bloom, as far as Fate will allow him, relieves by voyeuristic attention) may indicate the lack of interest in news that the eating of the lotus fruit caused (*Od.* 9.95), but it mainly shows that someone else is treated by Bloom as he often is by others. Marvin Magalaner long ago pointed out that M'Coy is Bloom's forerunner, an earlier version of him.[4] As M'Coy tries to wedge his way into the prestigious conversation of

Cunningham & Co., he obliges, unbidden, with physiological terms of the Bloomian kind ("Mucus," "thorax," *D* 158) but remains neglected very much as Bloom will be in the same company in the funeral carriage.

The Hades chapter assesses Bloom's place in society. Attention rarely turns to him and, when it does, it is against his will. This happens when Molly's concert tour is mentioned, and again when his unorthodox remarks on death, in a different key from accepted ones, clash with the appropriate ritualized formulae (95). But he is ignored or thwarted when he wants to contribute to the conversation, when he volunteers his story about Reuben J. Dodd and son. There is, however, also good rhetorical reason for the usurpation of Bloom's tale. He gets off on a risky start by announcing, twice, how "awfully good" the story is, and only a skilled storyteller can live up to such a promise. When he settles down to the unmistakable tone that is required ("There was a girl in the case, ... and he determined to send him to the Isle of Man out of harm's way..."), he is not too successful in keeping paternal and filial identities apart, and there are interruptions for clarification until Cunningham takes the story away from him and presents a reedited, and superior, version, which he insists on carrying to its climax. Clearly Bloom's narrative talent would not qualify him to negotiate "the funny part" (94–95).

As it happens, Bloom's story is launched just about when the carriage is closest to the newspaper offices off Sackville street. In general, Bloom stays away from the uncongenial role of a storyteller. The reader knows why in this case, after the sight of Blazes Boylan, and with a moneylender looming into view, he has deviated from his usual practice.

The episode in which Bloom fares best is the visual, projectional, reflective, and almost wordless scene on the beach. As a silent, dark, mysterious stranger he can appear attractive to a girl who is hesitant to move. He realizes that talk would not have improved the encounter. "Suppose I spoke to her. What about? Bad plan..." (370). He briefly considers gambits but shrewdly rejects them. A man like Boylan would not have any such qualms. A few sentences he throws out are enough to show that he hits upon the right tone with ease, in front of a shop girl or a barmaid. "What's the damage?" or "Why don't you grow" (227, 265) are not great aphorisms, but impressive enough to cause a blush or a sigh.

"Impromptu" (141)

With his commonsense approach and his commonsense vocabulary, and some business to attend to, Bloom walks into the newspaper office, where a rhetorical seminar is going on. For a moment he stops the stylistic analysis in progress by asking a few questions, short but to the point, "pertinent" (124) in fact. This word characterizes him, his speech and his acts; he "holds on to" whatever is at hand. His purposeful bearing and his simple statements set him off from the grandiose mannerisms of most others. His own words are trite, factual, polite, and unexciting. Yet his exit and his reappearance are decorated by theatrical gestures and elocutionary flourishes. As long as he remains peripheral he is treated with neglect, condescension, or mild ridicule, but as soon as he has to assert himself, he becomes a nuisance.

Joyce chose the rhetorical context of the Aeolus chapter, of all the possible settings, for a close-up view of Bloom in search of a pithy retort to Menton's recent snub. He moreover gives Bloom the advantage of a moment's unruffled leisure and the benefit of hindsight. If we try to imagine how some of the more sharp-tongued Dubliners would have reacted, or remember how Odysseus was able to deal with his adversaries, we can appreciate the endearing flatfootedness of Bloom's effort:

> I could have said when he clapped on his topper.... [No inspiration yet; the sting is slow in coming. So try again:] I ought to have said something about an old hat or something. No ... [Try once more:] I could have said. [The sentence without a pointed mot instill incomplete.] Looks as good as new now. (121)

As good as new? No "topper" is forthcoming, "old hat" is about right.

Cousin Bloom will never be an orator.[5] Nor, for that matter, was another figure who is featured more in this chapter than in any other one. Moses—who also at times found it hard to get his people's attention—was "not eloquent ... but I am slow of speech and of a slow tongue" (or "*impeditioris et tardioris linguae sum*" Exod. 4:10).[6]

To make up for a deficiency in brilliance, Bloom often has some pertinent factual information, for which, worse luck, there is not much of a market in his environment. One's reputation is based more on Aeolian luster, which, in the book, is glorified and mocked, but expansively displayed throughout. A later chapter will be devoted to the seduction (and the vacuity) of musical performances. Sirens through appropriate changes shapes words with regard to their sensuous appeal. Its overture is the most conspicuous example in the whole book of the celebration of pure aural entertainment, a matter of sound and phrasing and orchestration, an orgy of tonal rhetorics, before, secondarily, the sense can and will come through.

The music, to which Bloom listens, serves the same function to those present that talk does in Cyclops; it affords distraction. But in Barney Kiernan's pub Bloom imprudently tries to compete. Not a habitual pub crawler, he is lured by circumstances and a specific invitation into the locality, and because of his displaced aggression the otherwise silent observer becomes unusually talkative. He behaves with oddly un-Odyssean rashness; he distinctly does not resort to "words of guile" or "deceit" (as in *Od.* 9.282), but appears naively truthful and accurate in what he says and at times unnecessarily officious and intrusive, which aggravates his already precarious situation.

"that kind of talk" (302)

Cyclops, one of the gregarious chapters, develops traits and themes from Aeolus: coming and going, rambling and interrupted dialogue, discussion and parody of newspaper mannerisms, narrative disruptions, a shared cast (Lenehan, Lambert, O'Molloy, Hynes), and the application of oratory—a reasonably comprehensive list of rhetorical forms could be gleaned from this chapter too.[7] Again we have a group of some expert talkers and a few expert critics. The Citizen excels in one kind of invective and takes the opportunity to address the public in several set speeches.[8] Even the dog Garryowen holds the stage for a spell of cynical oratory. Bloom inadvertently maneuvers himself into the position of a public speaker. He is not comfortable in the role and breaks off his proclamation of love in a somewhat abrupt manner, obviously sensing that the audience is not quite with him. The scene is set for his second speech toward the end of the chapter, with the externals of a temporary rostrum and an expectant gathering. Rhetorical repetition characterizes Bloom's parting words (342), which clearly have a kinetic effect, but again this is not the occasion for a grandiose peroration. The burst of forensic eloquence is exceptional for Bloom (it becomes the rule in Circe, but Cyclops serves in many ways as a rehearsal for the later chapter), and remains a qualified success. The reader knows what unusual provocation has led to this singular tortuous climax.

All along in the chapter, Bloom has been a multiple transgressor. It is not his own fault, nor even quite strictly true, that ethnically he does not really belong to the group. He might know, however, that to avoid being treated and treating again is not good policy (though others manage to get around this one with impunity). But beyond all that, Bloom proceeds in the wrong conversational key. He informs and instructs, or argues, or voices *his* grievances—but he does not amuse. There is a tacit code that Bloom seems (or chooses) to be unaware of. The prevalence of such codes is signaled early on in an act put on between the Citizen and Joe Hynes when they go through the ritual of the passwords of the Ribbonmen, with all the required gestures (295),[9] as if to establish some of the rules of the game.

There are other violators present. Bob Doran, who bears his own understandable grudge against providence, irately seizes upon the literal sense of the word "good" in relation to Dignam's death and Christ and is instantly admonished—"they didn't want that kind of talk in a respectable licensed premises" (302). There are indeed "premises" that one had better observe. Remarks about the responsibilities or the ethnic background of divinity are clearly taboo, even if other blasphemies may be cheerfully applauded. Fittingly, an earlier verbal transgression of Bloom is worked into this chapter, his "giving lip to a grazier" (315). This observance of his own personal code above the socially accepted one led to his dismissal from a job.

The tacit rules are simple enough. You keep the party going by being wittily entertaining (which may amount to finding new permutations for old jocularities), and you play straight man to the Citizen and prompt him to his histrionics (though you may laugh behind his back). But you do not seriously argue or waste everybody's good time with explanations or technicalities. To define a nation, or love, or injustice, just does not make you popular. Who cares, anyway, about mortgages, insurance, or hoose drench?—except perhaps widows or cattle, but none of those are present. The nameless narrator is irritated by Bloom as he is also once by J. J. O'Molloy when he helps out with some legal point about the laws of libel: "Who wants your opinion? Let us drink our pints in peace," as though mere factual clarification were somehow to disturb that peace (321).

Bloom is a disturbance, and part of it is due to the sense that he has little value as an entertainer. His inauguration speech is exemplary. The floor at the moment is being held by Alf Bergan, one of Dublin's wits and one thoroughly familiar with the ground rules (he may break some other ones; surely the public reading of the letters received from hangmen is hardly professional etiquette for a civil servant—but the letters *are* amusing). He offers a report on naive Denis Breen as a diversion (Breen, taunted by the verbal insult "U.p.: up," promptly tries to bring a gravely different code, the legal one, to bear upon what has been designed only "for a lark" (299). Bergan appears impatient with serious talk about capital punishment and uses (what is no doubt Bloom's phrase) "deterrent effect" to broach the much more fascinating topic of the erection of a hanged man (304). To this there are, in neat instructive juxtaposition, two responses. The one, entirely in the spirit of the game, by Joe Hynes:

—Ruling passion strong in death.... as someone said

is a maliciously clever shift of a well-known line to a new, amusing context. The deviant response is, naturally, Bloom's

> —That can be explained by science.... It's only a natural phenomenon, don't you see, because on account of the ... (304)

We, the readers, can see how Bloom does not want to have the talk turn around erection at this particular moment, but scientific explanation has a way of spoiling the fun. Accounts are the last thing wanted, and Bloom's speech is, once more, rudely thwarted, this time by the narrator, who instantly substitutes a commentary on Bloom for Bloom's verbatim lecture. And a parodistic interpolation follows right away in which Bloom's characteristic approach and his interest in medical evidence are satirized. Bloom has started on the wrong foot; he comes out "with the why and the wherefore and all the codology of the business" (304). He wants to argue and only provokes arguments *ad hominem* and quips at his expense, often with anti-Semitic overtones—"Professor Luitpold Blumenduft" (304).

"Mr Bloom with his argol bargol"

The scientist Bloom, "Mister Knowall" (315), with his useful though tedious contributions about sheep-dip, rower's heart, discipline, insurance, or persecution, is out of place, "putting in his old goo" (310–11), "mucking it up" (313), a nuisance even if he had not mentioned, of all things, "the antitreating league" (311)—a rhetorical outcast as well. One of his favorite phrases is "as a matter of fact" when facts are the least interesting things anyone wants to hear. He may well be right about the racial origin of Marx or Spinoza,[10] or even the Savior, but such information would fail to rouse much interest at the best of times and, at this juncture, merely reinforces the prejudices against him. It matters very little that the Citizen and his faction are contradictory and inconsistent. For all the proximity of the courts and the thematic relevance of parliament and debates at the meetings about the Irish language or the cattle traders, no one wants an objective debate with pro and con. This is a gathering for having "a great confab," as we are warned early on (295), for drolleries like "don't cast your nasturtiums" (320), for clever impersonations ("taking off the old recorder," 322), where forms of "codding" are the order of the day, or "letting on" is expected as well as variations of "doing the rapparee" (295), "the weeps" (302), "the mollycoddle" (306), etc. Rhetorical compulsion requires the translation of Bloom's straightforward "cigar" into the code expression "Give us one of your prime stinkers," or at least some minor elaboration like "knockmedown cigar" (304, 305). This minor incident of Hynes forcing a cigar on reluctant Bloom is transformed by the narrator into "his twopenny stump that he cadged off Joe" (311), a bit of a distortion and a slightly more diverting story. Occasionally clarity demands the reverse translation from the coded allusion to normal terminology. "Wine of the country" and "Ditto MacAnaspey" are put into the vernacular—"Three pints" (295). We learn that "Half one ... and a hands up" amounts to "Small whisky and bottle of Allsop" (328).[11] Such terminological shifts within the dialogue are a realistic counterpart to the alternation of spoken (ordinary) and parodistic (written, histrionic) parts in the chapter.

Where everybody is expected to wield tropes divertingly, for the fun of it, Bloom remains, even in his most rhetorical moments, factual (whether he gets the facts right or not), sincere and truthful, devoid of Odyssean trickery. The Cyclops chapter exemplifies the free transposition of Homeric material, especially in the diversified distribution of epic roles, and it shows that many of the ill-termed "parallels" are often inverted. Homer's episode confronts the civilized Greeks with uncouth and lawless giants who rely on their muscular strength. Much of this is transferred straight. Humane Bloom is holding his own against opponents who are biased, prejudiced, or brutal. And yet it is also Bloom who does not abide by the laws of the place, and he is even, according to the criteria of the regular customers, a barbarian—he speaks a strange and different language, is not conversant with the rules and yet still speaks out. He is a spoilsport, a disquieting intruder.

Imprudently (and the reader knows why), he talks more than normally. This makes him, in an odd doubling of roles, also a Polyphemus, literally *poly-phemos*, from *pheme* (in turn derived from *phemi*, I speak; cognate with Latin *fama* and "famous"): voice, speech, word, report, renown—and rumor. In fact the whole chapter is *polyphemos*, full of voices, talk, resounding exaggeration, and rumor—with an empty biscuit tin thrown in for bad measure. Conversely, it is as though this episode of elaborate naming were also to utilize the only etymology of the name Odysseus in the whole poem: it connects him with *odyssamenos* (*Od.* 19.407), the participle of a verb "to be angry" ("in great wrath," Butcher and Lang). A surprising number of participants are angry about one thing or another, starting with the narrator, the debtor Geraghty and his contestant Herzog—"the little jewy getting his shirt out" (292), and on to Denis Breen, Bob Doran, Bloom, Garryowen, and the Citizen. Anger lends force to Bloom's two outbursts and his subliminal belligerence. Cyclops is suffused with "suppressed rancour" (312).

Straightforward Bloom is distrusted, but Lenehan (both glibly *polyphemos* and angrily *odyssamenos* about his gambling losses), whose sayings at all times would merit the least literal credibility, is believed immediately when he suspects Bloom to be the only man in Dublin to have won money by backing Throwaway. The reader knows that this *fama* primordially derives from Bantam Lyons projecting onto nongambling Bloom a rhetorical and allusive ingenuity that he neither has nor ever attempts. But it may well be that Bloom's factual bias makes it easier for the others to believe he may have had some inside knowledge, or to believe the other rumor attached to him, that he "gave the idea for Sinn Féin to Griffith" (335): he might well be the sort of person who would help the cause with pertinent specific advice. But not even that momentary patriotic halo bestowed upon Bloom by a tenuous political connection would make him any more popular.

Another interesting quasi-political parallel involves the absent hero Charles Stewart Parnell, who was not a gifted speaker either, and in his early parliamentary appearances even a notably poor one, with at times a stammer.[12] This un-Irish deficiency might have contributed to his cultivation of a pose of taciturnity and aloofness, a manner that would have stood Bloom in good stead when facing Parnell's talkative epigones.

"change the venue"

Bloom's talk, for reasons mentioned, is often cut short by the others, or else the narrator simply ignores the talk and replaces it with his own more racy paraphrases. In the narrator's opinion, Bloom would, and does, talk at length and "talk steady," monotonously so.

In the long run, this might well pall on the reader too. So, following the precedent of the nameless narrator of Cyclops, Joyce from now on does not allow Bloom—or anyone else, for that matter—to "talk steady" *in his own spoken words*. Instead he takes over more and more. The daytalk of *Ulysses* culminates in Barney Kiernan's noisy pub and then gives way to nocturnal transformations. Bloom's unappreciated miniloquence has been sufficiently established and needs no further illustration. But the novel itself becomes more and more extravagantly multiloquent; it begins to change its voices away from actual speech, even though the voices still remain a substratum that can be, on demand, dexterously extrapolated.

Direct transmission of spoken words after Cyclops becomes the exception. What is being said is translated, metempsychosed, reflected into new variations and stranger modes.

Nausicaa contains little dialogue. It is essentially silent and/or stylized according to its own laws. There is just one speech by Bloom, and reported indirectly, though still almost audible: "he said he was sorry his watch was stopped but he thought it must be after eight because the sun was set." Since his watch is not functioning at this point he cannot even do what he is best at, give accurate information, and he has to fall back on circumstantial evidence. Again the reader knows that Bloom's small audience does not really care about the facts offered. Gerty attends, not to what Bloom says, but to how a gentleman expresses himself. She registers the quality of his voice, "a cultured ring," "the mellow tones," or "the measured accents" (*U* 361). A turn like "measured accents" does not really have much denotative point to it; on the other hand, it characterizes, very literally, how heroes speak in epic poetry. Translators of Homer devoted much thought to imitating Greek *meter* by English *stress*. Gertyan diction strains to project the language back to the epic grandeur from which the realistic mode of the book deliberately removed it (note that "cultured ring," "measured accents," or "mellow tones," while wholly appropriate for any Victorian authoress, could all be equivalents of Homeric compound epithets). Bloom's simple speech is variously translated—or dislocuted. Cissy Caffrey, the most linguistically venturesome girl of the group ("jaspberry ram," *U* 353), in her report restates Bloom's words in jocular and more expressive paraphrase, "and said uncle said his waterworks were out of order." She is doing what the book is doing all along, changing the narrative key. The small paragraph is typical of all post-Cyclopian chapters, where actual words spoken tend to be submerged by translation, parody, or commentary. It is a long time till we can be certain we hear Bloom's own voice again.

In Oxen of the Sun dialogue surfaces only rarely verbatim, if at all, and is mainly refined into various literary impersonations. Only the last pages of the chapter look like a return to actual speech faithfully recorded (as if by a tape recorder), as though it were the real performance of a surprisingly articulate group of *ad hoc* orators. But we are not quite sure if this placental verbiage is meant to be the substance of what the students are really saying in precisely these words, in precisely those roles, or whether these spurts of instant ingenuity may not also be tampered with by a more and more manipulative intermediary. Even if the talk is just talk, it is of the kind that Mulligan, for one, can command, and not of the Bloomian variety. One might indeed describe the second part of *Ulysses*—all those chapters, that is, that do not conform to S. L. Goldberg's aesthetic dogmas[13]—as a taking over of the Mulliganesque features that prevailed in Telemachus.

In Circe dialogue is ubiquitous but only part of it is actually real and spoken aloud. And there is no way of dispelling doubt that anything in it might not be imaginary or at least metamorphosed by the governing magic. By now all appearances have become frankly deceptive.

Of the Nostos chapters, only Eumaeus reinstates direct speech, and plenty of it; it is a return to ground that is familiar. Bloom finally takes the opportunity to hold forth at great length, in compensation for all that has gone before. He pulls out all the stops and becomes rhetorically overambitious; he is figurative and metaphorical and engages in elegant variations—all to no avail, of course, as Stephen is only minimally interested in what Bloom says and not at all in the way he says it. But again, does Bloom really and extendedly speak like that, *verbatim*? Are the following Bloom's actual words, faithfully transcribed:

> —Spaniards, for instance.... passionate temperaments like that, impetuous as Old Nick, are given to taking the law into their own hands and give you your quietus double quick with those poignards they carry in the abdomen. (637)

There are his idioms, his recognizable cadences, and yet his diction, especially in this relentlessly concentrated form, may be tarred with the brush that is responsible for the stylistic idiosyncrasies of the whole chapter, which of course, in turn, merely exaggerate the potential of his own mind. Perhaps it just no longer makes sense to distinguish actual performance from what are no doubt oratorical aspirations and those, in turn, from the mode of the chapter. *Ulysses* also teaches us to let go—reluctantly, at times—some of those neat categories that our minds have been brought up on. In practical terms this might mean that, at this late stage, we may not even trust the dashes any longer, that typographical convention by which, so far, direct speech has been honestly set off from the rest of the narration. Sounds and speeches and dashes may be impostures in Eumaeus, a chapter of guises and subterfuges.

Clearly, both Circe and Eumaeus, in their own particular modes, hint at a distorted fulfillment of Bloom's rhetorical (and authorial) aspirations, as if in compensation for what he cannot bring off in his actual day by day performances. Yet in both chapters of wishful triumphs, Bloom's fumbles and blunders too are magnified correspondingly and grotesquely.

And again, it seems that Joyce removes the novel at this point from even these highly hypothetical excrescences of Bloomian ambitions with their semblance of direct quotation. In Ithaca direct speech has disappeared entirely and given way to pointedly oblique report, which is catalogued deadpan along with everything else, though we can, of course, try to reconstruct Bloom's and Stephen's actual spoken words by an empirical, inductive process.

The Peneloquence of the last chapter is unspoken, though based on spoken language, and *sui generis*. It does, however, reintroduce some of Bloom's sentences to Molly, spoken with effect and remembered with relish. Bloom undoubtedly is capable, at times. Even so, without the setting of rhododendrons and romantic wooing, "the sun shines for you" and you are "a flower of the mountain" (782) are not necessarily, by themselves, evidence of remarkable rhetorical potential.

"*various different varieties*"

In grammatical metaphor, Bloom's progress through his fourteen chapters is from the predominant indicative mood (corresponding to his acts, thoughts, and talk) into different moods like subjunctive or optative, expressing more the aspirations, imaginary achievements, fears, or wishful thinking. Much of Circe is written in a kind of conditional: *if* Bloom could get up for a stump speech, and *if* he could conjure up the right phrases on the spur of the moment, and *if* ..., then he might undergo such rapid changes and rise to glory and also suffer such ignominies. And if he had the resources of a Mr Philip Beaufcy (or, as he seems to think, of Stephen Dedalus, poet and man of letters), then he might be able to compose such figurative, parabolic, ornate, winged, fumbling, discordant, and alert (yes, alert) prose as the one of Eumaeus.

The rhetorics and tropes Bloom lacks in everyday life are lavished on the novel as a novel, with increasing boldness. The book as an event in language plays most of the roles, along with, and above, the characters. The smooth and sweet and cunning words that Odysseus contrives when he first addresses Nausicaa (*Od.* 6.143 ff.) are never even attempted by Bloom, but they inform the first part of the softly featured and mellifluent chapter. Beyond the reaches of any one person, the book becomes mercurial, myriadminded, multifaceted, histrionic, and polytropically all-round.

The mind around which all this mainly revolves is, like most minds, relatively pedestrian. Mr Bloom's own utterances can be improved upon by a good translation. So Joyce comes to his aid and more and more conspicuously runs the show on his behalf, with transformations, transmutations, transubstantiations, and metamorphoses, with different contexts and styles and parallactic systems of correspondences. It did not occur to the detractors of *Ulysses* that even its more elaborate features, whatever else, also work against the boredom of anything that is carried on for too long. That is all done with a purpose and with consideration for the reader, believe it or not, "to cheer a fellow up" (107).

Joyce puts poor Bloom, who endures many troubles and hardships (*Od.* 1.4), at one of the greatest further disadvantages, by depriving him of a quality that Homer, the Greeks, the Irish, and most lovers of literature and talk, value highly. But he lends him his sympathy, does duty as his own personal Muse and gives assistance by metaphrasing more and more of his words and by providing him (though Bloom would never know)—and us (and we had better know it)—with a course in remedial rhetorics.

NOTES

1. I discuss "Chrysostomos" as narrative deviation in the essay "Metastasis," reprinted in this volume.

2. "*Polytropos*, he [Antisthenes] argues, does not refer to character or ethics at all. It simply denotes Odysseus's skill in adapting his figures of speech ('tropes') to his hearers at any particular time." In W. B. Stanford, *The Ulysses Theme: A Study in the Adaptability of a Traditional Hero*, 2nd ed. (Ann Arbor: University of Michigan Press, 1968), p. 99. See my essay "Odysseeische Metamorphosen," in *James Joyce's "Ulysses": Neuere deutsche Aufsätze*, ed. Therese Fischer-Seidel (Frankfurt: Edition Suhrkamp, 1977), p. 44; and Michael Groden, *"Ulysses" in Progress* (Princeton: Princeton University Press, 1977), pp. 91–92.

3. "Yet [Bloom] must be separated from those about him, and by the gift of expression—the highest a writer can bestow on his creature.... But Bloom has to speak in ordinary language ... taking a keen pleasure in manoeuvring among common idioms, allusions, and proverbs. It is this power of speech, mostly inward speech, that inclines Bloom towards Odysseus." In Richard Ellmann, *Ulysses on the Liffey* (London: Faber and Faber, 1972), p. 30.

4. Marvin Magalaner, "Leopold Bloom before *Ulysses*," *Modern Language Notes* 68 (February 1953): 110–12.

5. But then, Bloom's first words spoken in "Aeolus" constitute the best all-time editorial advice that fits all occasions: "Just cut it out" (16).

6. The implication is that eloquence is not everything, and anyway, the Lord said, "Who hath made man's mouth" (Exod. 4:11). Intriguingly, Stephen, who has worked "mouth" into the semiplagiarized creation recalled in the chapter, speculates at length on the reverberations of this word. "Must be some" (138).

7. See also Phillip F. Herring, ed., *Joyce's Notes and Early Drafts for "Ulysses ": Selections from the Buffalo Collection* (Charlottesville: University Press of Virginia, 1977), p. 146; and Groden, *"Ulysses" in Progress*, p. 133ff. To all these lists might be added the parallel that in both chapters Bloom appears twice and on his return gets worse treatment each time.

8. The Citizen's "No music and no art and no literature worthy of the name" (325) follows, roughly, a pattern set in Taylor's speech (142).

9. Hugh B. Staples, "'Ribbonmen' Signs and Passwords in *Ulysses*," *Notes and Queries*, n.s. 13 (1966): 95–96.

10. In the roll call of great Jews in Bloom's enumeration (342), Mercadante is the odd one out, by no stretch of ethnic definition a Jew. What happened is that Bloom has been confusing two composers he likes for different reasons, Mercadante (82) and Meyerbeer (168). In "Sirens" he wrongly attributed *Seven Last Words* to Meyerbeer (290) and now, in his unrehearsed speech, seems to make up for it. He means Meyerbeer, whose opera *The Hugenots* is about religious persecution.

11. It is important to have no misunderstanding interfere with the order of one's drink, but these variations also comply to the avoidance of mere repetition in conventional rhetorics.

12. Pointed out to me by Wayne Hall, a former student at Indiana University, who mentioned this when an earlier version of this essay was presented as a talk.

13. S. L. Goldberg, *The Classical Temper: A Study of James Joyce's "Ulysses"* (London: Chatto and Windus, 1961); to this day still the best book ever written against *Ulysses*.

SUZETTE A. HENKE

Uncoupling Ulysses:
Joyce's New Womanly Man

There is only desire and the social, and nothing else.
(Deleuze and Guattari, *Anti-Oedipus*)

The unconscious ceases to be what it is—a factory, a workshop—to become a theater, a scene and its staging.

(ibid.)

In *Ulysses*, Joyce depicts an epic hero who is also a pacifist, a Jew, a *petit bourgeois* businessman, a commercial traveler, a voyeur, an exhibitionist, and an ostensibly inadequate husband. Because psychological positions are mobile and transferable in the landscape of the novel, Leopold Bloom is alternately powerful and obsequious, feminized and flagellated, politically exalted and socially humiliated. He emerges as a "new womanly man" and unconventional hero who seems, paradoxically, to inhabit those marginal spaces on the edge of social discourse usually reserved for women and for cultural deviants.

A connoisseur of the sensuous joys of polymorphous perversity, Bloom proves to be androgynous not only in terms of psychological temperament but in libidinal orientation, as well. He apparently retrieves the primordial erotic impulses rejected by Freud in *Civilization and its Discontents*—those

From *James Joyce and the Politics of Desire*. ©1990 by Routledge University Press.

primitive olfactory and tactile responses that the father of psychoanalysis ascribed somewhat speciously to the female of the species, in contrast to the supposedly visual and oculocentric sexual economy associated with the male.[1] Bloom manifests a curious infantile "cloacal obsession" with excrementa cast off by the body. He smells the pickings of his toenails, relishes the tang of urine in a fried pork kidney, and is obsessively preoccupied with menstrual excrescences. The Lacanian phallus is displaced in his symbolic imagination by a fetishistic concern with breasts and bottoms, feces, menses, urine, and other physical secretions. Throughout *Ulysses*, "Baby Bloom" finds himself tantalized by purportedly feminine pulsions that replicate infantile attachment to the imaginary body of a beneficent and powerful phallic mother: "Be near her ample bedwarmed flesh. Yes, yes" (*U* 4: 238–9). "A warm human plumpness settled down on his brain.... Perfume of embraces all him assailed. With hungered flesh obscurely, he mutely craved to adore" (*U* 8: 647–9).

Throughout the novel, most of the female characters take shape as vivid projections of Bloom's richly heterogeneous fantasy life. They are inscribed in *his* imagination as figures of physical need or sadomasochistic impulse, visceral pity or sensuous attraction. Despite the epicene aspects of his sexual proclivities, Bloom tends to assess women in his environment as amorous objects stoking playful vignettes of the dreaming mind. His farraginous interior monologue offers a pentimento portrait of Irish society that includes such diverse sources of titillation as the next-door girl with a strong pair of arms and "crooked skirt swinging, whack by whack ... behind her moving hams" (*U* 4: 164, 172) and a well-dressed lady, gloved and booted, haughtily mounting a carriage in front of the Grosvenor: "Watch! Watch! Silk flash rich stockings white. Watch!" (*U* 5: 130). In a moment of voyeuristic fantasy, Bloom speculates: "Women all for caste till you touch the spot.... Possess her once take the starch out of her" (*U* 5: 104–6). He admires Amazonian females like Lady Mountcashel: "Riding astride. Sit her horse like a man. Weightcarrying huntress.... Strong as a brood mare some of those horsey women" (*U* 8: 343–5); and like Mrs Miriam Dandrade "that sold me her old wraps and black underclothes in the Shelbourne hotel. Divorced Spanish American.... Want to be a bull for her. Born courtesan" (*U* 8 350–7). Women excite or repel him, tease or titillate him; but all of their figurations suggest that in the course of *Ulysses*, Bloom is rewriting the text of turn-of-the-century sex-role enculturation in the discourse of polymorphously perverse desire.

In the persona of Henry Flower, Esquire, Bloom conducts a clandestine epistolary affair with Martha Clifford, a lonely and pathetic working-girl who pines for release from the prison of dreary secretarial duties. Martha complains of boredom, and headaches, longs to consummate this illicit liaison with her would-be lover, and takes curious pleasure in his obscene communications. But, like the virtuous Edwardian lady she was raised to be, Martha protests, "I called you naughty boy because I do not like that other world" (*U* 5: 244–5). Too exhausted and bleary-eyed to correct her typographical error, Martha fails to recognize the contradictions implicit in her quest for the "real meaning of that word" she does not like. She assures Henry: "I have never felt myself so much drawn to a man as you.... O how I long to meet you. Henry dear, do not deny my request before my patience are exhausted. Then I will tell you all" (*U* 5: 249–54). Martha tantalizes her pen-friend with promises of forbidden sexual discourse, but her patience and confidence have, indeed, been misplaced in the cautious married man she unwittingly tries to seduce. Bloom, despite a professed interest in social justice, attributes her depression and physical discomfort to menstrual malady rather than situational angst: "Such a bad headache. Has her roses probably" (*U* 5: 285). In "Lotus-Eaters," a chapter of flowers, the exhausted Martha is too busy earning her bread to be greatly concerned about the roses denied her—though she does, apparently, take some kind of masochistic pleasure from the thorns of Bloom's pornographic letters designed to pique erotic curiosity.

In the "Nausicaa" episode, Bloom responds to Gerty MacDowell's sentimental striptease with a kind of Zola-esque naturalism. Aroused by her tantalizing display of exhibitionism, he gives the young woman the impression that his strange "dark eyes" are "drinking in her every contour, literally worshipping at her shrine" (*U* 13: 563–4). With a little help from Maria Susanna Cummins's *Lamplighter*, Gerty romanticizes this, exotic stranger, sanitizes his masturbation, and idealizes his worshipful attentions. As Virgin Mary of Sandymount, she invites the tribute of Bloom's profane ejaculations, reinscribed in adolescent consciousness by that "dream of love, the dictates of her heart that told her he was her all in all, the only man in the world for her for love was the master guide" (*U* 13: 671–2).[2]

This "sterling man, a man of inflexible honour to his fingertips" (*U* 13: 694) evaluates the scene with the same phenomenological accuracy one might associate with the comic caricature of Herr Professor Luitpold Blumenduft in "Cyclops": "Near her monthlies, I expect, makes them feel ticklish.... How many women in Dublin have it today? Martha, she.... Anyhow I got the best of that.... Thankful for small mercies. Cheap too. Yours for the asking. Because they want it themselves" (*U* 13: 777–90). Bloom's matter-of-fact interpretation of his onanistic encounter with Gerty is fairly mechanical: "My fireworks. Up like a rocket, down like a stick" (*U* 13: 894–5). His response may seem self-serving, if not brutal: "Did me good all the same.... For this relief much thanks" (*U* 13: 939–40). But his post-orgasmic thoughts about Gerty are also imbued with feelings of pity and tinged with paternal solicitude. Stunned by his recognition of her lameness, Bloom thinks: "Poor girl! That's why she's left on the shelf and the others did a sprint" (*U* 13: 772–3). He feels grateful to Gerty for reaffirming his sense of manhood and acknowledges that their erotic adventure involved some form of mutuality and communication, "a kind of language between us" (*U* 13: 944).

Bloom sees in this postpubescent girl a figure of his own developing daughter Milly, whom he tenderly recalls in nostalgic reverie now that she has left home for an apprenticeship in photography down in Mullingar and is about to burgeon into a "wild piece of goods": "O, well: she knows how to mind herself. But if not? No, nothing has happened. Of course it might.... Ripening now. Vain: very" (*U* 4: 428–31). He remembers Milly's childhood fear of being deserted and the terror she experienced at the first bloody sign of womanly/wombly maturation: "Her growing pains at night, calling, wakening me. Frightened she was when her nature came on her first. Poor child! Strange moment for the mother too" (*U* 13: 1201–3). Just as Molly will later think through Stephen to Bloom, so the husband moves from the incident with Gerty to memories of female fragility and his daughter's growing-pains and finally to that ever-present object of sexual desire dominating his obsessed imagination, the fascinating but elusive figure of Mother-Molly.

The majority of Bloom's reveries about sexual difference seem to circle around reproductive potential, and both mammary endowments and fleshly opulence are high on his list of sex-linked preoccupations. Hence his fascination with Molly's ponderous female bulk as he stares at "her large soft bubs, sloping within her nightdress like a shegoat's udder" (*U* 4: 304–5). Much of Bloom's attention is obliquely focused on imaginary projections of an idealized maternity which he associates with the female body/breast/womb/genitalia. Although he can crassly reduce women to figures of oral, genital, and anal absence ("Three holes, all women" [*U* 11: 1089]), he is the only male in the novel to empathize with "poor Mrs Purefoy" in the throes of a painful *accouchement*: "Three days imagine groaning on a bed with a vinegared handkerchief round her forehead, her belly swollen out. Phew! Dreadful simply! ... Kill me that would.... Life with hard labour" (*U* 8: 373–8). Bloom can imagine the pain of parturition in a vivid evocation of the obstetrical labors of women, and his fantasies later collapse into a dream of masculine couvade. "I so want to be a mother," he declares in "Circe," then metaphorically *"bears eight male yellow and while children ... handsome, with valuable metallic faces"* (*U* 15: 1817–24). Apparently,

Bloom tends to fear what he most desires: woman as mother and fertile creator, the figure of matriarchal power that he tacitly worships in Molly and concretizes in his expressionistic encounter with Bella/Bello the Circean circus-master.

When sex-roles are tested on the stage of language, as they are in "Circe," gender-linked scripts prove absurdly intransigent. Bloom's deepest and most repressed fears erupt in dramatic fantasies of erotic compulsion and sexual loathing in Bella Cohen's ten-shilling whorehouse. Power relations, culturally inscribed in Edwardian consciousness, remain surprisingly stable, as phallocentric authority passes from male to female in a transvestite drama that parodies the psychosexual scripts that dominate 1904 Dublin. Even the "new womanly man" acting out the feminine vulnerability of his epicene nature gives voice to iterations of female helplessness, subservience, and sexual humiliation.[3]

It is only within the heterogeneous representation of Bloom's masculine–feminine, active–passive character that gender identity becomes dynamic and reversible. As Shoshana Felman explains: "Masculinity is not a substance, nor is femininity its empty complement, a *heimlich* womb.... Femininity *inhabits* masculinity, inhabits it as otherness, as its own disruption. Femininity, in other words, is a pure difference, a signifier, and so is masculinity."[4] In the expressionistic world of "Circe," Joyce explores that specular icon of feminine gender that inhabits the male cultural imagination. Bella/Bello Cohen, as fetishistic embodiment of the phallic mother, serves as a screen image for Bloom's projected fantasy of his own somewhat willful and tyrannical spouse. He himself is transformed into a woman and then into a pig through a "substitutive signifying chain which subverts ... the clear-cut polarity, the symmetrical dual opposition, of male and female, masculine and feminine."[5] As Daniel Ferrer observes, "Bloom's masochistic phantasy paradoxically takes the form of a kind of breaking-in of Bella/Bello: the masculinization of the dominating woman is quite as important as the pseudo-feminization of the victim. The game is double-edged."[6]

What is in question in the "Circe" episode is Leopold Bloom's culturally constructed manhood and the phallic signifier that affirms or denies his status as male/father/husband in a twentieth-century Oedipal configuration—the "Daddy–Mommy–Me" triangle defined by Deleuze and Guattari in *Anti-Oedipus* and replicated in religious trinitarian models. In the course of the chapter, Bloom temporarily adopts a schizoid position characterized, in Deleuzian terms, by libidinal viscosity: "flows ooze, they traverse the triangle, breaking apart its vertices."[7] Exploring repressed bisexual drives that challenge traditional domestic arrangements, Bloom moves in and out of the restrictive frame of reproductive triangulation

dictated by culturally inscribed paradigms of masculine sexuality. The
chapter offers a plurality of signs confirming Bloom's psychological
androgyny. He is first male, then female; and, finally, at the "Bip" of a trouser
button, he regains his precarious sense of Oedipal identity.

The primordial sign of Bloom's maleness, his phallus, is first
symbolically present, then absent in a game of sexual metamorphosis and
phallic veiling that entails both cross-dressing and imaginary genital
transformation. Bloom is symbolically castrated by Bello, the imperious
semitic circus-master who, as priestess of a Levitican sacrifice mimicking
exaggerated circumcision, "debags" her timid victim.[8] In Circean fashion,
she porcines the obsequious male who admits to being a secret "adorer of the
adulterous rump" (*U* 15: 2839). A pagan devotee and worshipper of the
voluptuous female body, Bloom admires precisely those aspects of physical
form that Molly scorns as impersonal features of animal passivity, the "same
two lumps of lard" that fail to confirm personal attractiveness.

The phallic icon of Bloom's socially sanctioned manhood is present in
the mode of absence as he acts out a bizarre transsexual metempsychosis.
Paradoxically, when the prominent signifiers of Bloom's epicene
personality—his sympathy, gentleness, vulnerability, and solicitude—are
reinscribed in an ostensibly female register, they are radically transformed in
the context of cultural interpretation. With Bloom's metamorphosis into a
woman, his compassion and gentleness give way to masochistic subservience.
Although this modern-day Odysseus is recognizably androgynous, his most
sympathetic and endearing qualities take on absurd dramatic resonance when
the ground of gender changes from male to female. What is admirable in the
emotionally bisexual male becomes a sign of debilitating weakness on the
part of a defenseless, quaking "womanly woman" exploited by the "manly
man" of Victorian pornography. Bella/Bello has leapt from the pages of
Frank Harris, of Huysmans's *A Rebours*, and of titillating texts like Sacher-
Masoch's *Venus in Furs* to perpetrate lascivious acts of brutality on Poldy's
feminized body.[9] Hence Bloom's ignominious fall from manhood when Bello
orders:

> Down! (*he taps her on the shoulder with his fan*) incline feet forward!
> Slide left foot one pace back! You will fall.... On the hands down!

>   BLOOM
> (*her eyes upturned in the sign of admiration, closing, yaps*) Truffles!
> (*With a piercing epileptic cry she sinks on all fours, grunting, snuffling,
> rooting at his feet; then lies, shamming dead, with eyes shut tight,
> trembling eyelids, bowed upon the ground in the attitude of most
> excellent master.*)

BELLO

(*with bobbed hair, purple gills, fat moustache rings round his shaven mouth, in mountaineer's puttees, green silverbuttoned coat, sport skirt and alpine hat with moorcock's feather, his hands stuck deep in his breeches, pockets, places his heel on her neck and grinds it in*) Footstool! Feel my entire weight. Bow, bondslave, before the throne of your despot's glorious heels so glistening in their proud erectness.

BLOOM

(*enthralled, bleats*) I promise never to disobey. (*U* 15: 2847–64)

Joyce seems to be suggesting, like Deleuze and Guattari, that cultural laws of gender are constant insofar as they are manifest in contemporary social representation. The whoremistress acquires all the accoutrements of imperialistic power as soon as she dons male trousers and sprouts a moustache. As ringmaster and tyrannous phallic mother, Bella/Bello demeans, humiliates, and tortures her obsequious victim. A battered Bloom succumbs to ritual degradation and becomes the ham-holocaust to be slaughtered and skewered, then served up as "fat hamrashers" (*U* 15: 2896) in a sumptuous, non-kosher cannibalistic feast. Both Amazonian woman and effeminate male, enacting transvestite and transsexual roles of Edwardian pantomime, are inscribed in a melodrama of sadomasochistic catharsis.[10]

Bloom has given birth to the figure of Bello in his own tortured imagination, projecting his psychic need for punishment into the powerful *imago* of a manly woman, a carnivalesque embellishment of his generally supine spouse. Bella/Bello plays on Bloom's guilt and conjugal inadequacy—irrational responses evoked by his paternal failure to engender a viable male heir. "If it's healthy it's from the mother," he thinks. "If not from the man" (*U* 6: 329). Cross-dressing offers a mode of phallic veiling, a cover for his repressed sense of genital mutilation. If the child Rudy is metaphorically represented as a surrogate penis in Bloom's sexual imagination, then the grieving father must continually be punished for his son's death through psychological enactments of symbolic castration. Freud emphasizes in *The Interpretation of Dreams* the interchangeability of paternal and filial positions in the language of the unconscious. Having sired a son who was unable to survive, Bloom mentally changes places with the neonate and expresses his horror of filial loss through emotional rejection of phallic power. He internalizes both the guilt elicited by poor papa's suicide and the pain of little Rudy's death. Father, child, and phallus occupy the same psychological position in Bloom's unconscious, and all have become pathological symptoms of loss and bereavement.

The impotent Bloom, sonless and fatherless, is defined in terms of phallic lack: having nothing (but a daughter) to show for a lifetime of heterosexual engagement, he reverts to passive, homosexual, or feminized subject-positions that demand a posture of phallic subjugation. Unmanned by a socially defined pathology of male shame and sexual inadequacy, he adopts an ostensibly feminine persona. If "all is lost" in terms of traditional Oedipal triangulation, then the only hope of escape from psychic breakdown resides in the schizoid position of mental flow, process, viscosity, and disruption—a chaotic metamorphosis of shifting sexual identities enacted on the discursive stage of Circean pantomime.[11]

At this point in the carnivalesque fantasy, tropes are reified, and signifiers of sex and gender prove absurdly interchangeable. The swinish behavior of lascivious males is mythically hypostasized, first by allusion to the Homeric narrative of Circe the evil temptress, then in a Joycean expressionistic drama that allows Bloom to realize his most shameful, anarchic, and deeply repressed libidinal drives. The text of Joyce's pantomime reinforces those fetishistic signs attributed by the unconscious to the omnipotent phallic mother—an imperious female who sporadically offers nurturance but enjoys, at the same time, invidious power to demean, de-sex, and castrate the defenseless male. The phallic sign of masculine identity, once subverted or repressed, releases a flood of male fantasies depicted by the psyche in female guise. Traditional signs of gender-related authority seem indelibly inscribed on twentieth-century cultural consciousness, albeit in atavistic form.

In her male incarnation, Bella/Bello becomes authoritarian and violently sadistic, torturing Bloom to the point of absolute alterity. He is other, "*l'autre*"—first trembling in shame before his masterful captor, then enslaved to her dictates, and finally derided as a "maid of all work" trained to "fetch and carry" (*U* 15: 3086–8) in the chaotic bordello of Joyce's fictive imagination. As soon as Bloom's gender changes from male to female, his androgynous attributes are deracinated from their masculine context and conflated with cultural stereotypes of feminine, fragility. The new womanly man is reduced to the archaic subject-position of powerless womanly woman, as the female aspects of bisexual desire erupt in comic mockery. Compassion degenerates into impotence, androgyny into transvestite humiliation. The dramatic text is uprooted from realistic mimesis, and expressionistic drama gives rise to jubilant *écriture*. The narrative explodes in a riot of cathartic comedy, as "Circe" enunciates the polyphonic novel's "underlying unconscious: sexuality and death. Out of the dialogue ... the structural dyads of carnival appear: high and low, birth and agony, food and excrement, praise and curses, laughter and tears."[12] The poles of Joyce's dialogic imagination prove to be those of Bakhtin's carnival, as desire, unrestrained, flows through the schizoid gap between binary oppositional constructs: subject/object, male/female, death/birth, excrement/nurture, blood/milk.

In his/her female incarnation, Poldy/Paula manifests all the signs of feminine gender dictated by the ritual inscriptions of sex-role stereotypes. S/he colludes in his/her own victimization by meeting the erotic demands of the prostitutes and consenting to sadomasochistic practices. "O, it's hell itself!" (*U* 15: 2908) screams L. Paula Bloom, who nevertheless allows gestures of physical defilement to be perpetrated on his/her effeminate flesh by Bello, Zoe, Florry, and the bordello cook, Mrs Keogh. Bowing at the feet of Bello, Bloom acknowledges his/her authority as "Master! Mistress! Mantamer!" (*U* 15: 3062). Auctioned off to the highest bidder, s/he undergoes various animal metamorphoses as horse, cow, and chicken: "Fourteen hands high. Touch and examine shis points. Handle hrim. This downy skin, these soft muscles, this tender flesh. If I had only my gold piercer here! And quite easy to milk. Three newlaid gallops a day" (*U* 15: 3103–5). The defenseless Bloom is forced to give milk and lay eggs in agricultural postures that parody his/her mammary obsession and henpecked connubial role.[13]

It is clear from role-reversals in "Circe" that; in terms of cultural representation, female gender confers parodic marginality. Woman seems destined to play the part of *l'autre*, alienated other in the specular projections of the male libidinal imagination. When Bloom is auctioned by Bello in a satirical rendition of the bourgeois marriage market, his feminized genitalia become literal objects of commercial exchange. Feminine sexuality, represented as a hole or Freudian absence, absorbs a plethora of masculine fantasies that fill the castrated signature envisaged at the heart of female identity. Bello "*bares his arm and plunges it elbowdeep in Bloom's vulva*," exclaiming "There's fine depth for you!" (*U* 15: 3089–90) in mock imitation of heterosexual penetration and homosexual fisting. The victim's genitals are visibly mutilated as indelible signs of woman's enslavement to male phallocentric desire. "That give you a hardon?" (*U* 15: 3090) Bello inquires. Then s/he orders: "Let them all come.... Bring all your powers of fascination to bear on them. Pander to their Gomorrahan vices" (*U* 15: 3114–22). Bello savagely violates the vaginal hole denied the wholeness of sexual integrity. Every female orifice, it would appear, is for sale and on display; every hole can be purchased, raped, or penetrated for the purpose of phallic satisfaction.[14] And a good woman, raped, knows, like the disgraced cuckold, what to do: "Die and be damned to you if you have any sense of decency or grace about you" (*U* 15: 3204–5). In this expressionistic battle of the sexes, the power of an imaginary phallic mother manifests itself as monstrous and obscene. As textual icon of matriarchal authority, Bello assumes the right to debase and colonize Bloom's vulnerable, objectified, mock-female body.

As woman/Jew/victim; the hapless Poldy is reduced to little more than
a cipher of racial and sexual oppression. The male/female drama of courtship
and conquest unfolds as an age-old atavistic tale:

> Woman, undoing with sweet pudor her belt of rushrope, offers
> her allmoist yoni to man's lingam. Short time after man presents
> woman with pieces of jungle meat. Woman shows joy and covers
> herself with featherskins. Man loves her yoni fiercely with big
> lingam, the stiff one. (*he cries*) *Coactus volui*. Then giddy woman
> will run about. Strong man grapses woman's wrist. Woman
> squeals, bites, spucks. Man, now fierce angry, strikes woman's fat
> yadgana. (*U* 15: 2549–55)

This primitive tableau of meat and mating, of giddy flirtation and animal
friction, pornographically climaxes in sexual violence. Brutality inhabits the
underside of romantic courtship, and if the playmate of this behemoth lover
dares to arouse his lust, she must suffer the consequences of bestial cupidity.

When Bloom is transformed into a woman by Bella/Bello, he loses his
dignity along with the accoutrements of masculine pride. The repressed
feminine tendencies of this heroic androgyne erupt in a ludic play of erotic
madness. The bellicose matriarchal figure, usurping the male role that Poldy
is hesitant to enact, becomes a nightmare fantasy of the stereotypical
virago—a phallic mother invested with all the privileges of uninhibited
patriarchal authority. The semiology of gender remains unchanged, as
various *dramatis personae* appear in transvestite or transsexual guises. Even
the comedy of language cannot alter the binary codes of gender or the deeply
embedded sex-roles inscribed in societal consciousness. The text seems to
evoke the pervasive cultural fear that woman, granted phallic authority,
would persecute her mate with unbridled ferocity; and that man, bereft of the
kind of patriarchal power that buttresses an illusory sense of dominance and
mastery, would sink helplessly into sexual degradation.

BELLO

> What else are you good for, an impotent thing like you? ... Up!
> Up! Manx cat! What have we here? Where's your curly teapot
> gone to or who docked it on you, cockyolly? Sing, birdy, sing. It's
> as limp as a boy of six's doing his pooly behind a cart. Buy a
> bucket or sell your pump.... Can you do a man's job? (*U* 15:
> 3127–32)

When sex-roles are again comically reversed, a feminized Bella plays
the saccharine part of an ethereal nymph who incarnates the Edwardian

womanly ideal—an icon of grace and reverence, unsullied by either food or feces. "We immortals," proclaims the nymph, "have not such a place and no hair there either. We are stonecold and pure. We eat electric light" (*U* 15: 3392–3). This self-glorified, asexual image of the female is no more attractive than her opposite narrative number, Bello the sadistic ringmaster. "You have broken the spell," Bloom insists. "The last straw. If there were only ethereal where would you all be, postulants and novices? Shy but willing like an ass pissing" (*U* 15: 3449–51). Because sexual violence contaminates both ethereal and aggressive icons, the mirror image of Bloom's virginal seductress is a demonic succubus intent on castration. The saintly sprite, offended by Bloom's erotic indictment, grabs a poniard and strikes at his loins, then "*flees from him unveiled, her plaster cast cracking, a cloud of stench escaping from the cracks*" (*U* 15: 3469–70). Recognizing the antagonistic Bello emerging from angelic disguise, Bloom mimics abusive phallic authority and insults the transvestite (or hermaphroditic) impersonator: "Fool someone else, not me.... Rut. Onions. Stale. Sulphur. Grease.... Mutton dressed as lamb.... I'm not a triple screw propeller.... Clean your nailless middle finger first, your bully's cold spunk is dripping from your cockscomb" (*U* 15: 3477–93).

Joyce's polytropic man soon relinquishes this ill-fitting role of brutal *machismo* when he witnesses a dramatic enactment of his wife's seduction by that Dublin Don Giovanni, Blazes Boylan. Here the "coronado" [*cornuto*] husband wears a visible signature of cuckoldry, the antlered hat-rack of conjugal infamy.[15] He serves as eager flunkey to Molly's suitor, whose penile equipment is ostentatiously on show:

BOYAN

(*to Bloom, over his shoulder*) You can apply your eye to the keyhole and play with yourself while I just go through her a few times.

BLOOM

Thank you, sir. I will, sir. May I bring two men chums to witness the deed and take a snapshot? (*he holds out an ointment jar*) Vaseline, sir? Orangeflower...? Lukewarm water...?

KITTY

(*from the sofa*) Tell us, Florry. Tell us. What ... (*Florry whispers to her. Whispering lovewords murmur, liplapping loudly, poppysmic plopslop.*)

MINA KENNEDY

(*her eyes upturned*) O, it must be like the scent of geraniums and

lovely peaches! O, he simply idolises every bit of her! Stuck
together! Covered with kisses!

LYDIA DOUCE

(*her mouth opening*) Yumyum, O, he's carrying her round the room
doing it! Ride a cockhorse. You could hear them in Paris and New
York. Like mouthfuls of strawberries and cream.

KITTY

(*laughing*) Hee hee hee.

BOYLAN'S VOICE

(*sweetly, hoarsely, in the pit of his stomach*) Ah! Godblazegruk-
brukarchkhrasht!

MARION'S VOICE

(*hoarsely, sweetly, rising to her throat*) O! Weeshwashtkissinapooisth-
napoohuck? (*U* 15: 3788–813)

Bloom's gaze is transfixed before the scene of ritual conquest, as he yells
locker-room cheers through the keyhole and urges his sexual surrogate to
prodigious heights of erotic performance: "(*his eyes wildly dilated, clasps
himself*) Show! Hide! Show! Plough her! More! Shoot!" (*U* 15: 3815–16).

The presence-absence of Boylan's ithyphallic member signifies for the
excited onlooker both masochistic humiliations and scopophiliac *jouissance*.
In this outrageous enactment of caricatured cuckoldry, the timorous Bloom
relives the pain of conjugal loss in the mode of voyeuristic farce. He mentally
panders to the lascivious Boylan, whose virility signifies the kind of erotic
potency glaringly absent from Bloom's own sexual relations with his wife.
Participating as flunkey at the scene of Molly's infidelity, Bloom self-
consciously reinterprets the signs of connubial disruption from the
privileged perspective of dramatic choreographer. Acting as technical
director of the comedy, he symbolically sutures the wound of cuckoldry by
dramatizing marital transgression in the stylized frame of a turn-of-the-
century peepshow. The seriously embattled scenario of *Exiles* is here
replayed as *Commedia del'Arte*.

Like a clownish rendition of Richard Rowan, Bloom revises the text of
his wife's adultery in a grotesque fantasy that resembles French farce, not to
mention the titillating fabulations of Victorian pornography embodied in
Sweets of Sin. By imaginatively colluding in the subversion of marital stability,
by up-ending traditional expectations and putting his own phallic powers

deliberately under erasure, Bloom participates in the carnivalesque comedy not as unwitting victim, but as the author/actor/director of this play of infidelity. Through the dual role of playwright and spectator, he is able, like Sacher-Masoch's fictive Severin, to reduce his ignominious situation to an absurdly masochistic drama. In the course of "Circe," Bloom becomes author and reader of his own domestic narrative, gaining artistic control over emotional trauma by recreating the dread event in exaggerated detail on the stage of a highly charged erotic (and perverse) imagination.[16]

A projection of deeply embedded guilt, this preposterous dramatic fantasy offers Bloom the gratifications of both aesthetic mastery and psychological catharsis. In the dreamscape of "Circe," Bloom doffs the culturally inscribed role of irate cuckold to wear the costume of flunkey; but, like a dramatist who plays the Fool in a script of his own making, he asserts authorial primacy as godlike director of the scene. As playwright and participant, Bloom witnesses his wife's afternoon tryst from the standpoint of God, Shakespeare, and scopophiliac voyeur. He imitates that picaresque "playwright who wrote the folio of this world and wrote it badly, ... the lord of things as they are," the hangman-god who "is doubtless all in all in all of us, ostler and butcher, and would be bawd and cuckold too but that in the economy of heaven, foretold by Hamlet, there are no more marriages, glorified man, an androgynous angel, being a wife unto himself" (*U* 9: 1047–52). Playing bawd and cuckold onstage, Bloom strives to become in his own imagination a self-sufficient and, self-delighting "wife unto himself" by framing his spouse and her lover, gazing at them through a keyhole, and satisfying his own libidinous urges in masturbatory acts of playful postcreation.[17]

In "Circe," Bloom's polymorphous perversity and his masochistic longing for protection/punishment at the hands of a powerful woman have imploded in rich, hallucinatory, and schizoid images. The expressionistic drama depicts Bloom's repressed terror and obsessive fascination with the *imago* of a manly female, a fascistic figure of sensual domination. Libidinal desire gives rise to a polymorphous dissemination of sexual signifiers that destroy the univocal, phallocentric drives of masculinity and articulate deep-seated transsexual fantasies embedded in the psyche of Joyce's womanly man. "Circe" evokes what Hélène Cixous delineates as "a proliferating, maternal femininity. A phantasmic meld of men, males, gentlemen, monarchs, princes, orphans, flowers, mothers, breasts gravitates about a wonderful 'sun of energy' ... that bombards and disintegrates these ephemeral amorous anomalies so that they can be recomposed in other bodies for new passions."[18]

By the end of the "Circe" episode, Bloom has apparently been purged of both guilt and sexual humiliation in an odyssey that resembles Deleuzian schizoanalysis more than Freudian psychoanalysis.[19] Ready to reassert the feminine dimensions of his androgynous personality, he pursues the inebriate Stephen and rescues the nascent poet from the grasp of the Dublin watch, those ubiquitous policemen who signify the abuse of patriarchal power and the illegitimate authority of the threatening Father. At the conclusion of the chapter, Stephen lies semi-conscious and battered at the feet of his ersatz spiritual guardian. But the nature of the relationship between the two men is highly ambiguous. Is Bloom symbolically assuming the Homeric role of adoptive paternity, as critics have traditionally suggested? Or is he subverting the name and law of the Father in an act that replicates the movements of maternal nurturance and care? It might be argued that Bloom and Stephen come together not in Homeric filiation, but through a shared masculine bond that hinges on their mutual dread of maternal abjection.[20]

Bloom's ostensible reward at the end of "Circe" is a somewhat sentimentalized evocation of the lamb-like and erudite Etonian scholar little Rudy might have become:

BLOOM

(*Communes with the right*) Face reminds me of his poor mother ... (*he murmurs*) ... swear that I will always hail, ever conceal, never reveal, any part or parts, art or arts ...

(*Silent, thoughtful, alert he stands on guard, his fingers at his lips in the attitude of secret master. Against the dark wall a figure appears slowly, a fairy boy of eleven, a changeling, kidnapped, dressed in an Eton suit with glass shoes and a little bronze helmet, holding a book in his hand. He reads from right to left inaudibly, smiling, kissing the page.*)

BLOOM

(*wonderstruck, calls inaudibly*) Rudy!

RUDY

(*gazes, unseeing, into Bloom's eyes and goes on reading, kissing, smiling. He has a delicate mauve face. On his suit he has diamond and ruby buttons. In his free left hand he holds a slim ivory cane with a violet bowknot. A white lambkin pups out of his waistcoat pocket.*) (U 15: 4949–67)

As Cheryl Herr observes, the "highly artificial and bizarrely cross-coded Rudy needs to be understood by reference to the several discourses constituting him," since "the primary frame of reference is the pantomime: Rudy is both silent harlequin and the hero of the twentieth-century panto."[21]

Although the text embodies that phallic sign of Bloom's procreative powers, the male child he once engendered, the ghost of his dead son can be resuscitated only in the magical, inchoate fairy-world evoked by the pantomime's Grand Transformation scene. Because of the interchangeability of relational positions in the language of the unconscious, the specter evokes an aching reminiscence of paternal desire and filial loss—a final, enigmatic figure of the disappointed father gazing out through the unseeing eyes of a phantasmal, ever-living son.

In the concluding tableau of "Circe," Bloom the bereft father is coupled with the memory of a lost son in the presence of an adoptive surrogate whom he guards and protects with tender solicitude. But in some sense, Bloom has become more of a *mother* to Stephen than a substitute father. He symbolically supplants the terrifying specter of Mary Dedalus, whose withered hand points a finger of guilt as the ghost-mother counsels repentance and refuses to utter the word of love "known to all men."[22] Turning the Oedipal paradigm inside-out in a gesture of psychic couvade, Bloom enacts his longing for male motherhood through a fantasy that places the (surrogate) father at the origin and center of filial resurrection. Like the poet Mallarmé mourning at the "Tomb of Anatole," he plays out the parthenogenetic roles of both father and mother in a posture of male maternity that Hélène Cixous identifies with the legendary stance of Pygmalion: the "old dream: to be god the mother. The best mother, the second mother, the one who gives the second birth." The "death of the cherished son" gives rise in such cases to a "dream of marriage between father and son.—And there's no mother then.[23]

The conclusion of "Circe" stands the Freudian family romance on its head by amalgamating and shifting subject-positions in the domestic triangle "Daddy–Mommy–Me." Bloom adopts a maternal position *vis-à-vis* Stephen, who slips into an inebriate pose of infantile helplessness and resembles a narcissistic child. Substituting Stephen for Rudy, Bloom establishes a temporary homoerotic alliance with the younger man. Oedipal categories are further confused when, at the end of "Eumaeus," the two go off *"to be married by Father Maher"* (*U* 16: 1887) in a scene that parodies the kind of resolution dictated by conventional fiction."[24]

In a multi-layered, revolutionary narrative, Joyce deliberately subverts the expected codes of Aristotelian denouement. He tantalizes his reader to interpret Bloom's meeting with Stephen through the epic grid of Homer's *Odyssey* as the triumphant reunion of Odysseus and Telemachus. Such a reading, however, ascribes to momentary affiliation the kind of metaphysical meaning undermined by Joyce's richly experimental text. Although Stephen may relate to Bloom with openness and affection, any attempt to identify the older man as transubstantial, consubstantial, or even sub-substantial father founders on the rock of undecidability, since the father/son opposition is itself an Oedipal construct whose essentialist premisses refuse mimetic replication.[25]

The final chapters of Joyce's novel mock what Deleuze and Guattari identify as Oedipal imperialism by proposing an infinite regress of substitutability in the family's sex-stereotyped scripts. If Bloom assumes a maternal subject-position in his friendship with Stephen, he adopts a similar stance in relation to Molly, while simultaneously exacting nurture from his spouse in the role of benevolent phallic mother. The voyage of Bloom/Odysseus leads to Nostos, a nostalgic return to the bed of Mother-Molly and the womb/tomb of both conjugal and filial affection. Bloom goes home—in the company of a young man whom he offers as gift to a Penelopean figure who remains for him the symbolic center around which his dreams perpetually circulate. Molly inhabits Bloom's emotional world in the guise of maternal *imago* and Circean seductress—an archtypal projection of male need and erotic demand elevated to the wholeness and plenitude of imaginary (M)Other. "Ithaca" concludes the man's epic (his)story. Leopold Bloom is last seen in mythic motion, *en route* to a "square round Sinbad the Sailor roc's auk's egg in the night of the bed of all the auks of the rocs of Darkinbad the Brightdayler" (*U* 17: 2328–30)—in progress toward that enigmatic point of female/maternal origin associated with the mysteries of "bridebed, childbed, bed of death" (*U* 3: 396).

Bloom's polymorphously perverse delight in the comforting, voluptuous presence of Mother-Molly is nostalgic in the root-sense of the Greek word for "return." As Jane Gallop remarks, nostalgia refers to "a regret for a lost past that occurs as a result of a present view of that past moment." The word may connote either the languor of homesickness or the remorse evoked by unsatisfied desire. "Both the principal definitions relate to a return, the first in the wish to return to a place, ... the second in the wish to return to a time."[26] Bloom obsessively tries to go back to that far-off time of his inaugural love-making with Molly on Howth to reclaim a world and a place of amorous satisfaction, of erotic origins dissociated from the subsequent trauma of filial loss and paternal failure. Warm female flesh signifies a protective matrix of maternal and spousal love that once valorized Baby-Bloom in the position of an integrated subject and sheltered him from the confusions of psychic fragmentation.

The magic of Howth becomes for both Leopold and Molly a central axis for erotic nostalgia and impassioned fantasy. Each psychologically portrays the experience to him/herself in terms of emotional valorization by the other, an ecstatic self-mirroring that replicates the delights of pre-Oedipal bonding. The scene re-presents an imaginary fulfillment of the spiral of identity—a prelapsarian moment of Edenic happiness joyously recollected in Bloomian tableau and later embellished on the myth-making looms of Molly's Penelopean tapestries.

In a reverie framed by two copulating flies, Bloom celebrates those wondrous moments of tactile pleasure and infantile delight:

> Glowing wine on his palate lingered swallowed. Crushing in the winepress grapes of Burgundy. Sun's heat it is. Seems to a secret touch telling me memory. Touched his sense moistened remembered. Hidden under wild ferns on Howth below us bay sleeping: sky. No sound. The sky. The bay purple by the Lion's head. Green by Drumleck. Yellowgreen towards Sutton. Fields of undersea, the lines faint brown in grass, buried cities. Pillowed on my coat she had her hair, earwigs in the heather scrub my hand under her nape, you'll toss me all. O wonder! Coolsoft with ointments her hand touched me, caressed: her eyes upon me did not turn away. Ravished over her I lay, full lips full open, kissed her mouth. Yum. Softly she gave me in my mouth the seedcake warm and chewed. Mawkish pulp her mouth had mumbled sweetsour of her spittle. Joy: I ate it: joy. Young life, her lips that gave me pouting. Soft warm sticky gumjelly lips. Flowers her eyes were, take me, willing eyes. Pebbles fell. She lay still. A goat. No-one. High on Ben Howth rhododendrons a nannygoat walking surefooted, dropping currants. Screened under ferns she laughed warmfolded. Wildly I lay on her, kissed her: eyes, lips, her stretched neck beating, woman's breasts full in her blouse of nun's veiling, fat nipples upright. Hot I tongued her. She kissed me. I was kissed. All yielding she tossed my hair. Kissed, she kissed me.
>
> Me. And me now.
>
> Stuck, the flies buzzed. (*U* 8:897–918)

A glass of burgundy releases a physical memory of the pent-up "secret touch" associated in Bloom's mind with animal heat and bodily moisture, with flowers and defloration, and with an impressionistic riot of sensuous colors swirling around a sundrenched purple bay. In this joyous game of "laugh and lie down," it is Bloom who feels like a vulnerable Adonis ravished by the seductive Venus who lies throbbing and receptive beneath his trembling body. "Flowers her eyes were, take me, willing eyes" (*U* 8: 910). A younger Bloom-self regresses to a mode of infantile pleasure as he tongues "woman's breasts full in her blouse of nun's veiling, fat nipples upright" (*U* 8: 914–15). The perfume of flowers and the taste of food are mingled in the seedcake Molly shares with Bloom, like a mother feeding a child with predigested pablum or a bird nourishing its young: "Softly she gave me in my mouth the seed-cake warm and chewed" (*U* 8: 907). The "sweetsour" spittle suggests vaginal secretions, and Molly's "soft warm sticky gumjelly lips" offer a foretaste of the vulval "lips full open" that welcome her excited lover. This ritual exchange of eucharistic seedcake anticipates sexual communion with the mother/lover/wife of Bloom's amorous fantasies.[27] "Wildly I lay on her, kissed her: eyes, lips, her stretched neck beating," Bloom thinks, with a sense of wonder at the emotional pulsations that bring man and woman together in a timeless, rhapsodic embrace. The rhetoric of love proves metaphoric and oxymoronic: "lay" implies a passivity contradicted by the urgency of masculine libidinal drives, which are tempered, in turn, by sentimental feelings of tenderness and care.

In this lyrical reminiscence, Bloom is both ravisher and ravished, Molly both lover and beloved. The repressed romantic sensibilities of the novel erupt in a representation of male/female bonding that imitates, for both partners, the pleasures of pre-Oedipal, oceanic union and captures the reciprocity of ecstatic *jouissance*. The author titillates us with the thrill of sexual arousal, of highly charged emotion and about-to-be-satisfied desire. The actual moment of physical climax, however, is withheld from the scene of writing. Bloom's vivid recollection focuses on the tantalizing joys of foreplay, on anticipatory arousal rather than heterosexual release. In the textual frame before us, two buzzing flies copulate. Molly and Leopold do not (yet) come together—though they are always-already locked in a passionate embrace phantasmatically inscribed in the textual unconscious of Joyce's swirling, circular discursive matrix.

As Christine van Boheemen remarks, "the ideas of *coniunctio*, of communion, of the return to paradise ... do not just disappear from the consciousness of the text. They are incorporated into the consciousness of the characters as the presence of their absence," so that "the blissful happiness of resolution informs the text as permanent and unattainable desire."[28] Molly embodies, for Bloom, that figure of totalizing self-presence for which he perpetually pines—an unattainable object of romantic fulfillment sealed in the inaccessible world of the imaginary. From the point of view of Joyce's modern epic, Molly occupies the nostalgic place of mythic (M)Other, the "eternal feminine" that psychically centers male libidinal fantasy. By the time narrative focalization shifts to the female subject-position of "Penelope," Molly, portrayed from the standpoint of speaking/desiring subject rather than specular/desirable object, relates an entirely different (her)story of memory and desire.

NOTES

1. See Jane Gallop, *Feminism and Psychoanalysis*, p. 27. Gallop cites Michele Montrelay's Freudian critique that the "unbearably intense immediacy of the 'odor di femina' produces anxiety, a state totally threatening to the stability of the psychic economy ... because it threatens to undo the achievements of repression and sublimation, threatens to return the subject to the powerlessness, intensity and anxiety of an immediate, unmediated connection with the body of the mother" (ibid.)

2. As Wendy Steiner notes, "Bloom watches Gerty seated on the beach; Gerty watches Bloom watching her.... Each creates the other by creating the other's response, inducing him or her to display and to desire. Thus, Gerty, totally engrossed in her role as Bloom's voyeuristic object, imagines herself in the third person and composes Bloom's response to that objectified self.... Each character projects a fantasy of the other in the course of this subject–object interplay—Gerty through the fallen romance clichés of ladies' journals, Bloom through the primordial symbolism of femininity and the homely wisdom of his own experience.... Gerty and Bloom here demonstrate the problem of intersubjectivity through the model of vision common to painting and romance—the temporary appropriation of another solely by looking" ("There Was Meaning in His Look," p. 98). I have discussed Gerty more extensively in "Gerty MacDowell: Joyce's Sentimental Heroine."

3. In *Joyce's Anatomy of Culture*, Cheryl Herr offers a convincing interpretation of "Circe" as a "Joycean pantomime which plays out the confusing implications of how culture not only determines gender traits but also shapes concepts of selfhood," so that "sexual identity is largely a cultural or even a theatrical phenomenon" (pp. 152–3). "In *Ulysses*, there is ... no 'fully human' androgyny; there is only a perpetual rising to textual consciousness of gender traits that became rigidly entrapping labels, packages, and norms reflecting the culture's characteristic mechanism of binary encoding (male vs. female)" (p. 154). Although Herr and I both start from similar premises concerning the cultural construction of gender, we arrive at somewhat different conclusions about Joyce's transsexual play in "Circe."

4. Shoshana Felman, "Rereading Femininity," p. 42.

5. ibid., p. 31. It is not surprising that Joyce chose a brothel as the setting for the "Circe" episode of *Ulysses*, since, as Michel Foucault points out, the brothel and the mental hospital were two places which escaped the nineteenth-century injunction to silence that surrounded sexual discourse beyond the boundaries of the nuclear family. "If it was truly necessary to make room for illegitimate sexualities, it was reasoned, let them take their infernal mischief elsewhere: to a place where they could be reintegrated, if not in the circuits of production, at least in those of profit. The brothel and the mental hospital would be those places of tolerance.... Words and gestures, quietly authorized, could be exchanged there at the going rate. Only in those places would untrammeled sex have a right to (safely insularized) forms of reality, and only to clandestine, circumscribed, and coded types of discourse" (*The History of Sexuality*, p. 4).

6. Daniel Ferrer, "Circe, Regret and Regression," p. 136. In an interview with Frank Budgen, Joyce acknowledged "an undercurrent of homosexuality in Bloom as well as his loneliness as a Jew" (Budgen, *James Joyce and the Making of "Ulysses,"* p. 315).

7. Gilles Deleuze and Félix Guattari, *Anti-Oedipus*, pp. 51, 67. In his persona as Henry Flower, Bloom illustrates what Deleuze and Guattari celebrate as a Proustian "vegetal theme," the "innocence of flowers," which "brings us yet another message and another code: everyone is bisexual, everyone has two sexes, but partitioned,

noncommunicating; the man is merely the one in whom the male part, and the woman the one in whom the female part, dominates statistically.... Here all guilt ceases, for it cannot cling to such flowers as these" (p. 69).

8. For an informative discussion of Bloom's role as Levitican holocaust, see Beryl Schlossman, *Joyce's Catholic Comedy of Language*, Chapter 2, "Love's Bitter Mystery: *Blumenlied*." "The concept of the phallus and the castration complex," writes Jacqueline Rose, "testify above all to the problematic nature of the subject's insertion into his or her sexual identity" (*Sexuality*, p. 64). "The subject has to recognise that there is a desire, or lack in the place of the Other, that there is no ultimate certainty or truth, and that the status of the phallus is a fraud" (ibid.).

9. Richard Ellmann points out a number of similarities between the "Circe" episode and Leopold von Sacher-Masoch's *Venus in Furs*, which "tells of a young man named Severin who so abases himself before his mistress, a wealthy woman named Wanda, ... that she becomes increasingly tyrannical, makes him a servile go-between, and ... turns him over to her most recent lover for a whipping" (*JJ* 369). "Bloom's daymares of self-reproach," observes Stanley Sultan, "draw again and again upon Sacher-Masoch's book.... Bloom ... conforms to the pattern of the hero of *Venus in Furs*, the desire to be made to suffer by a woman to whose service he is dedicated ... because of his sense of guilt for failing to be that woman's true husband" (*The Argument of "Ulysses,"* pp. 315–16). Sultan notes, furthermore, that Krafft-Ebing, in *Psychopathia Sexualis*, "delineates a classic development of male perversion from passivity to masochism to feminization" (p. 317). For a provocative discussion of Circean masochism from a Deleuzian perspective, see Frances L. Restuccia, "Molly in Furs." For *fin-de-siècle* sources of the Bella–Bloom encounter, see my earlier articles on "James Joyce and Joris-Karl Huysmans" and "James Joyce and Krafft-Ebing."

10. As Catherine Clément suggests in "The Guilty One," the scenario of the circus depends on the "institutionalization of hysteria.... The history of the sorceress and the hysteric rejoins the history of spectacles: *the fusion of public child's play with private sexual scenes*" (Cixous and Clément, *The Newly Born Woman*, p. 13). According to Cheryl Herr, "*Ulysses* argues that sexuality is sheer theater, at least on the social stage on which we dramatically construct the selves we play.... 'Circe' provides evidence that to change Bloom we would have to change his culture and to alter the structure of terms in which individuality is positioned" (*Joyce's Anatomy of Culture*, pp. 154–5).

11. In the Oedipal schema attacked by Deleuze and Guattari in *Anti-Oedipus*, "the libido as energy of selection and detachment is converted into the phallus as detached object, the latter existing only in the transcendent form of stock and lack" (p. 73). "Lack (*manque*) is," furthermore, "created, planned, and organized in and through social production" (p. 28). "Castration as a practical operation on the unconscious is achieved when the thousand break-flows of desiring machines ... are projected into the same mythical space, the unitary stroke of the signifier" (p. 61).

12. Julia Kristeva, *Desire in Language*, pp. 78–9. For a discussion of Joyce and the carnivalesque, see Patrick Parrinder, *James Joyce*; and Elliott B. Gose, Jr, *The Transformation Process in Joyce's "Ulysses,"* Chapter 9, "Comedy in 'Circe.'"

13. For an analysis of Bloom's purgings and bestial transmogrifications, see Gose, *The Transformation Process*, Chapter 10, "The Grotesque in 'Circe.'"

14. As Luce Irigaray declares in *This Sex Which Is Not One*, "femininity" is itself "a role, an image, a value, imposed upon women by male systems of representation. In this masquerade of femininity, the woman loses herself, and loses herself by playing on her femininity.... In our social order, women are 'products' used and exchanged by men. Their status is that of merchandise, 'commodities.'" (pp. 84–5).

15. In *James Joyce and Sexuality*, Richard Brown explains why Molly Bloom's malapropism "coronado" should actually read "cornuto" (p. 19).

16. Sigmund Freud notes in *Beyond the Pleasure Principle* that such "punishment dreams" tend to "replace the forbidden wish-fulfillment by the appropriate punishment for it; that is to say, they fulfill the wish of the sense of guilt which is the reaction to the repudiated impulse" (p. 61). The first German edition of this work was published in 1920; the first English translation, by C. J. M. Hubback, in 1922. Either could have been known to Joyce.

17. The strategies of Bloom's unconscious are similar to those employed by the child initiating the *Fort/Da* game analyzed by Freud as a paradigm for the compensations offered the psyche at play. Children tend to repeat in play anything that makes a strong impression on them in real life, and "in doing so they abreact the strength of the impression and ... make themselves master of the situation" (*Beyond the Pleasure Principle*, p. 36). Thus the child who symbolically casts away a spool at the end of a string, only to draw it back with exclamations of delight, enacts a pantomime of "instinctual renunciation," compensating for his mother's absence "by himself staging the disappearance and return of the objects within his reach.... At the outset he was in a passive situation—he was overpowered by the experience; but, by repeating it, unpleasurable though it was, as a game, he took on an *active* part. These efforts might be put down to an instinct for mastery that was acting independently of whether the memory was in itself pleasurable or not" (pp. 34–5). "Finally, a reminder may be added that the artistic play and artistic imitation carried out by adults ... do not spare the spectators ... the most painful experiences and can yet be felt by them as highly enjoyable" (p. 37). For a discussion of "scopophilia," see Chapter 2, note 30.

18. Hélène Cixous, "Sorties," in Cixous and Clément, *The Newly Born Woman*, p. 84.

19. Most psychoanalytic readings of "Circe" agree that Stephen and Bloom are, to some extent, cognizant of the dramatic events enacted on Joyce's textual stage and are psychologically transformed by their confrontation with specters from the past. In *Joyce in Nighttown*, Mark Shechner analyzes the drama by drawing on Joyce's own biographical obsessions and interprets "Circe" as an extensive desublimation of Bloom's (and Joyce's) fantasy life. "The comedy," he tells us, "will be most hilarious wherever the fantasy is most revealing" (p. 151). Sheldon Brivic, in *Joyce Between Freud and Jung*, is somewhat pessimistic about the cathartic effects of Joyce's comedy and sees little hope for spiritual deliverance. In contrast, Elliott B. Gose, Jr, in *The Transformation Process of Joyce's Ulysses*, describes "Circe" as a "dialectic of purging. Both Bloom and Stephen have projected their deepest fears and desires into hallucinations which we share with them," and both are "cured" of neuroses by the end of the episode. Bloom "emerges as a more integrated and authoritative person after experiencing his worst *transformation*" (pp. 128, 162). See also my own discussion of "Circe" as psychoanalytic transformation in Joyce's *Moraculous Sindbook*, Chapter 9. Contemporary post-structuralist critics tend to assess "Circe" as static rather than kinetic—either a mock pantomime or a carnivalesque play of linguistic *différance*. In *The Book as World*, Marilyn French tells us that "Bloom and Stephen are not hallucinating. The hallucinations are hypostatizations of their hidden feelings ... production numbers staged by the author for the audience.... Circe is a nightmare sent by god Joyce to the reader" (p. 187). According to Hugh Kenner, the chapter contains a "plethora of episodes that resemble hallucinations, ... but are, in fact, either dramatized metaphors, ... or else expressionistic equivalents of states of feeling" ("Circe," p. 352). Nonetheless, Kenner describes "Circe" as "a nearly accidental psychoanalysis, wholly lacking an analyst" and believes that both Stephen and Bloom are "at least temporarily"

changed (ibid., pp. 359–60). Cheryl Herr observes that the chapter "shows us that we cannot burrow under a character's clothes to any essential nature, to any undiluted and potent identity, sexual or otherwise" (*Joyce's Anatomy of Culture*, p. 153). "Bloom's playing Bloom in 'Circe' describes his continuous adoption of one role or another, to the extent that we cannot distinguish character from role" (ibid., p. 155). My analysis of the episode in this chapter attempts to incorporate elements from both psychoanalytic and post-structuralist camps and, in so doing, swerves from the earlier psychoanalytic standpoint of Joyce's *Moraculous Sindbook*.

20. I use the term "abjection" both in the sense suggested by Julia Kristeva in *Powers of Horror* to connote the physical excrescences of the female body that tend to incite horror in the male imagination and in the psychoanalytic sense of an imaginative projection of the self/ego as an "abjected," cast off, and rejected product of the maternal body that serves, in fantasy, as an imaginary matrix of wholeness and cohesion. In "A Clown's Inquest into Paternity," Jean-Michel Rabaté suggests that in "Lacanian terms, Stephen is the phallus for Bloom even more than for Molly, the phallus as a signifier of absence; this representation triggers the movement of ellipse back to mother" (p. 91). Immediately before this book went to press, I discovered that Kristeva's theory of abjection had led Patrick McGee to some similar (and dissimilar) conclusions about "Circe" in Chapter 4 of his recent study *Paperspace* (pp. 115–49).

21. Herr, *Joyce's Anatomy of Culture*, p. 176. For a discussion of Rudy's appearance in terms of the "Grand Transformation" scene of theatrical pantomine, see ibid., pp. 173–9.

22. In the "Scylla and Charybdis" episode, Stephen thinks: "Love, yes. Word known to all men" (*U* 9: 429–30). These crucial lines were restored to the text in Hans Walter Gabler's 1984 edition of *Ulysses* and are discussed by Richard Ellmann in his introduction to the 1986 Random House publication of the Gabler text (*U* p. xii). See also my own commentary "Reconstructing *Ulysses* in a Deconstructive Mode." For "love" as a four-letter word known to all men, see *SL* 185. The dead mother has become for Stephen what little Rudy has long been for Bloom—an always-already absent object of desire, forever cast in a mold of paralyzed bereavement. As in Freudian dreamscapes, the child psychologically changes places with the dead or absent or spiritually defeated parent; psychic energies are constantly mobile because perpetually transferable. Identifying with the "lost one," the subject confuses guilt with grieving, consequence with cause. Stephen cannot forgive himself for a filial rebellion he associates with his mother's death, just as Bloom mourns for Rudolph the elder, for a dead son he could not succeed magically in keeping alive, and for his own diminished generative powers. For further discussion of the encrypted *imago* of the lost one, see Jacques Derrida, "Fors."

23. Hélène Cixous, "Sorties," in Cixous and Clément, *The Newly Born Woman*, pp. 65–6.

24. According to Christine van Boheemen, "*Ulysses* is a deconstruction of the family romance, a decreation that seems to suggest that epigenetic models are based on preconceptions of patriarchal presence" (*The Novel as Family Romance*, p. 171).

25. As Boheemen observes, Joyce self-consciously "refused to follow the tradition of clear-cut resolution, of recovery of origin, identity, or title. Leopold Bloom's return to the bed of his wife Molly is not a climactic *coniunctio*; the meeting of Bloom and Stephen is unconvincing as an emblem of permanent bonding.... With the characters in the fiction, the reader is denied the *catharsis* of a totalizing perspective. There is no closure, no resolution of contradictions" (ibid., p. 133). "Whatever *Ulysses* presents, creates, or constructs is immediately deprived of full self-presence and put 'under erasure'" (ibid., p. 146).

26. Jane Gallop, *Reading Lacan*, pp. 147, 150.

27. According to Sheldon Brivic, Bloom has placed Molly in "the role of nursing mother.... The situation of nursing is evoked by the infantile orality of this scene.... In making a God of woman, Bloom is really putting her in the place of the father. He continually plays a submissive, filial role with Molly" (*Joyce Between Freud and Jung*, pp. 137–8). In contrast, Richard Ellmann describes this memory as "an epithalamium; love is its cause of motion. The spirit is liberated from its bonds through a eucharistic occasion.... Though such occasions are as rare as miracles, they are permanently sustaining" (*JJ* 379).

28. Christine van Boheemen, *The Novel as Family Romance*, p. 158. Although her book was published after the completion of this chapter, I have tried to acknowledge the similarity of our enterprises (triangulated by Deleuze and Guattari, *Anti-Oedipus*) by both incorporating and responding to Boheemen's analysis.

VINCENT J. CHENG

Imagining futures: nations, narratives, selves

THE NEW BLOOMUSALEM IN THE NOVA HIBERNIA OF THE FUTURE

In the "Cyclops" episode, the Citizen had mocked Bloom as a "new Messiah for Ireland" and a "new apostle to the gentiles" (U 12.1642, 1489): The fantasies of "Circe" now allow Bloom the psychological (and therapeutical) space by which to counter and refute all the Citizen's innuendos and accusations, for in "Circe" Bloom does imagine himself as just such a Messiah, come to institute the New Bloomusalem according to his own ideals and in direct opposition to the Citizen's agenda. Although the fantasy—like all such passages in "Circe"—contains elements that are highly fantastic, parodic, contradictory, or just plain absurd, yet there is woven throughout the passage a certain coherence consistent with Bloom's brand of utopian vision, combining humanitarian concerns, socialistic agenda, impractical imagination, and practical reform within a redefinition of Irish nationhood. For "Circe" allows Bloom to play out in unrestricted imagination his ultimate utopian fantasies as an Irish Messiah and reformer.

This fantasy begins when Bloom is cheered as the "Lord mayor of Dublin!" (U 15.1363), and he responds with the practical solution to Dublin's traffic problem he had advocated earlier (U 6.400–2) in the funeral carriage: "better run a tramline, I say, from the cattlemarket to the river. That's the music of the future. That's my programme" (U 15.1367–69). Now he

From *Joyce, race, and empire*. ©1995 by Cambridge University Press.

launches into a speech outlining his agenda of reform; his speech is a mock-socialistic, neo-Marxist attack on the Orange (the "Dutchmen") ascendancy and the English nobility as a wealthy and lazy elite spending their time hunting and gambling while the Irish poor starve in "prostituted" servitude:

> (*impassionedly*) These flying Dutchmen or lying Dutchmen as they recline in their upholstered poop, casting dice, what reck they? Machines is their cry ... manufactured monsters for mutual murder, hideous hobgoblins produced by a horde of capitalistic lusts upon our prostituted labour. The poor man starves while they are grassing their royal mountain stags or shooting peasants and phartridges in their purblind pomp of pelf and power. But their reign is rover for rever and ever and ev ...
>
> (*U* 15.1390–97)

This speech elicits the applause of a large crowd of people bearing streamers reading "*Cead Mile Failte*" (Gaelic: a hundred thousand welcomes; still the slogan of the Irish Tourist Bureau) and "*Mah Ttob Melek Israel*" (Hebrew: "How goodly are [thy tents] King of Israel")—again equating the Celts and the Jews, for in Bloom's vision of an Irish nation they would both be welcome ("a hundred thousand welcomes") under his tents as King of Israel/Ireland. Thus, the procession of supporters which cheers him on is seen to include a broad representation of Irish people from all religions and walks of life ("newspaper canvassers," "chimneysweepers," "Italian warehousemen," and so on). Someone yells out: "That's the famous Bloom now, the world's greatest reformer. Hats off!" (*U* 15.1459); Parnell's brother (John Howard Parnell) proclaims him to be "Illustrious Bloom! Successor to my famous brother!" Bloom thanks them "for this right royal welcome to green Erin, the promised land of our common ancestors"—again underlining the common link between Irish and Jew, seeking their "promised land" in which all are welcome and can live in tolerant harmony, and in which a Jew can also be Irish (to prove the point "*He shows all that he is wearing green socks*"; *U* 15.1513–21). His patriotism (which had been questioned in "Cyclops") is now affirmed, with John Wyse Nolan (who had also defended him in "Cyclops") praising him as "the man that got away James Stephens"; in this world of heterogeneous harmony, even "A BLUECOAT SCHOOLBOY" yells out "Bravo!" (*U* 15.1534–36; the Bluecoat School was a fashionable Anglo-Irish Protestant school and a term that came to represent the values of the Protestant Ascendancy). Bloom, as Messiah to the promised land of Erin, proclaims the new nation (in appropriately Biblical language):

My beloved subjects, a new era is about to dawn. I, Bloom, tell you verily it is even now at hand. Yea, on the word of a Bloom, ye shall ere long enter into the golden city which is to be, the new Bloomusalem in the Nova Hibernia of the future.

(*U* 15.1542–55)

Asked by the crowd "When will we have our own house of keys?", Bloom spells out his reform agenda for the Nova Hibernia[1] as a Home Rule without hierarchy and without labels of difference:

I stand for the reform of municipal morals and the plain ten commandments. New worlds for old. Union of all, jew, moslem and gentile. Three acres and a cow for all children of nature. Saloon motor hearses. Compulsory manual labour for all. All parks open to the public day and night. Electric dishscrubbers. Tuberculosis, lunacy, war and mendicancy must now cease. General amnesty, weekly carnival with masked licence, bonuses for all, esperanto the universal language with universal brotherhood. No more patriotism of barspongers and dropsical impostors. Free money, free rent, free love and a free lay church in a free lay state ... Mixed races and mixed marriage.

(*U* 15.1683–99)

This is Bloom's reform manifesto, some parts of which seem clearly ludicrous in their mix of utopian idealism and mundane or inane specificities. And yet, under close review, even these latter contain appropriate and suggestive ideological significances based on Bloom's thoughts and experiences during the day. "Three acres and a cow for all" sounds like a fanciful Joycean absurdity—but in fact "Three acres and a cow" was a phrase that became "the rallying cry for Irish land reform" after its use by Jesse Collings in "a successful effort to force a measure of land reform on Lord Salisbury's conservative and reluctant government in 1886" (Gifford, *"Ulysses" Annotated*, 479). In other words, Bloom is advocating an equitable land reform program that redistributes Irish territory to the Irish; later we will learn that Bloom was an avid supporter of Davitt's Land League activism. "Saloon motor hearses" refers to Bloom's earlier suggestion (in "Hades") for motorized funeral carriages or for funeral trains as both more efficient and more humane (*U* 6.405–7). "Compulsory manual labour for all" suggests, by the logic of inversion, a shared redistribution of labour along socialist lines, rather than a capitalistic demarcation between labor and capital as social classes; more specifically, it speaks to Bloom's very recent condemnation (in "Cyclops") of human slavery in places like Morocco, where Jews were being bought and sold to do that society's servile, dirty work under the euphemistic title of "compulsory service." "Electric dishscrubbers" is typical of Bloom's practical ideas with humanitarian consequences, especially his thoughts during this day about the hard life of women in Irish society (no public toilets; difficult and frequent childbirths; and so on). Idealistic Bloom also wishes for a world without sickness ("tuberculosis"), "lunacy" (such as what poor Josie Breen endures in her husband), poverty ("mendicancy"), and—perhaps most importantly—"war" (the central topic of his argument with the Citizen about force and violence). The Citizens arguments for retributive violence are countered here by "General amnesty" and a policy of forgiveness. The language issue (Gaelic versus English) is also present in Bloom's advocacy of "esperanto the universal language," an attempt to step beyond a closed and binary Irish–English dialectic to a broader internationalist perspective; Esperanto (meaning "hopeful") was a popular hope among international idealists in Joyce's day. Even the sports issue (Irish versus English games in Phoenix Park) is indirectly hinted at here in Bloom's advocacy of parks being open to everyone without stated restrictions (reflective of his inclusive definition of a "nation"): "All parks open to the public day and night." Bloom also calls for a more honest and, true patriotism (such as Bloom's quiet, unboastful sort—as we will later see confirmed in "Eumaeus" and "Ithaca"), rather than that of drunken "impostors" like the so-called "Citizen": "No more patriotism of barspongers and dropsical impostors."

Interspersed with these suggestive if somewhat comic details are clearer, larger statements of Bloom's utopian vision of the Nova Hibernia as an inter-heterogeneous contact zone eschewing absolute hierarchies and homogenization of difference, in accordance with his earlier definition of "nation" ("the same people living in the same place"): "Union of all" of whatever religious persuasion ("Jew, moslem and gentile"). Bloom advocates a tolerant society of "universal language with universal brotherhood," not fractured by binary and exclusive allegiances (such as to language), a contact zone willing to acknowledge and accept its own ethnic/racial heterogeneities: "Mixed races and mixed marriage." As we see, then, the above manifesto for a New Bloomusalem is typically Bloom in its happy mixing of the idealistic and the mundane (the sacred and the profane)—but we have also grown to recognize its basic elements and tenets (as well as its "sacred/profane" mix) as Joyce's. Even in the "real world," one demanding pragmatics rather than idealistic fantasy, one could have a lot worse political agendas to believe in.

In "Penelope," Molly tells us of Bloom's stated opinion that Christ the carpenter, the advocate of "love thy neighbour," was a revolutionary and "the first socialist" (*U* 18.175–78). Bloom's own reform platform of "universal love" is, similarly, much too radical for his compatriots, and—like Christ—he ends up in "Circe" being persecuted and crucified, a new martyr/Messiah. And so at this point he gets scapegoated by the angry mob: "Stage Irishman!"; "Caliban!"; "Lynch him! Roast him! He's as bad as Parnell was. Mr Fox!" (*U* 15.1729–62). When in doubt, persecute Bloom: the accusations are resonant, for Bloom (who was a bit earlier accused of being "of Mongolian extraction" [*U* 15.954]) is now being persecuted and martyred as a racialized combination of Jew, stage Irishman, Caliban, a black man being lynched, the national martyr Parnell (an Anglo-Irishman, whose pseudonym was "Mr. Fox"), and the helpless fox hunted down as sport by the aristocratic establishment (as Oscar Wilde—who called fox-hunting "the unspeakable in pursuit of the uneatable," a quip often quoted by Joyce—had been by respectable Victorian England). Asked if he is "the Messiah ben Joseph or ben David," Bloom answers (like Christ to Pilate): "You have said it" (*U* 15.1834–36); we are now told in Biblical prose that he is dying for our sins: "And he shall carry the sins of the people to Azazel, the spirit which is in the wilderness, and to Lilith, the nighthag. And they shall stone him and defile him, yea, all from Agendath Netaim and from Mizraim, the land of Ham" (*U* 15.1898–901). Mizraim, or the land of Ham (i.e., Egypt), is identified in the Old Testament as the tribal homeland of the black race, the "sons of Ham" (Genesis 10:6); as messianic martyr, Bloom accepts his racialized status as Orientalized Jew, Irishman, black—as martyr for Everyman. Pronouncing that "Jewgreek is greekjew" (*U* 12.1097–98), Bloom is now turned into the second coming of Elijah in the New Bloomusalem, as "THE GRAMOPHONE" begins to play "The Holy City" ("Jerusalem! / Open your gates and sing / Hosanna") and a bursting rocket becomes a falling star *"proclaiming the consummation of all things and second coming of Elijah"* (*U* 15.2170–76).

In the fantasy pages when Messiah Bloom does finally seem to be killed in martyrdom, he is dressed in a priest's liturgical garment ("marked I. H. S."—which for Bloom had meant "I have suffered" [*U* 5.373]) and says ("amid phoenix flames"): "Weep not for me, O daughters of Erin" (*U* 15.1935–36)—again making the equation between Erin and Jerusalem (Luke 23:27: "Daughters of Jerusalem, weep not for me"); when he dies, his widow throws herself on a Hindu "suttee pyre" while "THE CIRCUMCISED" and Bloom's Jewish friends weep for him in Hebrew (*U* 15.3220–36). "COUNCILLOR NANNETTI" (who would in actuality, like Bloom in fantasy, become Lord Mayor) shows up to speak Robert Emmet's lines at the moment of patriotic martyrdom: "When my country takes her place among the nations of the earth, then, and not till then, let my epitaph be written. I have..." (*U* 12.3385–88). In short, Bloom as national martyr and Messiah is willing to take on (as Everyman) all heterogeneous identities—Jew, Moslem, gentile, Hindu, black, Irishman, Englishman, and so on—in a revolutionary statement of "universal brotherhood" and tolerance within a "Nova Hibernia" that would accept Jews like himself or Italians like Nannetti or Anglo-Irish like Parnell within its national sovereignty. Now *that* is an idea to die for.

NOTE

1. Joyce himself had, in his essays, spoken of "the new Ireland in the near future" (*CW* 228).

MARILYN REIZBAUM

Weininger and the Bloom of Jewish Self-Hatred in Joyce's Ulysses

James Joyce's connection with Judaism has been a source for some discussion since he made Leopold Bloom the "hero" of *Ulysses* (1922). The novel has received either praise or blame, and has been interpreted variously on the basis of conclusions drawn in this matter. Among those who have seen Joyce's representation of the Jew as antipathetic is Maurice Samuel, noted Jewish author and translator; in an article of 1929, citing passages from the "Circe" chapter, he asserts that Joyce treated Bloom in a loathsome and malevolent manner, and that he seemed to exhibit a "cosmic loathing for the little Jew, Bloom" (Samuel 1929, 14).[1] The notion that Joyce harbored hatred for the Jew and an extension from that to a consideration of Joyce as anti-Semite is voiced quite tellingly by Robert M. Adams: "Sentimentalists who simplify Bloom the Jew into a pathetic and admirable little man who forgives his enemies and so is apotheosized into the perfect Christian hero would do well to face the sizeable element of anti-Semitism in Joyce himself. This element is not distinct from powerful feelings of self-loathing" (Adams 1972, 104n.).

What is striking about both Samuels's and Adams's assessments of what are inherent and complex ambiguities in the presentation of Bloom are their assumptions about Joyce's own affinities in this regard. If we use the text of *Ulysses* to document Joyce's connection with Judaism, then we are faced with

From *Jews and Gender: Responses to Otto Weininger,* edited by Nancy A. Harrowitz and Barbara Hyams. ©1995 by Temple University Press.

what might seem to be irresolvable ambiguities; or we might be able to interpret them as artistically significant—Bloom as Jew or non-Jew or non-identifying Jew, Bloom as loathsome or heroic. A more profitable way of approaching these ambiguities and their significance is by examining a source that Richard Ellmann mentions in his biography of Joyce. Ellmann claims that this source—Otto Weininger's *Geschlecht und Charakter* (1903)—contains theories that Joyce generally believed, especially as they pertain to women (Ellmann 1982, 477). Ellmann does not make clear how well Joyce knew the book, and he does not discuss in any depth the relevance of Weininger's theories to Joyce's concepts of Jews. In fact, one cannot be certain from Ellmann's documentation that Joyce even read the book.[2] Nevertheless, the literature (by which I mean the intellectual documents exchange of the period) attests to the popularity of Weininger's ideas about Jews and women, as does the frequency with which the book was reprinted.[3] Assuming that Joyce used this source, I believe that it can be of at least heuristic value to examine Weininger's theories and how they might inform Joyce's work. For whether Joyce used Weininger, he plainly used the themes, and his development of them reveals an apprehension that adapts and departs from Weininger's own theories.

In his book Weininger expounds upon what he sees as the inferiority of women and the inhumanity of Jews. A kind of metaphorical link is set up between the two, and it is this link which Joyce gathered up to use in *Ulysses*. Weininger based his theory about the inferiority of women on what he saw as a fundamental relationship between sex and character. He saw every human being as a combination of both sexes, in which the male is the positive, productive, logical, conceptual side capable of genius, and the female is the negative side, incapable of any of these virtues. Woman has only two functions, according to Weininger—prostitution or procreation. The ideal woman accepts her role as being dependent on the phallus, and her only emancipation is achieved in the ending of coitus.

Since the Jew, according to Weininger's dubious yet historically informed anthropological observations, is "weiblich" (womanish or feminine), he theorizes that the Jew too is the negative side of every human being.[4] In the rest of his proof, Weininger rehearses the litany of discriminatory commonplaces about Jews: the Jews have no redeeming qualities; they believe in nothing and therefore are useless. Because they are undirected, they gravitate toward all destructive institutions and beliefs—communism, anarchism, materialism, and atheism. What is peculiar to Weininger's theories is the notion that Jewishness is a state of mind or being, a psychological constitution, rather than a religious or cultural attribute:

I do not refer to a nation or to a race, to a creed or to a scripture. When I speak of the Jew I mean neither the individual nor the body, but mankind in general, in so far as it has a share in the platonic idea of Judaism. My purpose is to analyze this idea.

That these researches should be included in a work devoted to the characterology of the sexes may seem an undue extension of my subject. But some reflections will lead to the surprising result that Judaism is saturated with femininity, with precisely those qualities the essence of which I have shown to be in the strongest opposition to the male nature. It would not be difficult to make a case for the view that the Jew is more saturated with femininity than the Aryan, to such an extent that the most manly Jew is more feminine than the least manly Aryan (Weininger 1906, 306).

The kinds of connections between race and sex that Weininger makes appear most prevalently and climactically in the "Circe" chapter of *Ulysses*, which in a way enacts the realm of the psyche. Bloom appears there in a series of stereotypes, some of which are directly associated with his Jewishness—as womanish, degraded—externalizations of a self-regard he exhibits throughout the novel. Rather than reproducing or representing Weininger's theories literally, however, the chapter dramatizes the psychodynamic of self-hatred, linked here with gender and race. The Jew, in this case, Bloom, internalizes the plight of being an outcast and accepts the sense of the self that others have determined and foisted upon him.[5]

If Joyce knew Weininger's book, he might also have known that Weininger was a Jew who converted to Christianity and then committed suicide at the age of twenty-three, in the very year the book was published. He might have seen Weininger as a man who, when confronted with his origins, theorized a way out that seemed to reinforce those origins and his dread of them. To Joyce, Weininger's philosophies may have appeared to be an expression of his subconscious. In fact, the study of Weininger's work has almost invariably entailed biographical investigation, seemingly mandated by the circumstances of his life and death. Since Theodor Lessing's ground-breaking work, *Der jüdischer Selbsthaß* (1930), Weininger has become the exemplar of the condition of Jewish self-hatred. His notions represent, by the example of his life as well as by history, a prevalent dynamic within a psychoanalytic framework that can be used, as the "Circe" chapter exhibits, both rhetorically and characterologically.

In the section of "Circe" where Bloom embarks upon his series of transformations, Dr. Dixon is reading Bloom's "bill of health:" "Professor

Bloom is a finished example of the new womanly man. His moral nature is simple and lovable. Many have found him a dear man, a dear person. He is rather a quaint fellow on the whole, coy though not feeble-minded in the medical sense" (Joyce, 1986, 1798–1801). Bloom is *weiblich*, but it is important to note that he is a "new womanly man." (It is equally important to note the double entendre in the word "finished." Just as Stephen is, according to his self-description later in the episode, a "most finished artist," at once polished and impotent, so Bloom here is exemplary of qualities that make him a "dear man" while he too is impotent. This may also be a clue to his rehabilitation within the context of the chapter; he is "finished" with the "old" womanly man and ushering in the new.) Joyce seems to rewrite the Weiningerian model that reproduces the historical figuration of racial or cultural inferiority in stereotypes of the feminine (just before Dixon, "Dr." Punch Costello has identified Bloom as Jewish by his smell—*"fetor judaicus"* while using B's urine to discover he's pregnant) not so much by using parody, but by decoding this series of condemnatory pronouncements upon Bloom.

One way that this decoding is achieved is through the use of the fantastic. This womanly man is about to give birth, an act of regeneration that Joyce's texts regularly celebrate and interrogate as the biological analogue of artistic immortality; it is an act so devoutly to be wished that it is embodied within the church's doctrine of the Trinity, allowing for the fathering of the wor(l)d and emptying the mother of the (pro)creative function. Thus another way to read Bloom's feminization or capacity for childbirth is as a symbolic enactment of this kind of appropriation, keeping in place the logical and conceptual side that a complete feminization would preclude in Weiningerian terms. But this description of Bloom as "coy though not feeble-minded in the medical sense" suggests that he is not governed totally by his intellect; to be coy is metonymically to be woman and therefore, in (not exclusively) Weiningerian terms, intellectually inferior. To be coy is also to be uncommitted and flighty, a stereotypically feminine disposition that here signals that stereotype as well as Bloom's gender position. What makes Bloom "dear" both as a man and as a person, a distinction that points to the gendering of attributes, is that the strength of his intellect could be said to be enfeebled by his emotional, or "other," capacities. In other words, the intellectual is devalued, or valued differently. We see this borne out later in "Circe" when Stephen and Bloom come together—when "extremes meet" (Joyce 1986, 15.2098). Lynch's "cap" invokes and disrupts the Arnoldian distinction between Hellenism and Hebraism—"Jewgreek is greekjew" (Joyce 1986, 15.2099)—and at once characterizes Stephen's analysis of this relation as tautological and illogical— "Woman's reason" (Joyce 1986, 15.2098). Finally Stephen's analysis breaks down in the face of this illogic and becomes elliptical; he cannot "finish." Here sex and race both become determinants of intellectual prowess. Logos, however, does not accommodate or account for the fantastic, the mystical, the cosmic, the realm of Stephen's and Bloom's meeting.

These extensions, which are not immediately logical, lead us to Joyce's notion of lineage. It is useful to note that "*geschlecht*" may mean "race" as well as "gender," allowing these concepts to collapse together in Joyce's (and Weininger's) creation of character. Bloom gives birth to a kind of mini-Europe, producing eight white and eight yellow (exotic or metallic) children, who run the economic world (Joyce 1986, 1820–31). But then "A Voice" questions the origins of Bloom and his brood: "Bloom, are you the Messiah ben Joseph or ben David?" "You have said it," Bloom answers "darkly" (Joyce 1986, 15.1833–36). This invocation of the messianic doctrine in which there are two messiahs—one who will prepare the way for the messianic age, another who will enact it—calls up the relationship between the Christian and Jewish messianic traditions, a relationship that is variously represented in the literature. Bloom's answer to this query repeats Jesus' answer to Pilate's question—"Are you the king of the Jews?"—which in turn had been prompted by the elders' report that Jesus had identified himself as the messiah of the house of David (Luke 23:3).[6] Bloom's response, like Christ's, makes the question into a statement, so that in this case either Messiah will do (Jew or Christian/Bloom or Jesus). Perhaps more to the point here, the only distinction is accorded by dogma rather than lineage.[7] With this distinction gone, Stephen and Bloom may become familial by virtue of a line of descent from Bloom that is comically disrupted by a sexual and linguistic error: "*Leopoldi autem generatio*. Moses begat Noah and Noah begat Eunuch and Eunuch begat O'Halloran and O'Halloran begat Guggenheim and Guggenheim begat Agendath..." (Joyce, 1986, 15.1855–69). This is Joyce's line—a sort of jumble of association that is more synchronic than linear, putting a new gloss on race. At the same time, an acknowledgment of the distinction made between races and religions points up the split within Bloom Jew and non-Jew, the self and the alien self, what is dogmatic is reproduced through internalization.

It is with these ideas of the "new womanly man" and the Joycean notion of lineage (sex and character, race and character) that we may most profitably look at Bloom's relation to the Circean Bella/Bello figures and at the final section of "Circe" in which Bloom meets his son, Rudy/Stephen. In "Circe" the sexes take turns being both dominant/sadistic and subservient/masochistic. These extremes are separated out and embodied in the figments Bella and Bello. Their interaction with Bloom in part dramatizes or (en)acts his relationship with Molly. Weininger's theory states that each person is made up of both female and male, and therefore both are always present. Joyce has, however, altered this distribution, and in doing so decodes as before the essentialism of certain kinds of gendering—what signals their sex are the accouterments of gender. Bella has olive skin, which signals the exotic (i.e., Jewish) element that Joyce so often evokes and that we associate with Molly; she wears a dress and earrings; and she has a "sprouting mustache." What establishes her sex is only the linguistic signal—"she." In her "fan's" (synechdochic) interaction with Bloom we see an inversion of roles in Bloom's relationship with Molly:

THE FAN
(*Flirting quickly, then slowly.*) Married, I see.

BLOOM
Yes ... Partly, I have mislaid ....

THE FAN
(*Half opening, then closing.*) And the missus is master. Petticoat government.

BLOOM
(*Looks down with a sheepish grin.*) That is so.
(Joyce 1986, 15.2754–62)

When the Bello side comes out, the positions are more than reversed. What was a characterization of Bloom's externalized submissiveness—the "sheepish grin"—and an externalization of his internal condition—"the missus is master"—now becomes literalized when the "man" (with "bobbed hair") takes over. Bello turns Bloom both into a woman (with "large male hands") and an animal ("pet"), the latter aligned with the former and, in the parallel with *The Odyssey*, emblematic of the submission to desire or seduction (Circe transforms the men into hogs and thus "unmans" them). In Bello's equation, to be unmanned or impotent/castrated is to be woman(ish)/inadequate. The Bello side of Bloom "finishes" him off, "embodying" his feelings of impotence and self-hatred:

BELLO
What else are you good for, an impotent thing like you? (*he stoops and, peering, pokes with his fan rudely under the fat suet fold of Bloom's haunches*) Up! Up! Manx cat! What have we here? Where's your curly teapot gone to or who docked it on you,

cockyolly? Sing, birdy, sing. It's as limp as a boy of six's doing his pooly behind a cart. Buy a bucket or sell your pump. (*loudly*) Can you do a man's job?

BLOOM

Eccles street....

BELLO

(*Sarcastically*.) I wouldn't hurt your feelings for the world but there's a man of brawn in possession there. The tables are turned, my gay young fellow! He is something like a fullgrown outdoor man. Well for you, you muff, if you had that weapon with knobs and lumps and warts all over it. He shot his bolt, I can tell you! Foot to foot, knee to knee, belly to belly, bubs to breast! He's no eunuch. A shock of red hair he has sticking out of him behind like a furzebush! Wait for nine months, my lad! Holy ginger, it's kicking and coughing up in her guts already! That makes you wild, don't it! Touches the spot? (*He spits in contempt.*) Spittoon!

(Joyce 1986, 15.3127–3144)

In both cases, Bella and Bello, the locus of desire/consequence is Molly, the woman. Bloom, the Jew, the voyeur, the displaced, confronts his stand-in—Blazes Boylan—and images the role he plays in the scenario, as Molly does hers later in the "Penelope" section. And in both cases what is revealed is the character(ization) of such historical linking of sex and race.

Furthermore, we can see another twist on *The Odyssey* that marks a departure from as well as a manipulation of Weininger's theories. Odysseus uses the drug "moly" to ward off Circe and to save himself and his men from destruction (from being "unmanned"). Here too Molly is transformative in Bloom's realm of desire and fantasy, although she represents, like Penelope within the Odyssean myth, both prohibition and antidote. Bloom's confrontation with his origins, his desire, and his "death" are staged, and this sets up a parallel between Bloom and Weininger in a personal and parodic sense. The Bello in him consigns him to death, and while it is suggested that it is his guilt that kills him (for sexual desire and apostasy), he is given a Jewish funeral (no flowers) by "The Circumcised" (which he tearfully attends), pointing to, as with the accouterments of gender, the signifiers of race (Joyce 1986, 15.3218–40). He seems to emerge absolved and, in a parody of resurrection, enlightened—"(*crawls jellily forward under the boughs, streaked by sunlight, with dignity*) This position. I felt it was expected of me. Force of habit" (Joyce 1986, 15.3241–3).

It seems at least ironic that Jewishness and womanishness become states of mind that destroyed Weininger yet save Bloom. And while Bello sends Bloom to his "death," Bloom puts Bello to his, or, in other words, banishes him from the text. It is within the realm of the textual that this can occur, although we may be reminded that it is the textualization of Weininger's fears and notions about race, sex, and character that prompted his suicide, or literalized his death.

Finally, what is proposed as possible within the Joycean outline of lineage and sexuality, ironically informed by Weininger's own theories—the reunion of Molly and Bloom with each other and with a lost son (Stephen takes the place of Rudy)—seems viable only in the fantastical realm of "Circe." The family epic is countered by a kind of anti-*nostos* (homecoming) in the last three chapters of the novel, in which the rhetoric of sexual and cultural difference takes on mythic proportions and comes between the characters. Joyce's probable adaptation of Weininger's ideas dramatizes both the illogic in and the historical power of those ideas, if not, as some of the critics have suggested, the psychobiography of these two writers.

Notes

This essay is a revised version of Reizbaum (1982). The author would like to thank Indiana University Press for permission to reprint it here.

1. "Cosmic" seems almost an apt description of the strength of Samuel's response to Joyce's portrayal of Bloom. I include here a bit more of the passage from which this characterization comes: "somehow Stephen emerges from all this undefiled in the eyes of the reader. His madnesses are those of poets. Bloom's are those of a wretched, indecent little person, none the less so because there is something pathetic in the way he clings to the young Irishman. Joyce's malevolence can do no more. By the time the scene closes the worst that can be revealed concerning human beings, the most loathsome, has been unfolded about the figure of Bloom. One should not be personal, but one cannot help feeling that for the character of Bloom, the Jew, Joyce harbors a mad, insatiable hatred. As he sees into the soul of Stephen with the mercilessness of great love, he sees into the soul of Bloom with the mercilessness of hate" (Samuel 1929, 14).

2. Ellmann writes that Joyce "borrowed" Weininger's theory that Jews are by nature womanly men (Ellmann 1982, 463); this view is endorsed and enlarged upon by Ralph Robert Joly, who points out that Italo Svevo, often cited as a prototype for Bloom, may have told Joyce about Weininger to whom, Joly claims, Svevo was often compared. Although their documentation for such claims is largely speculative, one can safely imagine that Joyce would have encountered Weininger's work, regardless of whether Svevo told him about it. *Geschlecht und Charakter* was reprinted eighteen times between 1903 and 1919, and many can attest to its popularity and the prevalence of these theories of "psychobiology." Further, Joyce's notebooks make reference to Weininger (VI, C.7–267), and while the date of this notation cannot be firmly established, it at least confirms without doubt that Joyce knew of Weininger.

3. As this collection attests, there has been a great resurgence of interest in Weininger's work among, for example, feminists and Germanists, *fin-de-siècle* Vienna and

Jewish scholars: Viola Klein's *The Feminine Character: History of all Ideology* (1946), Sander L. Gilman's *Jewish Self-Hatred* (1986) and *Difference and Pathology* (1985), and Peter Gay's *Freud, Jews, and Other Germans* (1978) are a few of the sources. And see my own "James Joyce's Judaic 'Other': Text and Context" (1985).

4. For example, Sander Gilman discusses this historical link of figuration of the Jew in stereotypes of the feminine in both *Jewish Self-Hatred* (1986) and *Difference and Pathology* (1985).

5. In an article on Jewish self-hatred, Allan Janik critiques the theorization around this "stock concept"; he sees it "not only as a form of decadence but a type of dangerous cultural pathology presaging, perhaps, the eventual triumph of Nazism" (Janik 1987, 75–76).

6. For this source, see Gifford (1988, 481 [entry 15.1836]).

7. The Messiah ben Joseph appears in the Talmudic writings as a herald to the Messiah ben David who will bring about the messianic age. Since the former is from the house of Ephraim, he is often represented in the literature as a symbolic embodiment of the reunification with the ten tribes of Israel. In the Book of Zerubbabel, written around the beginning of seventh century B.C., this martial figure is pitted against a satanic king of Rome whom the whole world—except the Jews—believe to be God. This is of course resonant of Christ's stand against Rome. Zerubbabel is from the apocalyptic literature from the Middle Ages. It is a pseudoepigraphical work of the last ruler of the house of David. It is collected in Adolf Jellinek's *Bet Ha-Midrash*, Jerusalem: Bamberger and Wahrmann, 1938. The set is in six volumes and it is the standard edition for these texts— rabbinic and post-rabbinic apocalyptics. The linguistic error here appears in the word "Agendath," which we first encounter in the "Calypso" chapter (Joyce 1986, 4. 191). It is part of the title, *Agendath Netaim*, which should read *Agudath Netaim*, translated from the Hebrew as "Planter's Company," an organization promoting land development in Palestine during the early years of the Zionist movement. Bloom reads of this company's propositions of land for sale in Palestine in the newspaper at Dlugacz's (The Porkbutcher) that he uses to wrap meat Bloom buys. There has been much speculation about this mistransliteration from the Hebrew (see Reizbaum 1990, 217–8n. 16). Dr. Fritz Senn has pointed to the word "agenda" within "Agendath" as perhaps having some import for Bloom's sense of history and identity; this idea works particularly well in the discussion of lineage.

PETER FRANCIS MACKEY

Contingency and Bloom's Becoming

In the previous chapter, I described the parallels between "Ithaca" and chaos theory and their larger potential consequences. This connection to one chapter of *Ulysses* suggests how ideas from chaos theory can advance our understanding of Bloom and *Ulysses'* metaphysical implications. I now will focus on Bloom's contingent relationship to his world. This relationship springs in large part from his rational temperament, as well as from his professional habits. If Bateson is right, that "'nothing will come of nothing' without information" (46) and information is vital to learning and change, Bloom's mind seems primed to learn and change. An adman trained to notice consumer reactions and habits, he often reflects on practical matters, such as the economics of Dublin's thriving bars (4.126), the preparation of corpses for burial (6.14), and the "codology" of capital punishment (12.451). He also considers such promising business ideas as using trams for shipping cattle and corpses (6.400; 6.405), recording the voices of the dead for posterity (6.963), employing science to relieve the expense and pain of childbirth (8.373), and applying x-rays to learn more about the human digestive tract (8.1030). He also speculates on equally intriguing if less capitalistic matters, such as the circumstances that might have driven Denis Carey to betray the invincibles (5.381), the mathematics of music (11.830), and women's feelings about, for example, menstruation (13.822). It is easy to suspect the passive

From *Chaos Theory and James Joyce's Everyman.* ©1999 by the University Press of Florida.

Bloom will not pursue any of the schemes he ponders or answer any of the questions he raises. His observant perspective originates in his carefully maintained distance from the world. This position replicates the fecklessness he feels about his impact on that world. He may check whether Aphrodite is anatomically complete, try to help Dignam's widow, and inadvertently get into an argument at Kiernan's. But most often, at least until he follows Stephen, Bloom watches: Dignam's funeral mass, the passing of Father Conmee's cavalcade, Gerty, the toasting at the Ormond Hotel, the rudeness of the young men at the maternity hospital, and of course the movements of Blazes Boylan toward his home, for example. To a small degree, he acts like the "intelligent Agent" (quoted in Soskice 37) that is Newton's God, analyzing the world in deistic fashion, "distant and diffident" (Soskice 37).

In his profession, Bloom seems to have found the perfect match for his inclination to fantasize rather than act. This work becomes the professional expression of his personal style—to *speculate* rather than do—just as his allegiance to vision becomes the habitual sign of the isolation he finally strives to overcome. Franco Moretti points out that advertising, like the stream of consciousness, is a medium of time-present, of immediacy, perfectly suited to the urban milieu, where "fascination does not lie in any specific promise, however seductive, but in the *many* choices that appear equally possible" (139). As Bloom's fleeting mental processes put him "at ease in the world of commodities," allowing "him to pick up hundreds and hundreds of stimuli, and play freely with them," they serve well his inclinations in a world of "fantasizing possibilism" (Moretti 140). His recirculating but idle wishes keep hope both at arm's length and ever-present. This habit finds a good match in his job, where he strives to bring further temptations to the world, such as in a Keyes ad. His *flânerie*, likewise, suits him: "During Bloom's walk, chance brings to light an endless quantity of things and ideas" (Moretti 141). So moving, he can pass by commodities, as he lets pass his idle wishes. As we will see, though, the state of remove adopted by this wishful, fantasizing, and canvassing *flâneur* is merely an embedded, and yearning, man's pose.

If Bloom's practical judgment, stream of consciousness, fantasies, profession, and walk offer nascent, if unexplored, opportunity in every encounter, his watchful attention to his culture does not always find a reward in accurate judgments. "Oxen of the Sun" tells us that "sir Leopold ... was the goodliest guest that ever sat in scholars' hall" (14.182–83), but the reach of *this* scholar's intellect sometimes exceeds its grasp. Bloom thinks that "[s]ulphate of copper" is the chemical compound "SO_4" (16.801). He not only is incorrect—copper sulfate is $CuSO_4$ but has named a thoroughly unstable compound (Gifford 545). At times, Bloom's formal knowledge seems equally unstable. For example, he struggles to recall Archimedes' principle (5.39–41), misinterprets I.N.R.I. and I.H.S. (5.372), confuses the Greek god Apollo with the Greek painter Apelles (6.959), and jumbles the history and legend of Cormac, St. Patrick, and high king Laeghaire (8.663–66). In a moment of self-defensive temper, he also describes three individuals as Jews when in fact one abandoned the faith (Marx), another was Catholic (Mercadante), and a third was excommunicated (Spinoza) (12.1804) (Gifford 378).

Even Bloom's errors, however, show that his cultural knowledge comes from experience in life, comes from encountering the world's stimuli and reflecting on them, rather than from innate tendencies or instincts. The signifiers of Bloom's formal learning have their source in an "objective" truth, the cultural context from which his recollections come. Bloom, after all, must contemplate the facts he ponders at a temporal distance, however indefinite, from when he learned them. Bloom's particular cultural facts stretch into his thoughts and away from their origins in the culture in two ways: via their symbolic constitution as signifiers of cultural signifieds, and via their temporal, recollected distance from when he first learned them. Precisely because it works to reach his consciousness again, such knowledge becomes vulnerable to the weaknesses of human recall, like strands of rope stretched until they begin unraveling. We, though, have the facts to assess Bloom's cultural, scientific, and practical knowledge, which is how his errors make themselves apparent and expose his dislocation from the truth.

Bloom's sensory responsiveness to his world, on the other hand, seeks not factual accuracy but instead vouches only for itself. It belongs to that stream of consciousness that manages to adjust to the stimulating commodity culture of his city. Arising from personal experience, these responses cannot be challenged. Their signifiers and signifieds inhabit the same context, Bloom's private sensory plane. His sensory experiences thereby provide a purely personal expression of his relationship to his world. These sensory experiences become, that is, the most personal element not only of Bloom's experience but also of *Ulysses*' stream-of-consciousness technique. "[N]o text can ever be read in isolation from its historical context," Patrick McGee observes (*Telling the Other* 15). Nor can Bloom be understood without the immediate experience— the lived historical moment—in which his consciousness lives and out of which it arises. His responsiveness to his world is both a constituent and a reflection of his identity. An inherent generative relationship exists, after all, between the stream of consciousness and the character whose consciousness it represents. As Georg Lukács says, in *Ulysses* "the stream-of-consciousness technique is no mere stylistic device; it is itself the formative principle governing the narrative pattern and the presentation of character" (17–18). To appreciate the significance of Bloom's responsiveness to his world, we need only compare the vividness and immediacy of his thoughts with those that inhabit the stream-of-consciousness technique in Woolf's characters, so relatively dry, and in Proust's, so relatively studious.

While there is no one accepted definition of "stream of consciousness," the technique usually is said to incorporate one or both of two narrative angles: "interior monologue," which refers to the representation in language of a person's immediate thoughts (that is, the contents of the perceivable consciousness), and "erlebte Rede," which refers to the stylistic convention that represents as reported speech any thought not spoken. Both depend upon the influence of a character's perspective on the language and topics of the stream-of-consciousness text. Robert Humphrey clarifies how narrative emphasis can change when a character's stream of consciousness is at work: one way that writers such as Zola and Dreiser differ from such stream-of-consciousness writers as Joyce, Proust, and Woolf, Humphrey says, is that for the earlier novelists, the subject matter is "motive and action (external man) and for the later ones, psychic existence and functioning (internal man)" (8). As this point emphasizes, a writer's use of the stream-of-consciousness technique entwines the text with the character's development. The technique becomes the voice of the character's inner life itself.

In Bloom's stream of consciousness, specifically, we see his inner life accrue much of its energy from his contingent relationship with his surroundings. This relationship provides the generative nexus out of which we discover who Bloom is. Put another way, his presence in the novel, his identity, forms primarily in the dramatic space where his consciousness and world overlap, like a geographic feature arising from the collision of tectonic plates. As Bloom comes into being, meanwhile, so does much of the novel—as the primary source of *Ulysses'* text, his stream of consciousness "produces" much of the book. So much of Dublin comes to us via Bloom's encounter with it that to imagine *Ulysses'* Dublin without him is to imagine it not at all. Similarly, so much of Bloom comes to us through his encounter with Dublin that to imagine him without those experiences is to imagine him not at all. This solipsism makes a point: *Ulysses* would not merely be a different book without a consciousness like Bloom's and its contingent relation to experience; a good part of the book itself would be missing. In these ways, as a practical matter, *Ulysses* and Bloom are born together. As Mary Anne Gillies notes, "The readers do not simply follow Bloom as he wanders around Dublin on this day; they join him on his trip and in his experiences. Indeed, they become the readers' experiences because the readers not only need to recreate them to understand them, but also to relate the different versions of the events in order to reconstruct them" (148).

Without Bloom's vivid and generative consciousness, Joyce would seem ridiculous rather than wryly hyperbolic in claiming that were Dublin destroyed, we could rebuild it out of *Ulysses'* detailed description of it (Budgen, *Making of "Ulysses"* 67–68). In effect, if Joyce is the painter, Bloom—or, specifically, his consciousness—often serves as the brush that Joyce uses to make the precise touch. Richard Kain, exploring the resemblance between *Ulysses'* city and the real Dublin, alludes to this valuable quality of Bloom's constitution: "The eager intelligence and keenness of perception of this alert little man allow no perception to pass unnoticed" (134). Moretti helps extend the point: "Unlimited possibilities [are] the experience of every paragraph [in *Ulysses*] ... [each paragraph offers] a horizon always open, which gives sense and colour to Bloom's day, *and which therefore binds him to the world despite everything*" (148)—and, we say as readers, "vice versa." *Ulysses'* thorough portrait of Bloom and his world does depend largely on the contingent relationship between his consciousness and that world.

Relationships between the complexity of consciousness and *Ulysses* again emerge. The intertwining of Bloom's responsive mind and his physical experiences, for example, makes John Searle's materialist remark in a book on complexity interesting: "The secret of understanding consciousness is to see that it is a biological phenomenon on all fours with all other biological phenomena such as digestion or growth.... In neither case are we talking about something spiritual or ethereal or mystical.... [It is a big mistake] to think that consciousness, because it is private, subjective, touchy, feely, ethereal, etc., cannot be part of the ordinary sordid physical world of drinking beer and eating sausage" (quoted in Coveney 280). The aboriginal liveliness of Bloom's mind gives it this biological quality. His consciousness certainly demonstrates it is part of his world, as that world is part of his consciousness. Kain correctly observes that Bloom possesses a "keenness of perception" and is "alert." To a degree, this perceptiveness makes ironic the identification Bloom feels with his world despite his disconnection from those who inhabit it with him. His sensitivities foreground the distance he otherwise feels from the social life he perceives.

The depth of this gap between Bloom and the very world to which his reactions pay witness becomes evident when we consider the position amid experience that sight in particular entails. Bloom's experiment with parallax (8.564–67) makes this clear, as I will discuss shortly. It suggests why vision fools us more readily than touch (Turbayne 128). When we touch our body to the contingent reality of which we are part, distance ends. To see something, though, we must be a certain distance from it. We know how things get fuzzy as they approach or dim as they depart. Sight clarifies our position outside the things we see, as we apply an instinctive geometry that assigns things a place in the scene around us. The eye's nerves, we might note, merge into the optic nerve. At their precise unity there, a blind spot, like a black dot on a white screen, occludes vision. Anything projected into that precise point cannot be seen. The skin, however, testifies without that muted site. Illusions become less likely as the contingency between body and world speaks in its own reliable voice.

Martin Jay's survey of twentieth-century French critical reactions against ocularcentrism explores the philosophical significance of this contrast between vision and touch. He notes that Guy Debord, Michel Foucault, and Michel de Certeau, among other critics of the cultural constructions of subjectivity, objected to Western culture's adoration of the spectacle, the image, and reification. They believed that this homage to "discrete images detached from life, separated from their original context, and reunited as an autonomous world apart from lived experience," such as in advertising, television, and the cinema, distances the individual from the world (*Downcast Eyes* 426–27). This gap, which Bloom enacts, resembles, interestingly, the divide between us, word, and world that Marshall McLuhan and Walter Ong found instigated by typography, as we saw in the previous chapter. Like print's materialization of the world, the reification of cultural objects objectifies the severing between us and world, even forcing "a separation and a fragmentation of the public and the private" (Duffy 6). The printed word, the distance necessary to vision, and reification each serve as related testimony before our eyes to our role as readers of the complex system of the world to which we belong. Each reification constructs a public image, that is, one that is not ours alone, affirming our distance from the world that speaks to us with its visible signs. Turbayne makes this similarity explicit: "like the marks on this page or their corresponding sounds, although they lack the dimension of depth in relation either to the things they suggest or to other visual data, it is clear that the visual data are outside us. That is to say, they are not in our eyes just as sounds are not in our ears" (128).

As writer and Aristotelian interpreter of physical reality, Stephen experiences this same separation. Bloom too undergoes it, by his immersion in the postal system, as alluded to in the previous chapter, and as we will see in detail in chapter 6. He also undergoes it via his attention to reified cultural images and objects, and as an ad canvasser. Moretti remarks, drawing upon the work of George Simmel, "If [advertising] were to last, it would lose its magic.... [It is meant] to be glimpsed out of the corner of your eye.... 'it is not possible to possess all the attractive (things)' around us. And so, while flirtation takes care of the human beings, advertising takes care of the things" (136–37). Vision leaves "all the things around us" in that distant space. Advertising, Bloom's business, one so often dependent on vision—on images of images—takes the real another remove away. More than this, as the "flirtation" Moretti mentions does not involve consummation, advertising makes the allure even more impersonal. Bloom's profession, like his personal life, and his idle observations—as well as his inability to move from lust for Gerty, Martha, or Molly to even the personal satisfaction of direct flirting—only accentuate his isolation. Bloom in fact lives out, serves, and perpetuates the influence of reifications. With reification, "the everyday loses any power to reach us; it is no longer what is lived, but what can be seen or what shows itself, spectacle and description, without any active relation whatsoever. The whole world is offered to us, but by way of a look" (Maurice Blanchot quoted in Jay, *Downcast Eyes* 432). As we shall see, applying this "look" to both things and people, Bloom makes clear his separateness from the objects and people around him, his aloneness in the world as husband, father, Dubliner, and professional. The truth to which his eyes lead him returns him merely to his own dilemmas, feeding back into the gap of his *dis*-illusionment.

Taking such looks, Bloom demonstrates that he has far more than a careful, logical vision of the world, despite what Kain's phrase, "keenness of perception[,]" may imply. That description could be taken to suggest that Bloom merely views life rationally, focuses on its discrete objects, or stands outside, viewing. But Bloom's outlook, despite the troubling signs it reveals, comes complete with his full and lively dimensions. His view is more than rational, is more than scientific, and is involved. It also possesses more than the mere sexual inclinations that Kain calls Bloom's "sensuality" (250). We see Bloom's sensory immersion in his world from his very entrance: "Mr Leopold Bloom ate with relish the inner organs of beasts and fowls. He liked thick giblet soup, nutty gizzards, a stuffed roast heart, liverslices fried with crustcrumbs, fried hencods' roes. Most of all he liked grilled mutton kidneys which gave to his palate a fine tang of faintly scented urine. Kidneys were in his mind as he moved" (4.1–6).

Leopold Bloom here enters our world indulging his hunger with carnivorous pleasure, tasting organs that his own body puts to use at both the episode's and the day's end. In the hours that stretch between these moments, as we learn, he more than indulges his tastes; he indulges all his senses. Joyce has created in Bloom a man finely tuned to the stimuli of his aboriginal world, a man, in fact, who affirms life and its aboriginal influences on him. As if to stress this trait, Joyce later reminds us of Bloom's entrance when Bloom eats at the Ormond: "As said before he ate with relish the inner organs, nutty gizzards ... bite by bite of pie he ate Bloom ate they ate" (11.519–22). This is the appetite of the same man who, when his first episode in the novel concludes, doesn't merely defecate but relishes his moment of release, and, when his final episode concludes, delivers what might be called a primal kiss—to his wife's derriere.

    While from morning to night Bloom's responsiveness to primal stimuli
asserts itself, its greatest incarnation comes in Bloom's identification with the
bestial in and about himself. Time after time, Bloom shows the contingency
that persists between his instincts and identity and the beasts of the world.
Although Kain says that one of Bloom's "dominant traits" is his
"[c]onsideration for animals" (199), Bloom is more than merely kind to
animals. He empathizes with beasts to the extent that he even enjoys
speculating what it would be like to be an animal—as he observes in
"Eumaeus": "Of course ... you must look at both sides of the question"
(16.1094–95). In this empathetic spirit, he responds strongly whenever he
encounters an animal. For example, immediately after entering our world,
reveling in his animalistic hunger, Bloom sees the cat approach: "Just how
she stalks over my writingtable. Prr. Scratch my head. Prr. Mr Bloom
watched curiously, kindly the lithe black form. Clean to see: the gloss of her
sleek hide, the white button under the butt of her tail, the green flashing
eyes. He bent down to her.... They call them stupid. They understand what
we say better than we understand them. She understands all she wants to.
Vindictive too. Cruel. Her nature. Curious mice never squeal. Seem to like
it..." (4.19–28).
    Note that Bloom more than studies the animals' features; he also
imagines the thoughts of the cat and its prey. This is symbolically important
because Molly's first words to Bloom on this day resemble a cat's meow—
"Mn" (4.57)—and in her last words in this episode she speaks to the cat with
self-referential suggestiveness—"Come, come, pussy. Come" (4.471). In
"Lotus Eaters," her adultery and the cat will merge in his mind: "Letter. Cat
furry black ball. Torn strip of envelope" (5.156).
    As these examples indicate, Bloom repeatedly sees people in animal
terms, projecting, it appears, his own tendencies to identify with beasts onto
others. As dusk falls, for example, he watches Gerty leave the beach without
glancing back at him and describes her as someone moving "[l]ike a cat
sitting beyond a dog's jump" (13.908–9). Shortly afterward, recalling the
time that Milly kept his change after purchasing stockings for Molly at his
request, he calls Milly a "[c]lever little minx" (13.922). Such metaphors,
arising from Bloom's empathy for animals, advance the argument that he
takes masochistic pleasure in Molly's adultery, as she, catlike, punishes her
husband, the man later mocked in one of his most troubling moments (in
Barney Kiernan's) as "that bloody mouseabout" (12.1579). In Bloom's
relationship to females, a key aspect of his identity, women dominate both on
human and on animal levels. When we learn in "Circe" that Bloom enjoys
Bello's sadistic dominance over him (he tells her: "Exuberant female ... I
desiderate your domination" [15.2777]), we already know that such

hallucinations are consistent with his sensibility. He thinks, regarding Gerty, "Like to be that rock she sat on" (13.1084–85), considers the girl graduates at the library with "[h]appy chairs under them" (13.1087–88), thinks "[c]haps ... would go to the dogs if some woman didn't take them in hand" (13.974–75), and, seeing the women who fox hunt as extensions of their mounts, judges them "[s]trong as ... brood mare[s]" (8.345).

Bloom's feelings about women's power over him originate in his relationship with Molly, which is not surprising given his sense of helplessness before her adultery. Darcy O'Brien's remark that Bloom is "both the manservant of his wife and the scorned admirer of other women" (113) hints at this causal connection between Bloom's awe of females and Molly's domination. The association in his mind between Molly and the cat therefore assumes special significance for his character. Since Bloom began his day by thinking of a cat killing a mouse—in the same hour when Boylan's eventual arrival becomes clear—it is fitting that he would associate his wife with a predator. For example, he recalls how "the cat likes to sniff in her shift on the bed" (13.1023–24) and observes "[t]hat half tabby-white tortoiseshell in the City Arms with the letter em on her forehead" (13.1136–37). Thinking of his morning encounter with M'Coy, he thinks, "M'Coy valise. My wife and your wife. Squealing cat" (11.972). He also ponders female authority with an allusion to Molly: "Her hand that rocks the cradle rules the. Ben Howth. That rules the world" (11.1183–84). Bloom's view of the relation between humans and animals arises from and gives further substance to his sensibilities.

Bloom's identification with the animal world, not surprisingly, also informs our understanding of his base sexual desires. Lusting for Woods's servant girl, he observes "her moving hams" (4.172), and seeing the woman on Grafton Street, he describes her as "[b]eef to the heel" (13.931–32), using appropriate metaphors for a sexual appetite that amounts to carnivorous consumption. This is confirmed by his onanistic lust for Gerty from a distance, when he makes her the object of his appetite with a passion that, as Gerty thinks, "had made her his" (13.692). No wonder, then, that Bloom repeatedly associates sexual desire with animal behavior. Considering how men court women, he thinks, "Always know a fellow courting: collars and cuffs. Well cocks and lions do the same and stags" (13.829–30). Such thoughts may explain Bloom's feeling of guilt when he recognizes the whore at the cabman's shelter, castigates her mentally, and then excuses her with this thought, "Of course I suppose some man is ultimately responsible for her condition" (16.731–32).

Bloom's resonant responsiveness to animals also affects his view of the world in other ways. For example, he empathizes enough with animals to know that they suffer from human appetites: "Pain to the animal too. Pluck and draw fowl. Wretched brutes there at the cattlemarket waiting for the poleaxe to split their skulls open. Moo. Poor trembling calves. Meh. Staggering bob. Bubble and squeak. Butchers' buckets wobbly lights. Give us that brisket off the hook. Plup. Rawhead and bloody bones. Flayed glasseyed sheep hung from their haunches, sheepsnouts bloodypapered snivelling nosejam on sawdust. Top and lashers going out. Don't maul them pieces, young one" (8.722–28).

If Bloom elsewhere compares women to bovines, we might argue from this passage that Bloom's lust for women is tempered by his empathy for them as victims of male appetites. This judgment, again, is substantiated not only by his empathy for other animals raised to satisfy our appetites—such as "Christmas turkeys and geese. Slaughter of innocents" (8.753–54), or fish, "Do fish ever get seasick?" (13.1162); "Silly fish learn nothing in a thousand years" (8.858)—but also by such attitudes as his sympathy for Dignam's widow and Mrs. Purefoy.

In a world in which Bloom seems forever an outsider, as observer as well as disregarded voice, his fellow citizens naturally greet his empathy for animals with derision. When the narrator of "Cyclops" criticizes Bloom's empathy for animals, he offers one of the most scornful passages directed toward Bloom in the novel: "So Joe starts telling the citizen about the foot and mouth disease and the cattle traders and taking action in the matter and the citizen sending them all to the rightabout and Bloom coming out with his sheepdip for the scab and a hoose drench for coughing calves and the guaranteed remedy for timber tongue.... Mister Knowall. Teach your grandmother how to milk ducks.... What's your programme today? Ay. Humane methods. Because the poor animals suffer and experts say and the best known remedy that doesn't cause pain to the animal and on the sore spot administer gently. Gob, he'd have a soft hand under a hen" (12.831–45).

While the empathy criticized here may evolve explicitly from Bloom's former work at Cuffe's butchery, it is also a sign that Bloom's deep feeling for the aboriginal world exacerbates his difficult relationship with others. Reaching out to animals with empathy, wanting to belong, Bloom even has his instinctual impulses scorned. Bloom's empathy for animals thereby increases our understanding of his isolation in *Ulysses*. Defending animals, he meets a very human meanness, and watching animals, he finds a meager humanness. Observing the gulls near the Liffey, he realizes that they have discerned between the bread and wad of paper he has tossed from the bridge and concludes that they are "[n]ot such damn fools" (8.59). Unable to leave without feeding these "poor birds" (8.73), he buys and tosses to them two Banbury cakes. Aware of their weaker human traits, "Aware of their greed and cunning" (8.77–78), and having given them sustenance, Bloom is pleased with himself, "They never expected that" (8.78–79). He is also disappointed, though: "Lot of thanks I get. Not even a caw" (8.84). Turning to animals in friendship, he finds not camaraderie, but ingratitude.

Bloom's empathy with animals even inspires him to think that they can be intentionally mean, suggesting the influence of his occasional experiences with people on this day. Knowing of human crudeness, for example, he infers a whimsical crudeness even in animal intentions with their bodily functions: seeing pigeons flying overhead, he thinks: "Their little frolic after meals. Who will we do it on? I pick the fellow in black. Here goes. Here's good luck" (8.402–3).

Bloom's responsiveness to the primal world, though, does not end with animals. While he eats, he identifies with a "[f]lea having a good square meal [while] Nosey Flynn snuffled and scratched" (8.799). He observes earlier, "Flies come before [a man is] well dead. Got wind of Dignam. They wouldn't care about the smell of it. Saltwhite crumbling mush of corpse: smell, taste like raw white turnips" (6.992–94). He understands, finally, that "[f]lie[s] picnic too" (8.167). In Bloom's day of difficult personal relationships—with Molly, Stephen, the Citizen, and Crawford, among others—the fleas are carnivorous, the flies ruthless. Even the bees enjoy the suffering they cause; typically presuming to understand other creatures, he thinks, "That bee last week got into the room playing with his shadow on the ceiling. Might be the one bit me, come back to see" (13.1143–45).

Even in the midst of death, when presumably he should be reflecting on the life of the spirit, Bloom continues noticing the liveliness of animals. Attending Dignam's burial, he grows curious upon sensing a rat's presence and watches it move about a crypt, recognizing its greediness: "Rtststr! A rattle of pebbles. Wait. Stop! [Bloom] looked intently down into a stone crypt. Some animal. Wait. There he goes. An obese grey rat toddled along the side of the crypt.... An old stager: great-grandfather: he knows the ropes. The grey alive crushed itself in under the plinth, wriggled itself in under it. Good hidingplace for treasure" (6.970–76).

Bloom's thoughts about rat society also vary little from his practical ideas about his world, leading to an explicit comment on the links between animals and humans: "Wonder does the news go about whenever a fresh one is let down. Underground communication. We learned that from them. Wouldn't be surprised" (6.990–92). It is an indication of how people affect Bloom on this day that he attributes human communication to the wisdom of rats. Though Bloom recognizes that the crypt the rat invades could well be his own, he nevertheless feels camaraderie with the creatures, perhaps enviously: "One of those *chaps* would make short work of a fellow. Pick the bones clean no matter who it was"

(6.980–81, emphasis added). Still, the mortal implications of the rat's work later reprise in disturbing tones, such as when Bloom thinks of Dignam, "And that old grey rat tearing to get in" (7.83), or when he is reminded of that crypt and thinks, "Wonder where that rat is by now" (11.1036).

Because his identification with animals is so pronounced, Bloom also envies those who seem to understand beasts better than he does. Regarding women, for example, he thinks, "Of course they understand birds, animals, babies. In their line" (13.903–4). He assumes as well that just as Molly can intuit the meaning of gibberish, others can "[u]nderstand animals too that way. Solomon did. Gift of nature" (11.1093–94).

It could be said, however, that the lively animal imagery in Bloom's descriptions of others is merely "an esthete's allusion" (14.1305), a function of Joyce's naturalism and his artistry in rendering vivid his fellow citizens as they move through Dublin. Moreover, we could describe such figures of speech as merely a function of *Ulysses'* fictional realism. John Rignall, for example, notes how such language plays a role in realistic fiction: "the descriptive energy expended in realist practice on appearances, clothes, buildings, interiors, is predicated on the assumption that to see, to observe closely the visible exterior is to gain access to the life or truth within. Seeing is knowing; description yields meaning; representation involves faithfully mirroring what is seen" (12).

These responses to Joyce's language, though, however legitimate, fail to account for what the animal imagery tells us about Bloom. It is Bloom's consciousness, rather than merely the author's text, that the imagery populates. This imagery is the instinctive product of a thoughtful man whose primal nature finds resonance at every turn, whose personal experiences and sensory imagination merge. This imagery reflects Bloom's deep connection with the aboriginal about him and informs us of his nature as someone immersed in, and responding with vivid feeling to, experience. If this resonance of the primal and the human in Bloom's consciousness suggests the depth of his contingent relation to the physical world, his keen observance of other things confirms it.

His first appearance in the novel, for example, begins, as we have noted, with a primal image, and it ends with a subtle auditory experience: "A creak and a dark whirr in the air high up. The bells of George's church. They tolled the hour: loud dark iron. *Heigho!* ... There again: the overtone following through the air" (4.544–49). Such aural sensitivity also characterizes his entrance into the press offices, "The door of Ruttledge's office whispered: ee: cree" (7.50). Moving back out of the offices, Bloom responds to olfactory stimuli, "Heavy greasy smell there always is in those works. Lukewarm glue in Thom's next door when I was there" (7.223–25).

Bloom proves how sensitive he is, how sensorially observant he can be, with his recollections of his morning visit to Molly's bedside. Though this encounter is brief, Bloom's recall is extensive, vivid, and visual—"No book. Blackened court cards laid along her thigh by sevens. Dark lady and fair man. Letter. Cat furry black ball. Torn strip of envelope" (5.155–56)—and both auditory and tactile, "Swish and soft flop her stays made on the bed. Always warm from her" (8.198–99).

If he is, not surprisingly, attuned to Molly, Bloom is also attuned to people that he passes in the city. Seeing a woman dressed in black, he observes, "a widow in her weeds. Notice because I'm in mourning myself" (5.460–61). He notices Bantam Lyons's "yellow blacknailed fingers.... Wants a wash too. Take off the rough dirt.... Dandruff on his shoulders. Scalp wants oiling" (5.523–25). Meeting Mrs. Breen, he observes "the eye that woman gave her, passing. Cruel. The unfair sex" (8.269). Recalling how Woods's servant girl next door cleans the carpets, he remembers, "The way her crooked skirt swings at each whack" (4.151). Then, walking home after his morning shopping, he notices a woman preparing to board a carriage in her "[s]tylish kind of coat with that roll collar, warm for a day like this" (5.101–2). Bloom is also, not surprisingly, the one observant enough to notice the ding in Menton's hat (6.1015).

Bloom's sensory nature and his primal feel for the world, of course, never affect him more than when he notices Boylan. He hears a single sound hail the usurper's approach, "Jingle" (11.212). Continuing his walk, he hears Boylan's echoes with greater clarity, "Jingle jaunty jingle" (11.245). About to enter the Ormond, he "eyed and saw afar on Essex bridge a gay hat riding on a jaunting car. It is. Again. Third time" (11.302–3). Once they're both inside, "Blazes Boylan's smart tan shoes creaked on the barfloor where he strode" (11.337–38). Typically alert, Bloom notices, "(flower in his coat: who gave him?)" (11.366). Finally, as Boylan departs for the tryst, Bloom hears, "Jingle a tinkle jaunted. Bloom heard a jing, a little sound.... Jingling. He's gone. Jingle. Heat" (11.456–58).

Though upset by Boylan's appearances, Bloom reveals explicitly how much he relies upon his senses. The first time he encounters Boylan, he is on the way to Dignam's burial in the carriage, and, as Simon Dedalus waves to Boylan, who is passing by on the street: "Mr Bloom reviewed the nails of his left hand.... I am just looking at them: well pared. And after: thinking alone.... I suppose the skin can't contract quickly enough when [a person dies and] the flesh falls off. But the shape is there.... Shoulders. Hips. Plump. Night of the dance dressing. Shift stuck between the cheeks behind" (6.200–208).

Bloom's attention to his nails, to one physical detail, gives him surcease from the implications of Boylan's stroll past by leading him to another satisfying detail, the treasured memory of Molly's behind. Similarly, when he sees Boylan again, he tries to distract himself with the tangible comfort of his bar of soap; feeling it, he declares, "Safe!" (8.1193). Seeing Boylan at the Ormond, Bloom purposefully expresses his hope that physical experience will distract him from the tryst blighting his day: "Wish they'd sing more. Keep my mind off" (11.914).

Such compulsions, especially in the moments when Boylan's presence and the tryst loom, corroborate the accuracy of our judgment about the depth and immediacy of Bloom's connection to aboriginal reality. The contingency of his thoughts and emotions to the world explains why, as Clive Hart notes, "[I]t is often [Bloom's] relationship with the gritty physical universe that provides potential salvation from personal attack" (Hart and Hayman 185). We understand, then, why Bloom turns to his senses when thoughts of his own mortality trouble him as he fights them off by reminding himself, "Well, I am here now. Yes, I am here now" (4.232–33), and indulging his sensory fantasies: "To smell the gentle smoke of tea, fume of the pan, sizzling butter. Be near her ample bed-warmed flesh. Yes, yes" (4.237–39). Recalling Martha's typographical error, suggestive of a fear of dying, he likewise thinks, "I do not like that other world she wrote. No more do I. Plenty to see and hear and feel yet. Feel live warm beings near you.... Warm beds: warm fullblooded life" (6.1002–5).

Bloom's senses are so resonant with the world that even imagined experiences have sensual power. Upon seeing sardines on a store shelf, he can "[a]lmost taste them by looking" (8.741). Imagining a trip to the East, he can see, feel, and hear it: "A shiver of the trees, signal, the evening wind. I pass on. Fading gold sky. A mother watches me from her doorway. She calls her children home in their dark language. High wall: beyond strings twanged. Night sky, moon, violet, colour of Molly's new garters. Strings. Listen" (4.93–97). Yearning to bathe, he can anticipate the experience with such feeling that it overtakes him: "He foresaw his pale body reclined in it at full, naked, in a womb of warmth, oiled by scented melting soap, softly laved. He saw his trunk and limbs ripprippled over and sustained, buoyed lightly upward, lemonyellow: his navel, bud of flesh: and saw the dark tangled curls of his bush floating" (5.567–70). In one of Joyce's most celebrated passages, Bloom stands before the silk merchant's store and is able to drift away upon a sense-filled imaginative experience: "Cascades of ribbons. Flimsy China silks. A tilted urn poured from its mouth a flood of bloodhued poplin: lustrous blood.... Gleaming silks, petticoats on slim brass rails, rays of flat silk stockings.... A warm human plumpness settled down on his brain. His brain yielded. Perfume of embraces all him assailed. With hungered flesh obscurely, he mutely craved to adore" (8.621–39).

In *James Joyce and the Making of "Ulysses,"* Budgen tells us of the pride Joyce took in describing Bloom's "hungrily abject amorousness" (20) with these last two sentences, "Perfume of embraces all him assailed. With hungered flesh obscurely, he mutely craved to adore." Joyce worked on this description for two days, explaining, "I have the words already. What I am seeking is the perfect order of words in the sentence. There is an order in every way appropriate. I think I have it" (20). Budgen adds, "Among other things," [Joyce] said, "my book is the epic of the human body.... [If my characters] had no body they would have no mind" (21). Joyce thus insists that physical experience produces consciousness.

Physical experience transformed into imaginative sensory indulgences also dominates Bloom's mind as he reads passages from *Sweets of Sin*. He feels, "Warmth showered gently over him, cowing his flesh. Flesh yielded amply amid rumpled clothes: whites of eyes swooning up. His nostrils arched themselves for prey. Melting breast ointments (*for him! for Raoul!*). Armpits' oniony sweat. Fishgluey slime (*her heaving embonpoint!*). Feel! Press! Chrished! Sulphur dung of lions!" (10.619–23). The allure of the physical likewise entrances him as he watches the patrons and barmaids in the Ormond listen to the whisper of a seashell; he is able to imagine all it expresses: "Sea, wind, leaves, thunder, waters, cows lowing, the cattlemarket, cocks, hens don't crow, snakes hissss. There's music everywhere" (11.963–64).

Sensory experience also overtakes Bloom at the close of "Nausicaa." Interestingly, the narrator's objective voice enters here only after Bloom has drifted into sleep, as if Bloom must surrender his mind's sensory engagement with the world for the narrator to assume control:

O sweety all your little girlwhite up I saw dirty bracegirdle made me do love sticky we two naughty Grace darling she him half past the bed met him pike hoses frillies for Raoul de perfume your wife black hair heave under embon *señorita* young eyes Mulvey plump bubs me breadvan Winkle red slippers she rusty sleep wander years of dreams return tail end Agendath swoony lovey showed me her next year in drawers return next in her next her next.

A bat flew. Here. There. Here. Far in the grey a bell chimed. Mr Bloom with open mouth, his left boot sanded sideways, leaned, breathed. Just for a few

> *Cuckoo*
> *Cuckoo*
> *Cuckoo*.... (13.1279–91)

Anyone as responsive to physical experience as Bloom—who, after all, began his day by eating animal innards, feeding his own body with another beast's death—of course realizes that the world shall pass. Its ephemeral nature becomes symbolized for him in the letters he begins to carve into the sand as a message to Gerty Having begun by writing "I.... AM. A.," he knows, "Tide comes here" (13.1258–64), and admits, "All fades" (13.1267). It is a metaphysical reflection that attains weight from his immersion in the tangible about him. The irony is that these tangible phenomena come to us through Bloom, and that through them Bloom's isolated identity comes to us, as *Ulysses* becomes something akin to a "chaffering allincluding most farraginous chronicle" (14.1412).

Not surprisingly, a man whose perceptions bring him so close to life's aboriginality experiments with his receptivity to stimulation. Early in "Lestrygonians," for instance, he performs that test of the optical effect of parallax. The first time, "He faced about and, standing between the awnings, held out his right hand at arm's length towards the sun. Wanted to try that often. Yes: completely. The tip of his little finger blotted out the sun's disk. Must be the focus where the rays cross. If I had black glasses. Interesting" (8.564–67). The work of the finger, so often touch's device, makes of the gap between Bloom and the sun an occlusion. This blotting out is possible because of that distance between himself and the sight he studies. In the gap, the confusions of disproportion can thrive. Bloom's efforts are, of course, as futile as his business ideas: even parallax using two people in different places on earth causes extreme problems of measurement (Ferris 126). Distance is not easily judged by the eyes alone. Bloom, alone along the human plane, cannot escape the restriction on knowledge sight imposes or his humbling circumscription within the aboriginal to which he belongs. There, whatever divine, transcendent views he wishes for yield to his mortality.

Yet Bloom's most extended reflections on sense experience arise when his mortal plane finds one route to discovery denied. This fact becomes obvious when he encounters the blindness of the piano tuner at the end of "Sirens." In this scene, again ironically, Bloom thoroughly explores his responsive contingent relationship to the world. It is as if in encountering someone unable to feel the full range of the world's potential sensory stimuli, Bloom most appreciates the senses that so heavily influence his own consciousness and identity. We should especially note the ease with which Bloom decides here to test his own senses and promptly considers the heightened powers that he presumes the blind develop in compensation. If "the dawn of the modern era was accompanied by the vigorous privileging of vision" (Jay, *Downcast Eyes* 69), Bloom's encounter with the blind boy enacts the modern man's encounter with his premodern ancestor. Bloom seems to believe that some basic and consistent level of sensory experience is necessary for human cognition and wants to be sure that he has it. With his offer to escort the blind boy across the street accepted, he immediately notices the fellow's clothes and begins to speculate about how blindness might be affecting the young man's other senses: "Stains on his coat. Slobbers his food, I suppose. Tastes all different for him" (8.1096–97).

Bloom proceeds to admire him, no doubt partly because the boy is like himself, "[s]ensitive," "[s]izing [Bloom] up ... from [Bloom's] hand" (8.1098), and able to figure out Bloom's gender from his voice: "Thanks, sir," he says, as Bloom realizes, "Knows I'm a man. Voice" (8.1101–2). Bloom also cannot help but marvel at how well the fellow moves about, a natural reaction given Bloom's reliance upon his senses. Impressed, Bloom observes, in metaphoric language that emphasizes his faith in sight, "[s]ee things in their forehead perhaps: kind of sense of volume" (8.1108–9) and considers "all the things they can learn to do. Read with their fingers. Tune pianos" (8.1115–16). Bloom concludes that these skills are possible only because other senses compensate: "Sense of smell must be stronger too. Smells on all sides, bunched together. Each street different smell. Each person too. Then the spring, the summer: smells. Tastes?" (8.1121–23).

With Bloom's sensory experiences repeatedly enriching his *flânerie*, it is also no surprise that he wonders how the fellow makes his way about the city: "Queer idea of Dublin he must have, tapping his way round by the stones" (8.1110–11). Bloom here invokes an analogy between sight and touch used by Simplicius in his commentary on Aristotle's *De Anima* and by Descartes, among others (Jay, *Downcast Eyes* 74). Jay observes, applying ideas from that familiar machine model, "The point of the comparison [between sight and touch] is that both reveal an instantaneous transmission of the stimulus through pressure, either seen or felt, to the sensory organ" (74). Bloom's classical assumption affirms his sensory dependence as much as it reflects his empathy with others.

The lustful Bloom also cannot help but invoke touch when he imagines what sex would be like without sight; "And with a woman, for instance.... Kind of a form in his mind's eye. The voice, temperatures: when he touches her with his fingers must almost see the lines, the curves. His hands on her hair, for instance. Say it was black, for instance. Good. We call it black. Then passing over her white skin. Different feel perhaps. Feeling of white" (8.1125–31).

Stimulated by these thoughts, Bloom experiments with his tactile sense and particularly enjoys the opportunity rational speculation gives him to touch himself, a notion that foreshadows his self-satisfying masturbation in "Nausicaa": "With a gentle finger he felt ever so slowly the hair combed back above his ears.... Then gently his finger felt the skin of his right cheek. Downy hair there too.... The belly is the smoothest.... Walking by Doran's publichouse he slid his hand between his waistcoat and trousers and, pulling aside his shirt gently, felt a slack fold of his belly. But I know it's whitey yellow" (8.1135–41).

Feeling himself, Bloom enacts a familiar trust referred to earlier, "It is probably the case that tactual illusions, although not nonexistent, are very rare" (Turbayne 125). Experience and memory then add qualities that sight has already noted—the "lemonyellow" of his trunk (5.569)—to the affirmation touch gave him, as if even with his hand on his body, the distance and separateness implicit in vision, implicit in the sense on which Bloom muses, cannot fail to assert themselves.

Perhaps the most interesting observation Bloom makes following his encounter with the blind piano tuner, though, comes when he wonders about the boy's dreams. This is significant because Bloom's mental life is so rich with sensory detail and his fantasies so reliant upon sensory appetites. Knowing how much those fantasies give him pleasure and how important his sensory experiences are to his consciousness and identity, we see that Bloom's empathy for the fellow's blindness is also a fearful imagining of what his own life would be like if he did not have his full sensory powers to enrich his world, distract him from the tryst, and fulfill, at least mentally, his desires: "Really terrible. What dreams would he have, not seeing? Life a dream for him. Where is the justice being born that way?" (8.1144–46).

While this encounter inspires Bloom to fear for and experiment with his sensory powers, it does not diminish his confidence in them. He is, after all, the man confident enough to deduce a universal truth from a singular sound: "Slit. The nethermost deck of the first machine jogged forward.... Almost human the way it slit to call attention.... That door too slit creaking, asking to be shut. Everything speaks in its own way. Slit" (7.174–77). Asserting the Aristotelian model of nature we saw Stephen introduce— "[e]verything speaks in its own way"—Bloom reads the world he watches and to which he belongs. His sense of close feeling for that physical universe explains the authority he assumes when Stephen shrinks from the force of thunder: "Master Bloom, at the braggart's side, spoke to him calming words to slumber his great fear, advertising how it was no other thing but a hubbub noise that he heard, the discharge of fluid from the thunderhead, look you, having taken place, and all of the order of a natural phenomenon" (14.424–28). Bloom knows, in classical form, that "[s]cience, it cannot be too often repeated, deals with tangible phenomena" (14.1226–27). These tangible phenomena continue to reverberate in Bloom's consciousness. As the night ends, Bloom himself affirms his powers of observation. Described as a man "with his practised eye" (16.229–30), he can only enjoy the idea, throwing "an odd eye at the same time now and then at Stephen's anything but immaculately attired interlocutor.... Being a levelheaded individual who could give points to not a few in point of shrewd observation" (16.215–20). Sitting with Stephen in the cab station, he criticizes Mulligan and observes with confidence, "Of course you didn't notice as much as I did" (16.283–84).

Even Bloom, a man closely aligned with the physical world, is not always as observant as he likes to think—as his errors in cultural knowledge hinted. It is only after he stands to leave the church, for example, that he realizes he did not finish dressing that morning: "Were those two buttons of my waistcoat open all the time?" (5.452–53). The exceptional omission, however, only proves again the rule of Bloom's more usual awareness of his world. If he misses a thing or two, he is often successfully and richly responsive to his world. We see this in the close connection he feels with the primal, in his responsiveness to things at their most aboriginal level, and in how the stimuli of the world thrive in his mind. We see in his day a person whose consciousness continually reveals how much of the world he sees, feels, tastes, and desires, his senses wide open and reverberating at every turn. As genesis for much of what we learn about Bloom and his world, this contingency is of fundamental importance to our understanding of the character as well as of Joyce's method and achievement. The ties between Bloom's consciousness and the world make his mind, and therefore *Ulysses*, vivid with color, texture, taste, echoes, and smells—vivid with life. It is a quality that reveals not only Dublin to us but also Bloom and his nature.

Applying Jay's assessment of the French antiocularcentric critique of the Enlightenment tradition to *Ulysses*, we might say the tradition finds its avatar in Bloom's responsiveness to his world. While he extends sensory vitality beyond Enlightenment ocularcentrism and deepens *Ulysses*' realist and naturalist qualities, Bloom does depend most upon his powers of sight. The Enlightenment tradition assumed that truth could be found through the eyes, and Bloom seems to agree. Whether living out Joyce's perspective or simply his own, he is a man for whom, beyond any other sense, "Seeing is knowing" (Rignall 12). How suitable his profession is, then, intended, via the bombardment of advertising, to offer images "to be glimpsed out of the corner of your eye" (Moretti 136). Bloom can ask Nanetti with some authority, however deferentially, to recognize the value of a Keyes ad layout that "[c]atches the eye, you see" (7.151). He has a right to believe he is a man "with a practised eye." We have seen how he notices people he passes, spots the dent in Menton's hat, and turns to visual concentration when Boylan's proximity threatens, preferring "to observe, to see and not be seen" (O'Brien 145), to have the power attendant to perception at his disposal. No wonder he feels "glad I didn't go into the room to look at [my dead father's] face" (5.207–8). In his vibrant reaction to the blind boy, we have witnessed the trust in sight that leads him to imagine other senses alleviate the loss. Two particularly potent moments in his day, further revealing his valuation of sight, indicate a line that in fact links his most highly employed sense to his ultimate heroic actions in *Ulysses*. These actions come when he chooses paths he cannot see due to his lack of foresight—he can only hope they will turn out as he desires. Since those actions center on his relationship with Molly, it is no surprise that for the lascivious, lonely, and yearning Bloom, the scenes in question involve women.

In "Nausicaa," Bloom of course brings himself to climax through voyeuristic study of the willing object of attention, Gerty. Her willingness emerges in such moments as when she prefers to be gazed at herself rather than to join the others in watching the church fireworks: "if they could run like rossies she could sit so she said she could see from where she was. The eyes that were fastened upon her set her pulses tingling. She looked at him a moment, meeting his glance, and a light broke in upon her" (13.688–91). Light of Bloom's gaze penetrating her, she leans back to expose her legs, exchanging a look in the eye and accepting herself as object, "bent so far back that he had a full view high up... and she wasn't ashamed ... he couldn't resist the sight ... and he kept on looking, looking" (13.728–33). Admiring the fireworks, knowing she is being watched, she has surrendered to "the uncanny experience of being looked at [that] completely blots out the possibility of returning the gaze" (Jay, *Downcast Eyes* 288). Significantly for Bloom, "[T]he one who casts the look is always subject and the one who is its target is always turned into an object" (Jay, *Downcast Eyes* 288). Happily for our desperate hero, this power relation is one both he and Gerty accept, to the end of the visual dialogue, when "[t]heir souls met in a last lingering glance and the eyes that reached her heart, full of a strange shining, hung enraptured on her sweet flowerlike face" (13.762–64).

Gerty knows and accepts the object she has been for him. Now, the gaze broken, she turns her back to Bloom and walks away "without looking back" (13.766). His sex act complete, his view of her eyes severed, her physical imperfection suddenly apparent, Bloom's rapture ends. With his declaration, "Tight boots? No. She's lame! O!" (13.771), we break from Gerty as object and return to Bloom's thoughts, where he self-consciously informs us, "Glad I didn't know [of her deformity] when she was on show" (13.775–76). The imagination of perfection that had made her such a worthy object of lust would have been ruined by reminders of frail physiology. What he saw and wanted to see had been unified—he feels fortunate to know— long enough in Gerty's display that he could read titillation into her.

Broached by his imagination, the gap between her body and his had disappeared in the fever of his hand. When his imperfect object of lust becomes an object of pity, a "[j]ilted beauty" (13.774), it is at least not a moment too soon.

Identifying with the print era's "glorification of observation as the only valid way of knowing the world" (Jay, *Downcast Eyes* 67), our canvasser finds this return to distance and self-consciousness troubling. He and Gerty "know, alas, only the meeting of eyes" (O'Brien 158–59). Still, the encounter at least offers our Everyman the greater satisfaction of viewing flesh than of "[s]igns on a white field": "Damned glad I didn't [masturbate] in the bath this morning over [Martha's] silly I will punish you letter" (13.786–87). To us, Gerty is silly, but Bloom only knows what his eyes offer and his mind projects, unlike what Martha's writing tells him about her. If nature is a language, Bloom still much prefers the aboriginal presence of it, visions food of the flesh, even as object, than the additional remove from satiation of Martha's words. It is, in fact, as if our canvasser of ads, like the seagulls, reaches out, nevertheless, to choose the bread of life over paper and its merely typographic images. Empathetic toward women as always, Bloom therefore cannot help but wonder whether other voyeuristic pleasures they miss are the real thing, "Pity they [women] can't see themselves. A dream of wellfilled hose. Where was that? Ah, yes. Mutoscope pictures in Capel street: for men only. Peeping Tom.... Do they snapshot those girls or is it all a fake?" (13.792–96).

When Boylan joins Molly for sex in Bloom's "Circe" hallucinations, Bloom again observes with resonant symbolic reactions. Peering through the keyhole of their door, he shouts as they copulate, "Show! Hide! Show!" (15.3815). On the simplest level, he is of course rooting to see Boylan's phallus in action, replicating the deed he suspects was committed earlier. On another level, he is responding to the adultery of the hallucination and requesting both exposure to and protection from the truth. He also is seeking authority over the adultery, commanding the lovers to fulfill his voyeuristic fantasies and yet cease because it pains him. Similar drives lurk in his discreet reading of the pornographic *Sweets of Sin* and his gentle inquiries about Boylan's letter to Molly. Teresa Brennan writes, "In the case of the gaze, the fantasy is projected onto the other. It is an aggressive projection because, in Freud's terms, active seeing, the type of projective, external focusing Lacan was to call the gaze, is an expression of the drive for mastery" (222). Turbayne notes, further, that all seeing is in fact active, as the language model clarifies: "vision is much more than mere listening and receiving instruction. It is a dialectic or a game of question and answer that we play with visual language. Most of our metalinguistic answering back is in the form of questions, often silent questions of the form: 'What does this *mean* to me?' 'Is this to be called "a lake" or "a mirage?"' ... It involves the invention of hypotheses, the search for counter examples, then their rejection, revision, or retention" (136).

In "Circe," this process of inquiry—a model of our search for reinforcement of belief, it seems—*loops back* against Bloom with a disturbing self-image. There, what interrupts the gaze through which Bloom actively seeks visual discernment and mastery is an occurrence which, like Gerty's limping departure, forces him to notice his position as subject—to become the incomplete object of his own look: Lynch steps in and "(*points*) 'The mirror up to nature.' ... [and, the stage directions tell us,] (*Stephen and Bloom gaze in the mirror* ...)" (15.3820–22). This return to self-awareness resembles what happened when Bloom found his view of the woman entering the coach obscured by a passing tram—a frustration which, not surprisingly, only Gerty's pleasing objectification relieves, "Made up for that tramdriver this morning" (13.787–88). Yearning earlier to see the woman enter the carriage, he naturally was pleased that "gazing far from beneath his vailed eyelids" (5.110–11), "Clearly I can see today. Moisture about gives long sight perhaps" (5.112–13). Emphasizing how sight affects Bloom, these moments also show Bloom becoming an object of his own reflections. He resumes his position as an object in the world rather than as solely a surveyor of all he encounters. It is as if the instinctual questions Turbayne's viewer asks of the world suddenly feed back, like "Ithaca's," on Bloom's own life. Gerty's deformity thrusts him back upon his position as subject and body. Lynch's "mirror of nature" forces Bloom to see himself. When with the blind boy Bloom finds himself unseen, he touches himself instinctively, confirming that he is as physically present as the world to which he wants to belong. He can only sense that the closest he can come to warmth is in his own hands.

Such *self-conscious* actions assure Bloom of his place in the world, however alone. They involve a habit he applies, with a difference, to the end of his day. He earlier imagined the boy compensating for blindness with touch ("when he touches her with his fingers must almost see the lines, the curves" [8.1128–29]). As the night closes, now himself blinded by the dark of his bedroom, Bloom finally offers a kiss that affirms "warm fullblooded life." His lips touch her skin. Molly is there. Object of his renewed desire, centerpiece of the actions he risks to alter his life's trajectory for the better, subject of his "infatuation" with her "effulgent fleshliness" (O'Brien 113), she receives his kiss, the flesh of her buttocks affirming she is present and within reach. The posterior on which she has spent most of her day in touch with the world shares the aboriginal reality Bloom knows he inhabits and into which, as a member of it, he might insist, however gently, his will. He then lays his toes to her head, completing the yin and yang of their sleeping posture. It is on his feet that he has spent most of his day in the world, and so they remain bound to one another, as Bloom wishes, by what links any *flâneur* to aboriginality. In enacting that ritual again, though, he has come to bed with a difference, which *we* witness and are asked to understand.

On one level, he reaches a familiar symbolic and figurative physical union with her. On another, on the level of their behavior toward one another every day, he has instituted small changes in their lives at least through Stephen. "In the *tai chi* circle," it has been said, "the famous Taoist symbol of the fundamental energies of yin and yang—the opposing yet joined expressions of the universal force, Tao—we see that the seeds of disorder reside within the very heart or center of order and vice versa" (Bütz 323). The seeds of change, as chaos theory tells us, do spring from randomness, or apparent disorder at the heart of order. Returning to his familiar posture, Bloom returns with a difference that may yet make all the difference, to borrow Bateson's terms. Lying there with her, having made arrangements with Stephen, Bloom may also be expressing a freer thought, that Molly may yet return his loyalty and fatherly behavior by kissing his feet too and abiding his hopes for communion and love.

Thus goes to rest Bloom and the consciousness that has never ceased allowing the seemingly trivial to escalate in importance. Contingent with its world, it has ever been open to the world's influence. Its openness means that Bloom never stops unfolding to us as the day proceeds, stimuli of the world resonating in his consciousness and in his life as aboriginal creature. The level of Bloom's contingent responsiveness to his world suggests that it is not simply important for what he knows of his world—his epistemological development—but also for who he is—his ontological development. It can be suggested, knowing as we do of Joyce's commitment to making Bloom his representative Everyman, that if Bloom's consciousness comments upon the nature of our epistemology, his life on this day comments upon our ontology. Cheryl Herr has observed that in *Ulysses* "we are asked to agree that life is like art, that our own thoughts emerge just as spontaneously as those of Joyce's characters not out of a void of preverbal desire but out of the fictive discourses and received ideas among and through which we live" (Newman and Thornton 24). We might add that we are also asked to agree that if "life is like art," then our beings themselves and not only our thoughts emerge out of the world "through which we live." Herr says as much: "One of the things that Joyce's insistent alluding makes clear is that thinking, the streaming of consciousness, the content of interior monologue, the very shape of the self are woven from the materials of one's culture" (Newman and Thornton 25).

Herr has reminded us that insofar as we are concerned, Bloom and the world of the novel that emerges through his consciousness are born together. In this respect, Joyce told Budgen two relevant and interesting things. First: "Most lives are made up like the modern painter's themes, of jugs, and pots and plates, back-streets and blowsy living-rooms inhabited by blowsy women, and of a thousand daily sordid incidents which seep into our minds no matter how we strive to keep them out" (quoted in Power 25). This statement invokes Joyce's appreciation of the aboriginal world's impact upon individuals, an idea fully enacted during Bloom's *flânerie* amid Dublin's relentless, chaotic sensory influx—by Moretti's count, Bloom's observing mind, in his first three chapters in the novel alone, depicts three thousand stimuli (155). Along the way, despite what he might imagine, Bloom absorbs and is affected by what he sees: "people [like Bloom] are constantly receiving impressions and images within their minds that they cannot understand or predict.... [and] Joyce recreated this psychic influx with phenomenal success" (Brivic 187). At the same time, "the hero of *Ulysses* is learning a new art: to see and not to see" (Moretti 137). He is learning what deserves a response, what trivialities might burgeon into a new pattern in his world.

In the second key statement, Joyce told Budgen: "the modern theme is the subterranean forces, those hidden tides which govern everything and *run humanity counter to the apparent flood*: those poisonous subtleties which envelop the soul, the ascending fumes of sex" (quoted in Power 54, my emphases). Expressing a Freudian sensibility, this statement combines with the first to juxtapose phenomenal experience with subconscious presence and reveal the nexus of contingency between Bloom's world and his private being. It is an intercourse that is not uni-directional. For *Ulysses* not only shows how the world and Bloom's "subterranean forces" stand separate from each other, a mind retreating "into a more strongly fortified and isolated private world" (Kern 191); the novel also shows them rubbing against one another. Bloom's being is affected by his experience, twisting and turning with it, filled with its dross, touched by its drape. As with any surfaces in direct contact with one another, the overlap here opens the way for each surface to affect that which it touches—for the world to affect Bloom, and for Bloom, he finally understands, to affect his world.

David Wright says that in *Ulysses*, "From lost and isolated souls seen from outside ... we move to characters whose minds we inhabit and whose environment is increasingly determined by the way they see it" (11). Noting how our Everyman employs reification to satisfy his lasciviousness and preserve an empowered or at least safer distance from a threatening world, we watch him watch from outside and, to his loss, largely remain there. Yet, just as the responsive contingency of Bloom's consciousness allows the most trivial recollection or happenstance to stimulate a whole new series of ideas in his mind, it also insinuates that he can "run counter to the apparent flood" and affect his environment and even the course of his life. At the hospital, Mulligan notices Bloom studying the Bass label's red triangle and opines, "Any object, intensely regarded, may be a gate of access to the incorruptible eon of the gods" (14.1166–67). If any minor element might reveal the greatest secrets, such as to us, about Bloom's "hidden tides," it also might reveal one to him, about the world he inhabits. Maybe a trivial decision can blossom like an epiphany into the fulfillment of his greatest hopes.

In this chapter, I have focused on the qualities of Bloom's consciousness that reflect his openness to the "thousand sordid incidents" that seep into his mind and invite such a learning experience. In the next two chapters, I will explore how Bloom's encounter with his world's specific trivialities reveals his identity and inspires his hopes. Perhaps, as stimuli resonate in his psyche, he learns that he too can generate change in his world. The emergent potential in this reciprocal relationship between mind and world offers us at least a new understanding of Bloom. It also expands our appreciation of the significance of his day for us.

KAREN R. LAWRENCE

"Twenty Pockets Arent Enough for Their Lies": Pocketed Objects as Props of Bloom's Masculinity in Ulysses

Abstract. The male characters in *Ulysses*, Leopold Bloom, in particular, play a shell game in the many pockets of their suits. Way stations between the public and the private, Bloom's pockets provide a safe haven for the objects that he cherishes, ritualistically transfers from place to place on his person, and occasionally imports from and exports to others. From the outside the suit helps consolidate the bourgeois masculine image of self-possession and restraint; it provides hidden spaces in which resources are kept close to the body, available for use but hidden from view. Bloom's pocketed objects buttress the performance of his masculinity. The fondled amulets and fetish objects, such as his talismanic potato, arm him in his encounter with the public world and serve as props in the construction of his private sense of manhood. They enable him as well to bend commodity culture to his own idiosyncratic desires. For unlike Marx, who viewed the fetish worshiper as deluded into believing that an inanimate object would "comply with his desires," Joyce presents a fluid view of the flow of desire between an individual and society's commodities as he represents the mysterious process in which masculine subjectivity is constructed amid commodity exchange.

We are all familiar with the famous photograph of Joyce taken by C. P. Curran when Joyce was twenty-two.[1] Joyce adopts a stance of studied casualness: hips slightly forward, hands in pockets, head cocked slightly to one side, he mildly challenges the camera with an expression that gives

From *Masculinities in Joyce: Postcolonial Constructions*, edited by Christine van Boheemen-Saaf and Colleen Lamos. © 2001 by Rodopi Press.

nothing away. The gesture of the hands in the pockets is an integral part of the stance of self-containment, composing the subject in a closed circuit. His hands and his thoughts are hidden from view. The pose teased the photographer into asking what was on Joyce's mind. A viewer might wonder what is in his pockets.

As we all know from Richard Ellmann, Joyce was reported to have replied to the photographer's question, "I was wondering would he lend me five shillings" (caption under plate VIII), suggesting that the mind may be full of schemes but the pockets are almost empty. In the hypothetical afterlife of the photograph, Joyce will attempt to con the photographer. His wits will have to compensate for his empty pockets. In contrast, the mock-priest, Mulligan, does perform a coin trick in the first chapter of *Ulysses*. The old woman delivering tea to the tower needs to be paid, Haines reminds them. The cost of the tea is two shillings twopence.

> Buck Mulligan sighed and, having filled his mouth with a crust thickly buttered on both sides, stretched forth his legs and began to search his trouser pockets.
> —Pay up and look pleasant, Haines said to him, smiling.
> Stephen filled a third cup, a spoonful of tea colouring faintly the thick rich milk. Buck Mulligan brought up a florin, twisted it round in his fingers and cried:
> —A miracle! (*U* 1.446–53)

Mulligan is a magician, a miracle maker who can pull a rabbit out of a hat, a florin from a habitually empty Irish trouser pocket. As we know, much is made in *Ulysses* of what is not found in men's trouser pockets. Money, especially, is scarce. Latchkeys, too, are absent or misplaced: Bloom begins his day by remembering that he left his latchkey in the pocket of another pair of trousers; Stephen begins his day by momentarily pocketing the "huge key" to the tower (*U* 1.530), only to relinquish it soon after. Money and keys, of course, signify one's stake in society's property and one's claim to a proper share of its commodities. Mulligan's sleight of hand allows him to mystify the origins of money in colonial labor in a show of shamanistic powers.[2] In contrast, Stephen eschews Mulligan's pretense of magical powers. After pocketing the coins he has been paid by Mr. Deasy, he thinks: "A lump in my pocket: symbols soiled by greed and misery" (*U* 2.227–28). The telltale bulge in the trouser pocket only *seems* to symbolize the potency of possession; indeed, shortly after this Stephen emphasizes his sense of impotence, with a phrase that resonates beyond its specific reference in the chapter: "The lump I have is useless" (*U* 2.259).

A whole performance of "to have and to have not," of bulging pockets and useless lumps, pervades the multiple references to pockets in *Ulysses*. The novel is full of ritualized performances in which all sorts of everyday objects are hoarded, relinquished, exchanged, and transferred via male pockets. Mulligan's magic act underscores the way pockets function as repositories of props for the performance of character in general and masculinity in particular, props that are invested with magical powers. The "20 pockets" in the male suit, suspiciously viewed by Molly as not enough "for their lies" (*U* 18.1236–37), contain resources for charming the world. Yet Mulligan's hocus pocus disguises the phallic anxiety attached to the performance of the self and the characters' nagging suspicions that the lumps in their trousers are indeed useless.

Fetishism provides the link between everyday objects and the magical investments of desire; it provides as well a clue to the compensatory functions of material objects for the characters that circulate through Dublin in *Ulysses*. In an essay in *Fetishism as Cultural Discourse*, an excellent collection coedited with Emily Apter, William Pietz explains that the word "fetishism" originally referred to the primitive religious practice of worshipping "terrestrial, material objects."[3] Through Marx and Freud, the older anthropological discourse came to highlight the investments of desire in objects that circulate and are exchanged in modern society, with Marx focusing on the collectively valued commodity and Freud on the more personal and idiosyncratic projections of desire. In both Marxist and Freudian discourse, however, "[o]bjects are revealed as provocations to desire and possession," as Apter puts it.[4] It is, of course, in classical psychoanalysis that the fetish object is viewed as a substitute phallus, revealing and concealing the "fact" of maternal castration. Yet, as revisionary work on fetishism has shown, "the idea stipulated by classical psychoanalysis that virtually any object—fur, velvet, chair legs, shoelaces, apron strings, hatbands, feather boas, etc.—can become a candidate for fetishization once it is placed on the great metonymic chain of phallic substitutions ultimately undermines the presupposition of a phallic *ur*-form, or *objet*-type."[5]

Bloom's thought, "no key, but potato," captures the way he props up his sagging masculinity with the magic charms in his pockets. An updated version of Odysseus's moly, the potato is associated with Bloom's mother. It is his talisman, the fetish object that he endows with all the powers of possession that he lacks. "Potato I have," he reassures himself, as he embarks on his circulation through Dublin (*U* 4.73), and in "Circe," after a near miss with the sandstrewer, the stage directions tell us that Bloom "feels his trouser pocket" for comfort in "poor mamma's panacea" (*U* 15.201–02). In the same chapter, Zoe asks Bloom, "How's the nuts?" (*U* 15.1299), and puts her hand in his pocket and feels instead the potato, which she calls a "hard chancre" (*U* 15.1304), bawdily linking the tuber and syphylitic phallus.[6] Although he lacks the patriarchal keys to Dublin society, most of the day Bloom gains authority and confidence from his protective amulet. In his classic study *The Psychology of Clothes*, J. C. Flugel describes the carrying of amulets on the person to ward off evil spirits: "it is extremely convenient," he says, "to carry about some amulet which can be trusted to ward off the evil influences without the necessity of active intervention. For this purpose various objects, supposed to possess magical properties, were hung or otherwise attached to the body."[7] "Without the necessity of active intervention," Bloom arms himself for passive combat, one could say; in the modern suit, however, the amulet is pocketed conveniently rather than hung on the body. In returning magical properties to things, the fetishist locates a potency that he otherwise lacks.

In a way, all the small objects that Bloom carries in his pockets are amulets, for pockets in *Ulysses* are reservoirs of possessions and self-possession, the daily arsenals with which the male characters leave their houses, armed for circulation in society ("A potato, don't leave home without it," one might say). Pockets are temporary havens for the characters' private property as they navigate their way through city streets. We might think of pockets as the material counterparts of the interior monologue, containers that harbor and construct the domain of the private. In being temporary and portable, pockets contain objects that contrast with the more official and societal "secrets" of the drawer inventoried in the "Ithaca" chapter of *Ulysses*. Birth certificate, bank passbook, stock certificate, insurance policy, graveplot purchase document and official records of a name change—these contents of Bloom's second drawer establish the more permanent record of Bloom as a stakeholder in society. Coins, rather than bankbooks; cards with pseudonyms, rather than official records; daily newspapers and advertisements of paradisal communities; food and soap—these are the more perishable and vulnerable commodities protected in the portable pouches of the pockets. As Flugel puts it, "[C]lothes, like the house, are protective; but, being nearer the body and actually supported on it, they are (unlike the house) portable. With their help, we carry—like snails and tortoises —a sort of home upon our backs, and enjoy the advantages of shelter without the disadvantage of becoming sessile."[8]

According to Anne Hollander in *Sex and Suits*, the man's suit—Bloom's suit, with waistcoat, trousers and vest—consolidated the "modern masculine image," a consolidation virtually in place by 1820. In contrast to women's fashion, the masculine suit, she says, "suggests probity and restraint, prudence and detachment."[9] This image of prudence and self-possession is an important part of Bloom's self representation of his bourgeois masculine image; pockets allow for the careful arrangement and concealment of one's personal effects (think of Bloom's self-conscious gesture of "prudently pocketing" Molly's photo in the cabman's shelter [*U* 16.1644]). Pockets provide cover for Bloom's elaborately constructed rituals of docking imports and exports momentarily on his person—elaborate shell games in which he receives fondles, transfers, and replaces objects. Things virtually appear and disappear into the separate compartments of Bloom's "inner pocket," "handkerchief pocket," "sidepocket," "heart pocket," and "trouser pocket." These pockets provide ordering and circulating spaces in a private economy under Bloom's control. Martha's flower and Molly's soap are punctiliously rearranged and separated on Bloom's person, allowing for the literal compartmentalizing, one might say, rationalizing, of his desires ("Change that soap now. Mr. Bloom's hand unbuttoned his hip pocket swiftly and transferred the paperstuck soap to his inner handkerchief pocket" [*U* 6.494–96]). Indeed, Molly herself focuses on the number of secret chambers enabling male deception: "I'll see if he has that French letter still in his pocketbook I suppose he thinks I don't know deceitful men all their 20 pockets arent enough for their lies" (*U* 18.1235–37). Slipping Martha's letter and his own Henry Flower card into his sidepocket, Bloom carefully arranges an alibi, a screen, for his deflowering of Martha's letter: "His hand went into his pocket and a forefinger felt its way under the flap of the envelope, ripping it open in jerks" (*U* 5.77–78). Martha's letter is a kind of prophylactic (or French letter); the penetration of the envelope in the pocket is safe and prudent sex, a honeymoon in the hidden hand.

Yet if they harbor the domain of the private, Bloom's pockets house as well his passports to the public sphere. As a middle man between the economic base and the superstructure, as Jennifer Wicke has put it in describing Bloom's job as an ad canvasser, Bloom is a willing and active participant in the circulation of commodities.[10] Unlike Stephen, he welcomes commercial exchanges. Indeed, his pleasure in the accumulation and manipulation of the objects in his pockets distinguishes him from the more critical and parsimonious Stephen, whose gestures include divestment more than inventory. This commerce with the world is crucial to constructing Bloom's bourgeois masculinity, his participation in the public sphere.

Thus, as way stations between private and societal domains, pockets are portable spaces that facilitate Bloom's illusion of controlling the exchanges in which he participates. He buys a kidney—"His hand accepted the moist tender gland and slid it into a sidepocket. Then it fetched up three coins from his trousers' pocket and laid them on the rubber prickles. They lay, were read quickly and quickly slid, disc by disc, into the till" (*U* 4.181–83). The sensuous symmetry between the gland sliding into his pocket and his own coins sliding quickly into the till conveys the tactile, even sexual, pleasure that Bloom derives from his role in commodity culture, in the rituals of buying and selling. We might remember Apter's idea that all sorts of objects can function as fetishes if they exist on the metonymic chain of phallic substitutions, as "moist glands" are wont to do. Yet, what the tactile pleasure of the fetish suggests in the above example is the way in which pockets are the spaces where characters struggle to personalize commodity culture, to invest the objects in circulation with their particular desires and magical projections. As Pietz observes, Marx saw the fetish-worshipper as deceived into believing that an inanimate object would "comply with his desires."[11] Joyce seems to have a more fluid view of the flow of desire between an individual and society's commodities and represents a more mysterious process in which subjectivity is constructed amid commodity exchange.[12]

So Bloom's' private rituals depend on and attempt to refashion commodities, for example, as when the daily newspaper—a symbol of the urban everyday—serves Bloom as a detachable phallus, his own fetish object for masculine display. To gird himself for his trip to the post office to see if Martha Clifford has responded to him, Bloom draws the *Freeman* from his sidepocket, in a bravura show of his masculinity: "As he walked he took the folded *Freeman* from his sidepocket, unfolded it, rolled it lengthwise in a baton and tapped it at each sauntering step against his trouserleg" (*U* 5.48–50). Imitating the wide-hipped sauntering girl who purchased sausages, no less, in Dlugacz's earlier in the morning, Bloom orchestrates his performance of masculinity with the prop of his "baton," wearing the phallus on the outside. As with Martha's unpocketed letter, the unpocketed *Freeman* shows how Bloom commandeers circulating language, fetishizing textual objects, investing them with his own desire.

Yet Bloom's ritual management of masculine props cannot protect him from exposure and humiliation. Such exposure comes when M'Coy interrupts him and asks, "How's the body?" (*U* 5.86), and "Who's getting it up?" (*U* 5.153), questions that remind us of the lack the fetish object is deployed to conceal. Another moment comes when Bloom, unexpectedly spying Boylan, desperately inventories his ammunition, like a turtle who retreats into its shell:

> Look for something I.
> His hasty hand went quickly into a pocket, took out, read unfolded
> Agendath Netaim. Where did I?
> Busy looking.
> He thrust back quick Agendath.

Afternoon she said.

I am looking for that. Yes, that. Try all pockets. Handker. *Freeman*.
Where did I? Ah, yes. Trousers. Potato. Purse. Where?
Hurry. Walk quietly. Moment more. My heart.
His hand looking for the where did I put found in his hip pocket
soap lotion have to call tepid paper stuck. Ah soap there I yes.
Gate.
Safe! (*U* 8.1182–93)

The analogy between pockets and consciousness is never clearer than here;
Bloom's anxious thoughts and his things spill willy-nilly about, the syntax
unable to compartmentalize effectively the disparate contents of and on his
person. "Try all pockets," Bloom vainly instructs himself. In this passage,
Bloom anticipates Beckett's Molloy, who performs the most famous pocket
ritual in modern literature—the distribution into four pockets of sixteen
sucking stones, individually sucked and deposited.[13] Molloy's stripped down
version of appropriation and self-possession seems a far cry from Bloom's
bourgeois delight, yet the futility of trying to control the placements,
replacements, and displacements of desire is poignant in both cases—and
comic.

It is in "Circe" that this futility is dramatized in theatrical spectacle as
Bloom's inner pockets are picked, his privacy anything but inviolate: "Beware
of pickpockets" (*U* 15.245), Bloom warns early in the chapter. The objects
prudently pocketed or relinquished now speak their own desires rebelliously,
like Molly's soap or the watch which Bloom has earlier drawn from his
pocket in embarrassment, caught in the act of masturbation by Cissy Caffrey.
It is emphasized in "Circe" that Bloom's pocketed objects are mostly fetishes
associated with women: Molly's "wandering soap," his mother's "potato
preservative," Molly's *Sweets of Sin*.[14] These commodity fetishes, in Marxist
fashion, literally take on a life of their own, refusing to sit still for Bloom's
displacements. Indeed, the metonymic "slide" of phallic substitutions reaches
its apotheosis as sticks, "stiff" legs, a "stiff walk" (*U* 15.207), and
"stiffpointed" tails (*U* 15.1252) abound in the chapter. The prosthetic baton
Bloom has made of the *Freeman* is now replaced by Cissy Caffrey's "the leg
of the duck," which she distributes to Molly and to Nelly to strap on
wherever they please. The phallic mothers have their revenge. Indeed, the
sexual differentiation that pockets signify—women carry their objects in
their purses, men carry them in their pockets—is itself undermined. After
Tommy and Jacky run into Bloom at the beginning of the chapter, Bloom
"pats with parcelled hands, watchfob, pocketbookpocket, pursepoke, sweets
of sin, potatosoap" (*U* 15.242–43), trying to remain in possession of his

possessions, which form unnerving combinations and substitutions within his pouches. The pocket is now a "pocketbookpocket"; "purse" and phallic "poke" are combined in "pursepoke." It is in "Circe" most of all that the "thing itself," the phallus, is revealed as a prop. The pocket, by day associated with the masculine suit, by night reveals its female properties, specifically, its pouchlike, womblike function. The props of masculinity and femininity circulate and combine in the heated compression of the chapter. The fetishes, provocations to desire and possession, reveal the way desire is an errant thing not possessed or pocketed but always misplaced and displaced. Finally, for all Bloom's intimate and fond contact with the possessions he harbors, his elaborate pocket rituals can neither conceal his sense of lack nor make commodities conform to his own desires. The comic animism of the fetish in "Circe" signals the slippery slope of substitution, once the metonymic chain of displacement begins.

It stages as well a certain demystification of the artist's conjuring act, a resistance to his magical powers. There is a link between the talismanic potency of the fetish and the seduction of details that contribute to realism's power. It is a connection implicit in the following description in Hugh Kenner's *The Stoic Comedians*: "But Joyce tended to fondle data which comes in finite sets, and to enumerate these sets, and when the data is as protean as the life of a great city, he avails himself of various delimiting devices—single day, a city directory, a newspaper—to give at least the appearance of a finite set."[15]

In *Ulysses* the narrative fondles, invests, and inventories data in the manner of Bloom. In the narration of *Ulysses* we are made to see the sleight of hand performed in all representation—the conjuring of the "things" of the world, "the hidden hand ... again at its old game" (*U* 15.975). Watch carefully as the baton waves—take your mind off the narration and a scene has been moved, objects magically appear without being properly introduced. Anti-realism and realism merge in this fiat, this performance. But if we are careful, we must see through the deliberate mystifications of pulling rabbits out of hats, that is, the aesthetic of art's autonomous creation out of the "deep pocket" of the author's mind; for if the fetish reminds us of the mysterious workings of fantasy and desire, it also reminds us of the material object and its putative value in circulation. The fondling of data and the investment of everyday objects with desire, provide a corrective to the view that art is cut off from the world.

NOTES

1. The photograph is reproduced in *JJII*, plate VIII.

2. This sleight of hand, what Marx called the capitalist "trick" of commodity fetishism, mystifies the connection between labor and capital. I will discuss fetishism in more detail below.

3. William Pietz, "Fetishism and Materialism: The Limits of Theory in Marx," in *Fetishism as Cultural Discourse*, ed. Emily Apter and William Pietz (Ithaca and London: Cornell University Press, 1993), p. 131.

4. Emily Apter, "Introduction" in *Fetishism as Cultural Discourse*, p. 2.

5. Apter, p. 4.

6. After writing this essay and delivering it as a talk at the Joyce Symposium in Rome, I became aware of Peter Sims's fine article entitled "A Pocket Guide to '*Ulysses*,'" *JJQ* 26 (Winter 1989): 239–58.

7. J. C. Flugel, *The Psychology of Clothes* (New York: International Universities Press, Inc., 1930), p. 72.

8. Flugel, p. 83. See Vincent Pecora's description of the persistence of an archaic "oikos," or "noble household," in modern literature and philosophy, which includes a discussion of Bloom's household property, specifically, his potato. Pecora concentrates on the way in which a certain tradition of thought from Durkheim to Mauss viewed fetishism, with its nostalgic magic, as potentially liberating "things deadened by rationality, profit [and] utility" (Vincent P. Pecora, *Households of the Soul* (Baltimore and London: Johns Hopkins University Press, 1997), p. 47.

9. Anne Hollander, *Sex and Suits* (New York: Alfred A. Knopf, 1994), p. 55.

10. See Jennifer Wicke, *Advertising Fictions: Literature, Advertisement, and Social Reading* (New York: Columbia University Press, 1988), p. 128.

11. Pietz, p. 136.

12. Pietz attributes this view of the fetish as an expression of subjectivity to Hegel, whose view countered the more "objective" view of the fetish from Kant: "In contrast to Kant, Hegel emphasized the importance of random association and contingency in fetishism, which he viewed as the first spiritual expression of human subjectivity per se, in the form of arbitrary caprice and particular desire, projected and objectified as power in some (any) material object" (p. 124, n. 14).

13. "I distributed them equally among my four pockets, and sucked them turn and turn about. This raised a problem which I first solved in the following way. I had say sixteen stones, four in each of my four pockets these being the two pockets of my trousers and the two pockets of my greatcoat. Taking a stone from the right pocket of my greatcoat, and putting it in my mouth, I replaced it in the right pocket of my greatcoat by a stone from the right pocket of my trousers, which I replaced by a stone from the left pocket of my trousers, which I replaced by a stone from the left pocket of my greatcoat, which I replaced by the stone which was in my mouth, as soon as I had finished sucking it. Thus there were still four stones in each of my four pockets, but not quite the same stones" (Samuel Beckett, Molloy, in *Three Novels by Samuel Beckett: "Molloy," "Malone Dies," "The Unnamable"* [New York: Grove Press, 1955], p. 69). In this ritual performance, Molloy appears as a wildly exaggerated incarnation of Bloom's punctiliousness and obsessiveness.

14. Sims says that in "Circe" Bloom's pockets "play an important role as sources of comfort and prophylactic protection.... The potato, soap, and condom form a trinity of hygienic talismans, each addressing a different requirement of the phallus' protection" (245). My point is that in "Circe" Bloom's pockets are turned inside out in a risky gesture of exposure.

15. Hugh Kenner, *The Stoic Comedians: Flaubert, Joyce, and Beckett* (Berkeley, Los Angeles, and London: University of California Press, 1962), p. 105.

ZACK BOWEN

Millennial Bloom

After a seventy-seven-year vacillation between the lower (comedic) and the upper (intellectual) Bahktinian moieties, and after rising from being banned to the top of the publisher's list, *Ulysses* has entered into its own unique millennium. Bloomusalem, a new golden city situated in Hibernia, Joyce's comic resolution of the apocryphal discord of political and social ungodliness, unbridled lust, and sin in general is about to arise from the ashes of the known dissolute world. Having entered the new Y2K era with its own prophesied apocalyptic inception, let us consider the meaning of the words of Ben Bloom Elijah and their association with the concept of the millennium per se.

The present connotations of the term *millennium* as a watered-down concept of the span of one thousand years did not always apply. The earlier Hebraic idea of the word embraced a one-thousand-year period immediately preceded by an apocalyptic discord and the ascension of a messianic figure to cast out evil and to rule in peace and harmony over the righteous—separated from their evil counterparts—for one thousand years. After that, the messiah would bring back the evil for another encounter, when ultimately the permanently revanquished evil would give way to general celestial bliss. As initially conceived, the notion, like other Jewish Biblical symbology, was political in that it addressed the need for a safe, prosperous home in which

From *James Joyce Quarterly* 39, no. 1 (Fall 2001). © 2001 by The University of Tulsa.

133

the living as well as the righteous deceased might be gratified. It lent tradition and prophecy to the founding of a beatific hiatus for a Jewish people continually dispossessed by history and their monotheistic creed.

The notion also proved an effective soporific for beleaguered first- and second-century Christians, who applied the Messianic role to Christ and whose sectarian ascendancy to religious prevalence was slow and painful in coming. The more sects and the more nations that adapted it, the more variations were applied to the mythology. Most noteworthy was Augustine's idea that the millennium had already begun and that we were on the ecclesiastical road toward ultimate salvation. As the centuries passed, the idea of making some kind of prophecy regarding the afterlife more immediately available to living people continued the political aspects of the myth's Jewish forebears, and contemporary historical events, disastrous as well as benign, gave rise to a plethora of interpretations, revised and revitalized through time and place over the intervening centuries. Yet the idea of apocalypse persists right down to contemporary evangelism and its dire prophecies.

Joyceans are no doubt acquainted with W. B. Yeats's description of an era when the falcon no longer hears the falconer,[1] when, even in Joyce symposia, the best lack all conviction, while the worst are full of passionate intensity. Surely the Second Coming is at hand. And so it was on that night of 16 June 1904 in Mabbot Street.

Nowhere in the discourses of Jesus is there a hint of a limited duration for the messianic kingdom. The apostolic epistles are equally free from any trace of chiliasm.[2] In Revelations, chapter 20, however, it occurs in the following shape:

> After Christ has appeared from heaven in the guise of a warrior, and vanquished the anti-Christian world-power, the wisdom of the world and the devil, those who have remained steadfast in the time of the last catastrophe, and have given up their lives for their faith, shall be raised up, and shall reign with Christ on this earth as a royal priesthood for 1000 years. At the end of this time Satan is to be let loose for a short season; he will prepare a new onslaught, but God will miraculously destroy him and his hosts. Then will follow the general resurrection of the dead, the last judgement, and the creation of new heavens and a new earth.[3]

Joyce gave Bloom the necessary baptismal credentials to be the messiah to everybody. His establishment as a Jew has been made manifest in a half dozen fine works on the subject[4] and his more suspect references and appearances in Catholic houses of worship during the June day confer a limited Catholic grace on him. He also works the margins of his announced Irish nationalism all day long, a nation of which he is an avowed competent, keyless citizen; and his schemes—social, humanitarian, and commercial—for the betterment of his fellow citizens are everywhere evidenced in his stream-of-conscious thought. Thus, Joyce has created throughout Bloomsday an unlikely, if realistic, Messiah to lead Dubliners and, by extension, the rest of Ireland and civilization through the millennium, both politically, as in the case of the Hebraic millennium provision of a new home, and morally, as in the representation of the conscience of the Irish race.

Joyce's choice of Bloom to ply Stephen's announced trade to "forge in the smithy of my soul the uncreated conscience of my race" (P 253) adapts comic realism to an exalted purpose. In this sense in *Ulysses*, the newly created fictive character (Bloom) supersedes the ironically portrayed self of its author (Stephen Dedalus). Stephen tells us in "Proteus" that he has been reading the works of Joachim Abbas in Paris and in the next paragraph refers to Dan Occam. Both of these scholars contributed mightily to a twelfth-to-fourteenth-century resurrection of millennial and apocalyptic mythology in their efforts to destabilize church dogma by reinstating apocalyptic prophecy.

Beginning with the songs of love, the "Sirens" episode proceeds through the music of war, destruction, and betrayal to close on Robert Emmett's own Irish millennial prediction: "*When my country takes her place among ... [the] Nations of the earth.... Then and not till then.... Let my epitaph be.... Written. I have.... Done*" (U 11.1284–94). Reading Emmett's last words in Lionel Mark's window, Bloom affords them a religious association: "Robert Emmet's last words. Seven last words. Of Meyerbeer that is" (U 11.1275). He confuses the Jewish Giacomo Meyerbeer with the Christian Giuseppe Mercadante, whose oratorio, "The Seven Last Words of Christ," was exceptionally popular at the time and well known both to Molly and to Bloom. The conflation of Christian and Jewish saviors leads to Bloom's own dual and even tripartite religious identity, positioning him for his role of messiah of the new millennium. Emmet's final inspirational message identifies the millennium with the emerging nationhood of Ireland, while Bloom, under the cover of the passing tram—associated with his own scheme for Ireland's social betterment—trumpets a trio of flatulent variations as his own unique last contribution to the musical finale. The farts both presage Bloom's role as comic savior and recall the sound of Gabriel's horn at the last judgment.

Bloom's credentials both as a Jew and as a humanitarian leader are further established in the next episode, "Cyclops," where he exhibits the sort of charity associated with Christ and takes on the Citizen's own brand of satanic intolerance and evil before the episode's reenactment of an apocalypse, one so great that "[t]he catastrophe was terrific and instantaneous in its effect. The observatory of Dunsink registered in all eleven shocks, all of the fifth grade of Mercalli's scale, and there is no record extant of a similar seismic disturbance in [Ireland] since the earthquake of 1534, the year of the rebellion of Silken Thomas" (*U* 12.1858–62). The effect of linking apocryphal cataclysm with Irish political rebellion carries the old association of the creation of a new state linking the righteous with their maker.

The conversation in Barney Kiernan's takes many turns but keeps coming back to Irish nationalism. Bloom faces the same hostility as Stephen in the last chapter of *A Portrait*, since both characters are thought of by the mob as suspect because of their otherness. When Bloom links persecution and nationhood, he faces a sort of prosecutorial inquisition by the bystanders:

> —But do you know what a nation means? says John Wyse.
> —Yes, says Bloom.
> —What is it? says John Wyse.
> —A nation? says Bloom. A nation is the same people living in the same place....—Or also living in different places....
> —What is your nation if I may ask? says the citizen.
> —Ireland, says Bloom. I was born here. Ireland....
> —And I belong to a race too, says Bloom, that is hated and persecuted. Also now. This very moment. This very instant....
> —Are you talking about the new Jerusalem? says the citizen.
> —I'm talking about injustice, says Bloom.
> —Right, says John Wyse. Stand up to it then with force like men....
> —But it's no use, says [Bloom]. Force, hatred, history, all that. That's not life for men and women, insult and hatred. And everybody knows that it's the very opposite of that that is really life.
> —What? says Alf
> —Love, says Bloom. I mean the opposite of hatred. (*U* 12.1418–85)

That is, of course, as close as Joyce will ever come in his fiction to a serious pronouncement of creed.

In this highly political episode, Joyce conflates several themes of Ireland's salvation: Joe's concern about talking to the citizen about hoof-and-mouth disease, reminiscent of Mr. Deasy's bid to be the savior of Ireland; "The Resurrection of Hungary," which provided an impetus for *Sinn Féin*; and Bloom the ubiquitous Jewish messiah:

—Is he a jew or a gentile or a holy Roman or a swaddler or what
the hell is he? says Ned....
—He's a perverted Jew, says Martin, from a place in Hungary and
it was he drew up all the plans according to the Hungarian
system....
—That's the new Messiah for Ireland! says the citizen....
—Well, they're still waiting for their redeemer, says Martin. For
that matter so are we. (*U* 12.1631–45)

Then Joyce reintroduces another motif, the father/son search, to add
to his fictive millennial edifice: "—Yes, says J. J., and every male that's born
they think it may be their Messiah. And every jew is in a tall state of
excitement, I believe, till he knows if he's a father or a mother.... —O, by
God, says Ned, you should have seen Bloom before that son of his that died
was born" (*U* 12.1646–51). As Bloom comes closer to looking for a messianic
son in Stephen by the end of "Circe," he also approaches a sort of
consubstantiation with Stephen's creator, Joyce, who, like Shakespeare, was
his own father and grandfather (to paraphrase Mulligan's observation) thrice
removed; how ever, he is offstage paring his fingernails while the conscience
of his race is dissected.

After the citizen issues his derisive "Three cheers for Israel" (*U*
12.1791), Bloom, ensconced in the cart, begins, like Odysseus, to taunt the
ranting cyclops with the names of five famous Jews, culminating with Christ
and Christ's father, an attribution that even Cunningham cannot abide:

—Mendelssohn was a jew and Karl Marx and Mercadante and
Spinoza. And the Savior was a jew and his father was a jew. Your
God.
—He had no father, says Martin. That'll do now. Drive ahead.
—Whose God? says the citizen.
—Well, his uncle was a jew, says he. Your God was a jew. Christ
was a jew like me. (*U* 12.1804–09)

Confirming the conjunction between Bloom and Christ, the Citizen
vows to crucify Leopold on the spot. But, after escaping the thrown biscuit
tin, Bloom is described as the Prophet Elijah and only secondarily as Christ,
as he calls out to his celestial father:

When, lo, there came about them all a great brightness and they
beheld the chariot wherein He stood ascend to heaven. And they
beheld Him in the chariot, clothed upon in the glory of the

brightness, having raiment as of the sun, fair as the moon and terrible that for awe they durst not look upon Him. Ant there came a voice out of heaven, calling: *Elijah! Elijah!* And He answered with a main cry: *Abba! Adonai!* And they beheld Him even Him, ben Bloom Elijah, amid clouds of angels ascend to the glory of the brightness at an angle of fortyfive degrees over Donohoe's in Little Green street like a shot off a shovel. (*U* 12.1910–18)

While the connection has been made among Bloom, Christ, and Elijah in his ascending chariot, the cataclysmic or apocryphal event was meant to conflate them all, the final inflation of the episode. Bloom, like Elijah, can see clearly the sin of his nation embodied in its mean-spirited anti-Semitism and, in a sense, calls down the wrath of the Almighty. Elijah had only a nominal relationship to the millennium myth. The earliest of the most celebrated prophets of polytheistic downfall, along with the nations who practiced it, Elijah later became increasingly, if loosely, identified with the apocalypses associated with the millennium, and Joyce goes out of his way to further that conjunction throughout the book. As Ben Bloom Elijah goes off and up in his cart to the bright beyond, his "*Adonai!*" brings in a conjoined variation on the father/son motif as it comprises two-thirds of the Trinity. The scene from "Cyclops" sets the stage for a multipersoned persona for Bloom in "Circe" made up of prophet, messiah, and scapegoat.

Before we get to that, there is another Elijah-associated figure we have to consider—John Alexander Dowie, the evangelical preacher on tap for the Merrion Hall sermon, whose throwaway contributes to the apocalypse of "Cyclops" when it is confused with the Gold Cup winner at 20 to 1. When Bloom reads the throwaway, he initially and prophetically interpolates himself into the role of sacrificial victim. My reading of the actual verbiage on the throwaway is as follows:

> Heart to heart talks [the title for the series of inspirational protestant messages]....
> Blood of the Lamb....
> Are you saved? All are washed in the blood of the lamb.... Elijah is coming. Dr John Alexander Dowie restorer of the church in Zion is coming.
> Is coming! Is coming!! Is coming!!!
> All heartily welcome. (*U* 8.07–16)

At first, Bloom thinks that the message either refers to or is addressed specifically to him ("Bloo.... Me? No"—*U* 8.08). Then he speculates on

God's demand for restitution and, after finishing the throwaway, speculates on the money to be made from business enterprises peripheral to the whole prophecy of doom.

As Bloom does indeed throw away the throwaway, he gives it his own benediction: "Elijah thirtytwo feet per sec is com" (*U* 8.57–58). The main point to be made here is that, for the next hundred pages, particularly in the "Wandering Rocks" episode, Bloom's personification of the throwaway as Elijah takes on cosmic prophetic proportions as he/it drifts down river toward day's end, the apocalypse sermon, and the Mabbot Street cataclysm.

Elijah surfaces once more before the "Circe" millennial, this time in the plain language of the old elixir salesman, Dowie, as he shows us the way out of the verbal Armageddon of contemporary dialectical jargon at the end of "Oxen of the Sun." Compared to the rest of the episode, and particularly the scene in Burke's, the understandable words of Dowie's sales pitch fall like sweet rain on parched earth. Assuming the dual role of prophet (Elijah) and personal savior, Alexander J. Christ Dowie sells his salvational elixir to early-rising, would-be, Almighty-God diddlers. Wedded to Bloom in advertising vocation and in proposals of approach to personal and national Salvation, Dowie too has a role to play in the climactic millennial hijinks of the next episode. If he did not convert a single soul in the Merrion Hall, his throwaway certainly left its mark on Bloom's mind, winning the preacher a place in the libidinous activities projected in "Circe."

Bloom's rise to power and subsequent scapegoating has as much to do with political power and martyrdom as it does with spiritual matters. At the crowning ceremony, the Bishop of Down and Connor presents him as the "undoubted emperor-president and king-chairman, the most serene and potent and very puissant ruler of this realm. God save Leopold the First!" (*U* 15.1471–73). Bloom swears on his testicles to uphold law and mercy in all his judgments on Ireland. As supporters and detractors—including Dowie—raise their voices on all sides, Bloom declares the millennium at hand:

> My beloved subjects, a new era is about to dawn. I, Bloom, tell you verily it is even now at hand. Yea, on the word of a Bloom, ye shall ere long enter into the golden city which is to be, the new Bloomusalem in the Nova Hibernia of the future.

> (*Thirtytwo workmen, wearing rosettes, from all the counties of Ireland, under the guidance of Derwan the builder, construct the new Bloomusalem. It is a colossal edifice with crystal roof, built in the shape of a huge pork kidney, containing forty thousand rooms*). (*U* 15.1542–49)

Bloom appears in the guise of social, moral, judicial, and political leader and of Irish folk hero, advancing his ideas and speaking to the crucial issues of the day ("What about mixed bathing?"—*U* 15.1702). The end of this millennial sequence comes after "THE END OF THE WORLD" (*U* 15.2180) says something in a Scottish accent as earlier described by AE, and Elijah, now assuming the American evangelical accent of Dowie, proclaims for "A. J. Christ Dowie and the harmonial philosophy" (*U* 15.2205), inviting all to join in metempsychotic consubstantiality.

The accompanying theme song, "The Holy City," draws on the original millennial narrative for its theme. In the first stanza, the holy city is a nice, happy place, while in the second, a dark night of error includes the clouds of crucifixion on the horizon. Then, in the third, there is a restoration in which the sun shines again and the children sing hosannas. "THE GRAMOPHONE" (*U* 15.2210) captures the final exuberant moments of the millennium as it comes to the inhabitants of the Mabbot Street whorehouse, before the tune is choked off, "Whorusalaminyourhighhohhhh ... (*the disc rasps gratingly against the needle*)" (*U* 15.2212–13).

This metamorphosis is succeeded by a second one that has been much critically commented on,[5] when Bloom and Stephen meld into Shakespeare's mirror image, before the strains of the second major musical theme, "My Girl's a Yorkshire Girl," are taken up to begin the final political and psychological apocalypse; here, Stephen, adopting the guise of Siegfried, breaks the chandelier with his ashplant during the PIANOLA'S Yorkshire "Dance of Death." An era in the order of gods is concluded with Stephen's "*Nothung!*" as "*[t]ime's livid final flame leaps and, in the following darkness, ruin of all space, shattered glass and toppling masonry*" (*U* 15.4242, 4244–45). As Stephen escapes into the street to confront Privates Carr and Compton, echoes of the song pursue him. The "Yorkshire Girl," first heard in "Wandering Rocks" as martial music from the highland laddy soldiers, now accompanies a mock battle between the British privates and Stephen. It is about whose girl the Yorkshire girl is, when two young Brits who claim her for their own both go to her house to settle the claim and find a husband in charge who claims that his girl is a Yorkshire girl too. Stephen's military altercation begins over Cissy and ends with him being knocked down. After settling Bella's breakage demands, Bloom, in the guise of Haroun al Rachid, affects Stephen's release and stands guard over the prostrate young man, who assumes for Bloom the persona of his dead son, a resurrection to culminate in the climactic millennial sequences of the book.

After the denouement of doubt, the comically obfuscated subterfuges of "Eumaeus," and Bloom's settling down, rancor- and vengeance-free, between the "smellow melons" of Molly's behind (*U* 17.2241), peace has come at last over Bloom's existence. Molly's final pronouncements in this regard are nothing more than a comic affirmation that we have already entered into a blissful existence.

NOTES

1. See W. B. Yeats, "The Second Coming," *The Collected Works of W. B. Yeats*, ed. Richard Finneran (London: Macmillan Publishers, 1990), p. 187.

2. The term "chiliasm" refers to Christ's expected return to earth to reign for one thousand years.

3. See the *Encyclopedia Britannica*, 14th ed., p. 496.

4. See, for instance, Ira B. Nadel, *Joyce and the Jews: Culture and Texts* (London: Macmillan Publishers, 1989), and Harry Girling, "The Jew in James Joyce's *Ulysses*," *Jewish Presences in English Literature*, ed. Derek Cohen and Deborah Heller (Montreal: McGill-Queen's Univ. Press, 1990).

5. See Stuart Gilbert, *James Joyce's "Ulysses": A Study* (1930; New York: Vintage Books, 1958), p. 337, William York Tindall, *James Joyce* (1958; New York: Noonday Press, 1971), p. 206; and Zack Bowen, *"Ulysses," A Companion to Joyce Studies*, ed. Bowen and James F. Carens (Westport, Conn.: Greenwood Press, 1984), p. 528.

ANDREW GIBSON

Only a Foreigner Would Do:
Leopold Bloom, Ireland, and Jews

'What about the Jews?'

Critical accounts of the Jewish theme in *Ulysses* have often not been sufficiently historically specific. Alternatively, they have been so in one way but not another: precise about Jews and anti-Semitism in the modern Europe in which Joyce composed his novel, much less exact about the same subjects in the Ireland in which Joyce grew up, the Ireland of *Ulysses*. Neil Davison and, above all, Dermot Keogh have recently started to redress the balance.[1] But even Keogh's reading of *Ulysses* veers away from the implications of the historical material he provides. Neither scholar can break with a well-established structure which counterposes Bloom as a supposedly more or less representative European Jew to the emergence of a generalized, modern anti-Semitism. As far as the Jewish theme is concerned, it would seem that Joyce can only be either a paradigm of liberal tolerance and decency and a defender of humanist principle against dark forces of reaction, or a humanist in principle but given to lapses, for historical and cultural reasons. At this juncture, no other reading seems possible.

The problem with the critical tradition is its reluctance to think Jews and Irish together. Thus Marilyn Reizbaum's recent *James Joyce's Judaic Other* casts a Bloom- and Europe-centred reading of the novel precisely against one centred on Stephen and Ireland.[2] Yet when the citizen asks

From *Joyce's Revenge: History, Politics, and Aesthetics in* Ulysses. © 2002 by Oxford University Press.

Bloom what his nation is, in 'Cyclops', Bloom replies 'Ireland ... I was born here. Ireland' (12. 1431). The repetition is emphatic and, on one level, the fact is simple but crucial: Bloom is an Irishman, and Joyce intended him to stand as both Jew and Irishman at once. To think this double identity, however, between 1882, the year of Joyce's birth, and 1922, the year in which Ulysses was published, is to think an extremely specific phenomenon. Critics have addressed the question of the historical and cultural specificity of the Irish Jew in Ireland only in relation to the abstract structure just described. But this limits any formulation of the Irish–Jewish relation, for the structure in question tends to cast Bloom as modern European Jew in opposition to a benighted Ireland. More often than not, Bloom becomes a gauge of the unregenerate backwardness of the Dublin Catholic community. Indeed, Joyce's profound sympathy with Jews has frequently been linked to a tendency to denigrate his own people, for whom the critic him- or herself sometimes has at best a limited feeling (the case with Davison, for instance). What Joyce took to be the analogy between two traumatic histories was crucial to his interest in Jews. But his critics have often tended to treat the Jewish catastrophe with due respect, whilst hearing an emphasis on the Irish historical catastrophe as merely nationalist griping or sentimental self-indulgence. In effect, at the heart of what it understands to be Joyce's philo-Semitic humanism, criticism has repeatedly placed an extraordinary indifference to the long history of suffering and injustice about which he knew most. In this respect, Ulysses has been read as a post-Holocaust rather than as a post-Famine novel.

Without questioning or diminishing Joyce's stature as an opponent of anti-Semitism, I would argue for quite a radical departure from the critical tradition. This does not mean that I want to dismiss the more established emphases. Instead, I want to position them differently, to take them less for granted, to place them in a complex Irish historical context, and thus to see them as outcomes of an arduous, winding, difficult process of thought. The most significant and arresting features of Joyce's treatment of his Jewish theme are historically particular to late nineteenth-and early twentieth-century Ireland. His Jew is a historically specific Irishman. The anti-Semitism with which he deals is a historically and culturally specific anti-Semitism. Most importantly of all: in Ulysses, both Jew and anti-Semitism exist in a culture that is European but also colonial, that is, in a culture to which a politics of race is historically endemic and where it is pervasive in social relations. The position of Jewish people and the emergence and persistence of anti-Semitism within such a culture ask to be thought quite differently. So, too, do literary and political responses to Jews and resistances to anti-Semitism, like Joyce's in Ulysses.

In late nineteenth- and early twentieth-century Ireland, Jewish issues always insert themselves into an already existing politics. They form part of that politics and cannot properly be separated from it. In dealing with Jews and the Jewish theme, *Ulysses* necessarily also engages with the politics in question. It is therefore a much more complicated and sophisticated—or, better, more cunning—response to the situation of Irish Jews than has so far been recognized. The complex political formation at issue here can be addressed in various ways. My chief example—the Limerick pogrom—is familiar, but nonetheless representative. Its relevance to *Ulysses* has long been noted.[3] Both Davison and Keogh have recently reminded us of it in fresh contexts. The pogrom was a significant outbreak of Irish anti-Semitism historically close to the date at which the novel is set. There would seem to be no explicit mention of it in *Ulysses*. But certain references in the novel show that Joyce was well aware of it and had read about it in newspapers. Indeed, the instances of anti-Semitism which punctuate Bloom's day have a precise, historical character. Many of the characters in *Ulysses* reveal a heightened awareness of Bloom's Jewishness. This is partly the result, not only of the events in Limerick, but of the coverage of those events in the Irish and, to a lesser extent, the English press. Indeed, as we'll see later, such an awareness is also the consequence of a particular kind of concern about Jews that was widespread at the time in England and Ireland.

The disturbances in Limerick started in mid-January 1904, and then rumbled on for quite a long time afterwards. So did the press coverage. Arthur Griffith's *United Irishman*, for example, was still pursuing the issue energetically—and arguing with pro-Jewish nationalists—through April and May.[4] *Ulysses* responds to the Limerick pogrom, the climate that was its aftermath, and other kinds of manifestation of anti-Semitism in early twentieth-century Ireland. But Joyce was not directly concerned with a pure, unmediated manifestation of racial hatred. Insofar as he knew of the pogrom, he knew of it precisely through the newspapers, as involving questions of representation and discourse. Furthermore, terms like 'bigotry', 'tolerance' and 'intolerance' that were in circulation in discussions of Limerick were already contested and the site of a political and ideological struggle. The Limerick pogrom often made the news (quite literally) alongside two other Irish issues, the University question and the question of the Handbook of the Catholic Association. The three issues tended to get mixed up in Irish and English newspapers and in people's minds. In the first instance, during this period, the question of a separate university for Irish Catholics had re-emerged. Amidst expectations that the Balfour government would at long last deliver, January saw numerous meetings throughout Ireland in support of a Catholic university. But it also saw growing Unionist resistance to what, speaking to an Orange demonstration in Belfast, the government minister Lord Londonderry called this 'retrograde movement'.[5] For Catholics—and indeed many enlightened, liberal Protestants—the establishment of a separate university was simply a question of equality and right.[6] It meant redressing a historical injustice and bringing an end to the 'racial distinctions' in education with which, as I noted earlier, Lord Dunraven claimed the walls of Trinity College were 'saturated'.[7] In the terms of the *Freeman's Journal*, any refusal to establish a Catholic university would be an anachronistic perpetuation of a colonial politics, a 'continuance in the twentieth century of the spirit and principles of the Penal code of the eighteenth'.[8] On the other hand, Unionists declared that the case for a Catholic university was rooted in an illiberal sectarianism. This argument barely concealed Protestants' anxieties at the erosion of their cultural power. In certain quarters, at least, there also lurked within it a consciousness of race and class. The Unionist *Daily Express* in Dublin, for example, repeatedly argued that a Catholic university would mean 'an absolute lowering of the educational standard'.[9] J. P. Mahaffy later expressed a similar contempt with reference to the University question, describing Joyce himself as 'a living argument in favour of my contention that it was a mistake to establish a separate university for the aborigines of this island—for the corner-boys who spit in the Liffey'.[10] By early February, Unionist pressure had led to a statement in the Commons from George Wyndham, the Chief Secretary for Ireland. The Tory government, he announced, would take no steps to legislate for a Catholic university in the current parliament.[11]

The Catholic Association of Ireland had been formed in 1902 for the promotion of Catholic interests. In R. F. Foster's terms, it was out to 'destroy' Protestant influence.[12] In Catholic terms, it was intent on disputing the long history of the 'monopolies and privileges', the 'unjust and overwhelming prerogatives of ascendency'.[13] Its handbook had appeared late in 1903, to Protestant alarm, in that it struck a newly belligerent note. On the one hand, Catholics claimed that the sole aim and object of the Association was to give them the means to defend themselves against at least certain Protestant elements, 'to protect Roman Catholics from the bigotry and intolerance of the other side'.[14] Protestants retorted that the Association was itself a vehicle for bigotry. This accusation is fired back once again at Protestants by Catholics, not least in the nationalist press. The crucial point, here, is that, in this respect, a manifestation of Catholic anti-Semitism was a gift to the ideological cause of Unionism. Thus in Protestant accounts, the alleged bigotry of the Catholic Association was repeatedly linked with the Limerick Catholic 'attacks on and the persecution of the Jews'.[15] *The Times* in London made the same connection, associating Catholic anti-Semitism with nationalist anti-Englishness.[16] Catholics had claimed that the British and Unionist attitude to the University question was a form of persistence in 'a cruel persecution'.[17] But Protestants, Unionists, and their press claimed that Limerick offered ample evidence of the Catholic will to persecute.[18] This latter had simply been 'peculiarly vindictive in the case of the Hebrews'.[19] With the University question, Limerick, and Irish anti-Semitism all in mind, Bishop O'Dwyer of Limerick asserted that Catholic Irish shortcomings were the result of 'a defective, if not vicious education'.[20] But for many Protestants, in the words of James Stanley Monck, any claim made for the tolerance of 'the Roman Catholic proletariat' could from now on be summarily disposed of 'by asking the very simple question: "What about the Jews?"'. Belfast was allegedly a stronghold 'of Protestant bigotry and intolerance'. But its Protestants had willingly appointed a Jew as their mayor.[21]

This was not the only way in which Unionist Ireland and (less frequently) England used the case of the Limerick Jews. If only the inhabitants of Limerick had been 'as hardworking as the Jews', lamented one of the prosecuting lawyers at the trial of some of those responsible for the offences, 'Limerick would be a great deal more prosperous'.[22] The 'industrious, honest and law-abiding Jew'[23] swiftly became the implicit countertype of the slothful, feckless, deceitful, unruly and, indeed, sometimes still savage Irish Catholic worker or peasant. To a correspondent in the *Daily Express*, for example, Irish anti-Semitism made it seem hardly surprising that 'some English people think the Irish but little removed from barbarism'.[24] Jewish cleverness, too, became the countertype of Irish stupidity, as when E. H. Lewis Crosby, head of the Church of Ireland Mission, suggested that the ease with which the Limerick Jews had outwitted them demonstrated how 'very foolish or ignorant' a set of people 'Father Creagh's flock' were.[25] More generally, Unionists asserted that the Limerick Catholics had displayed a characteristic Irish 'inflammability', that their anti-Semitism showed how medieval they still were (as opposed to England, where anti-Semitic violence had supposedly died out in the Middle Ages).[26] What is remarkable is how far a Protestant, Unionist, and to some extent English rhetoric identifies the Jewish with the English and Protestant cause, especially in opposing the Catholic Irish.[27] Lewis Crosby argued that, historically but to their own detriment, it had been Catholic countries that had banished Jews. Over the centuries, Protestant countries had welcomed Jews and benefited from their talents, business acumen, energy, and thrift.[28] Protestants even asserted that, like the Irish Jews, they themselves were now vulnerable to Catholic persecution. Like the Jews, they depended on—and must have—British justice and fair play, the protection of the British government; in other words, the Union. In a strange twist of affairs—especially given the tradition of nationalist use of the Irish–Jewish analogy, of which more shortly—'To your tents, O Israel' even becomes a Protestant battle-cry.[29]

House of Bondage

The most significant contexts for the political discourses concerning the Jews in early twentieth-century Ireland are perceptible here. This formation—exemplified in but not confined to responses to the Limerick pogrom—is the dominant discursive formation with regard to Irish Jews in 1904. It should be clear from the start that Joyce's attitude to the Jews in Ireland must be sharply distinguished from the tradition of modern, Anglo-Saxon, liberal tolerance. Joyce had a very precise sense of how far that tradition could be specious; how far, in Ireland, especially in Unionist hands, it could be betrayed in being placed at the service of political calculations. Readily resorted to in certain cases (like the Limerick Jews), it was also categorically left out of account in the case of other Irishmen. The problem that then arises is a familiar one which Joyce confronts repeatedly: how to broach difficult questions for those Stephen addresses as 'his people' (14. 367–400) without disavowing what is also a fundamental identification with them. As far as the Jewish theme is concerned, in *Ulysses* as a whole, Joyce evolves a range of complex and subtle practices. In doing so, he seeks to repudiate and counter the Scylla of Irish Catholic anti-Semitism without identifying with the Charybdis of an 'enlightened' English and Anglo-Irish tolerance. For in this context, the latter is inseparable from a demonization of Irish Catholicism per se. As both Davison and Keogh have pointed out, Catholic and nationalist anti-Semitism was not confined to Creagh and his Limerick flock. According to Keogh, it had begun in the 1880s, with the sudden influx of Jewish immigrants fleeing Russian pogroms, the result being a rapid expansion of the Jewish population in the larger Irish towns and cities.[30] This produced anti-Semitic poster campaigns and letters to the press.[31] The most decisive instances of nationalist anti-Semitism before Limerick, however, came from Arthur Griffith in the *United Irishman* from 1899 and, a little later, D. P. Moran and other contributors to *The Leader*. During this period, for the first time, significant voices in Catholic and nationalist Ireland were raised in numbers against Jews in general and Irish Jewry in particular.

The newness of this phenomenon is very important for an understanding of the Jewish theme in *Ulysses*. Keogh argues convincingly that in Ireland, unlike other European countries, although the theological, liturgical, and intellectual foundation for anti-Semitism were certainly present, Catholicism was 'not characterized by a hostility to the Jews'.[32] The reasons for this are not altogether proud ones: as a colonized people, the Catholic Irish were preoccupied with their antagonism towards the colonizer. But throughout the nineteenth century, there had nonetheless been an honourable tradition of Catholic *and* Protestant nationalist identification of the Irish with the Jewish people. It ran from Tone to Parnell through O'Connell. There was of course a tradition of allegorization of the Irish as the Jewish people awaiting their redeemer or, more commonly, their Moses to deliver them from captivity. But the identification of Irish and Jews was more than an abstraction or a biblical trope. It also involved an insistence on the resemblances between Irish and Jewish histories: oppression, persecution, victimization, immiseration, demonization, disempowerment, diaspora. At times, it was a political matter: O'Connell allied himself with English Jews on questions of religious emancipation.[33] Indeed, the nationalist identification with the Jews was to some extent reciprocated: in the earlier nineteenth century, Jews had often felt a common bond with Irish Catholics precisely because of the extent to which areas of public life were closed to both races on religious grounds.[34] Jews worked on behalf of victims of the Irish famine,[35] and were themselves lauding Irish society for its racial tolerance until late in the nineteenth century.[36]

What happens then, disastrously, is that, in certain nationalist quarters, as Jews enter Ireland in greater numbers, the Irish–Jewish identification traditional within the culture breaks down. Griffith, Moran, and others begin to identify the arriving Jews with invaders and thus with the colonizer. Not only do they appear wilfully to ignore the dire injustice of this conflation. They also seem oblivious to the fact that it effectively subscribes to the structure of a mythology (identifying Protestant and Jewish causes) that was being promoted by Unionism. For the nationalists in question, the Jew is a 'parasite', like the Irish landlord and his agents.[37] Jews are 'prosperous' and therefore privileged.[38] They threaten to 'plant their heels' on the people's necks and impose a worse 'slavery' than did Cromwell.[39] They are 'grinders' of the poor and in conspiracy with the English.[40] Nationalist discourse on Jewry thus splits. Griffith, Moran and others become anti-Semites. Nationalists like John Redmond, Fred Ryan, and, above all, Michael Davitt continue to condemn anti-Semitism in itself, outright, and to insist on both the allegorical significance and the material substance of the more traditional Irish–Jewish analogy.[41] In the terms of this discourse, the denunciation of Jews is not required by nationalist opposition to English rule. It is rather the result of a pathetic, even cowardly reluctance to face the realities of colonial power and the logic of the Irish predicament. This above all is Davitt's argument.[42]

Remembering Thee, O Sion

Ulysses responds to this situation in various and complex ways. First, Joyce repudiates the English and Anglo-Irish construction which opposes reasonable, enlightened England and Unionist Ireland to bigoted, benighted Catholic Ireland. He knew it was a myth, not just where questions of tolerance in general were concerned, but where anti-Semitism itself was at stake. The first two major instances of anti-Semitism we encounter in the novel come from an Englishman and an Ulster Unionist. Joyce literally gives priority to English examples of anti-Semitism, or an anti-Semitism that refers back to an English context. This anti-Semitism was evident enough at the time. Haines's version of it echoes English worries about 'undesirable aliens' which led to the Aliens Act of 1905.[43] Jews (East European, rather than German) figured largely among the 'aliens' in question.[44] Balfour—who wanted to keep Britain 'Anglo-Saxon'—spoke of 'the undoubted evils which had fallen upon portions of the country from an alien immigration which was largely Jewish'.[45] Deasy echoes the same 'xenophobic attitude to the supposed "alien menace" threatening Britain' as expressed (according to Loughlin) by turn-of-the-century Ulster Unionists.[46] Here, again, the attitude was chiefly focused on Jewish refugees.

Joyce presents this English and Unionist anti-Semitism as the larger, determining frame for the Catholic anti-Semitism which will later emerge in the novel. Within a certain English and Unionist discourse, the Jews, like the Fenians, are the enemy of or at the very least a problem for the nation and state. They are 'the signs of a nation's decay', says Deasy: 'Wherever they gather they eat up the nation's vital strength. I have seen it coming these years. As sure as we are standing here the Jew merchants are already at their work of destruction. Old England is dying' (2. 347–51). But the most significant instance of Deasy's anti-Semitism comes at the end of 'Nestor': 'Ireland, they say, has the honour of being the only country which never persecuted the jews. Do you know that? No. And do you know why? ...— Because she never let them in, Mr Deasy said solemnly' (2. 437–42). From O'Connell to Davitt, what Deasy ironically calls Ireland's 'honour' in this respect was a nationalist boast.[47] It was famously echoed by the Chief Rabbi of the British Empire, Dr S. Hermann Adler, when consecrating the new headquarters of the Dublin Hebrew Congregation in 1892.[48] Davitt himself cited the Rabbi in denouncing Creagh and defending Irish and Limerick Jewry.[49] Deasy is clearly also citing Rabbi Adler but with Davitt in mind, mocking and distorting both the Catholic claim and the Irish-Jewish analogy in the process. But the historical irony rebounds on him: as Joyce surely knew, Deasy's jest and his anti-Semitism in general also flagrantly contradict the *Unionist* claim then current to solidarity with the Irish Jews. The chapter leaves it to the young 'fenian' Stephen Dedalus (2. 272) to defend the cause of the Jews as best he can. In fact, 'Nestor' as a whole returns us to an established nationalist alignment: Catholic and Jew on the one side, Protestant and Unionist on the other.

The irony, of course, is that, amongst Catholics, it is Bloom who must insist on the same alignment: 'And I belong to a race too, says Bloom, that is hated and persecuted. Also now. This very moment. This very instant' (12. 1467–8). Throughout the day, and above all in 'Cyclops', in the Catholic community, Bloom encounters the contemporary betrayal of the Irish–Jewish analogy. He comes up repeatedly against the anti-Semitism of the new nationalism. He likewise confronts the nationalist identification of the Jew with the colonial invader or the colonial exploiter evident in the writings of Griffith, Moran, and others. In the citizen's diatribe, the new Jewish arrivals in Ireland are not merely 'nice things ... coming over here to Ireland filling the country with bugs' (12. 1141–2).[50] They are also 'swindling the peasants ... and the poor of Ireland' (12. 1150), 'We want no more strangers in our house', the citizen continues (12. 1151–2): '—The strangers, says the citizen. Our own fault. We let them come in. We brought them in. The adulteress and her paramour brought the Saxon robbers here' (12. 1156–8). The Jews fleeing from the European pogroms are conflated with English despoilers. The citizen has only one type for the incoming arrival or alien intruder, and it is colonial. It is thus no accident that the two principal objects of the citizen's vituperations in 'Cyclops' are Jews on the one hand and British imperialism on the other. The coincidence of the same two targets was evident enough in Griffith's *United Irishman* and Moran's *Leader*. But the commonplace suggestion that Joyce understood both kinds of attack as informed by a similar racism is absurd. What he recognizes is a kind of colonial pathology according to which the invader's pitiless refusal to imagine otherness may be reduplicated and even intensified in the invaded. The capacity for any imaginative leap has been swallowed up by the polarized antagonisms of the colonial context. The other from elsewhere can only be the enemy.

Such intellectual paralysis left Anglo-Ireland and England free to appropriate the Jewish identification. In *Ulysses*, however, Joyce powerfully reasserts the traditional Irish–Jewish analogy. In effect, he reclaims it for a people in danger of disavowing and thereby surrendering it. The most obvious example of this is MacHugh's rendering of John F. Taylor's speech in 'Aeolus' (7. 828–70). The anti-colonial, Parnellite intensity of the speech emerges very clearly in the mimicry of the conqueror's voice:

> *—Why will you jews not accept our culture, our religion and our*
> *language? You are a tribe of nomad herdsmen: we are a mighty people.*
> *You have no cities nor no wealth: our cities are hives of humanity and*
> *our galleys, trireme and quadrireme, laden with all manner*
> *merchandise furrow the waters of the known globe. You have but*
> *emerged from primitive conditions: we have a literature, a priesthood,*
> *an agelong history and a polity.* (7. 845–50)

The speech goes on to insist on the need to continue with the proud, indomitable, Parnellite tradition of resistance, not least as couched in '*the language of the outlaw*' (7. 861–9). The passage is extremely important for the novel as a whole. It was so important for Joyce that, when he was asked to record some of *Ulysses*, he selected this passage.[51] In doing so, he repeated Stephen's self-effacing homage to the tradition Taylor represents ('me no more', 7. 883). He also chose, not only to give a privileged place to Parnell and Parnellism, but also to give the same privilege to the Irish–Jewish analogy. In effect, he was underlining the centrality of the latter to his larger project. But this is by no means the only moment at which *Ulysses* reasserts the Irish–Jewish analogy in more or less its traditional form. It reappears sporadically throughout the book, with Kevin Egan, for example: 'They have forgotten Kevin Egan, not he them. Remembering thee, O Sion' (3. 263–4); or with Stephen's injunction to '[his] people' to 'look forth upon the land of behest' in 'Oxen', whilst, as both Irish bard and scapegoat, he is left alone with the 'Egypt's plague' of 'the adiaphane in the noon of life' (14. 375–86).

   But Joyce does not just reassert the Irish–Jewish analogy. He also makes it his own. He deepens it, as in Stephen's recollection of the Jews at the Bourse (2. 364–72). 'Not theirs', thinks Stephen, 'these clothes, this speech, these gestures' (2. 367). The Parisian Jews' condition echoes that of an Irish bard dressed in 'castoffs' whose earlier avatar asserted of the English Dean of Studies that 'his language, so familiar and foreign, will always be for me an acquired speech' (*P*, 205). So, too, intermittently throughout *Ulysses*, the Irish–Jewish analogy is expanded into a sustained meditation on the psychology and politics—the trauma—of cultural alienation and self-dividedness. Still more importantly, in 'Calypso', Bloom calls the Dead Sea to mind: 'It bore the oldest, the first race. A bent hag crossed from Cassidy's, clutching a naggin bottle by the neck. The oldest people. Wandered far away over all the earth, captivity to captivity, multiplying, dying, being born everywhere' (4. 223–6). That the Irish hag, the poor old woman should cross Bloom's path at this moment is doubly significant, reminding us of how far Jews and Irish are engaged in parallel struggles with a burden of history and historical consciousness. At the end of the passage, Bloom briefly experiences a sentiment of 'desolation' and 'grey horror' (3. 229–30). Quickly, comically, he also bounces back from it: 'Morning mouth bad images. Got up wrong side of the bed. Must begin again those Sandow's exercises. On the hands down' (3. 233–4). Here, in miniature, the issue of catastrophe and recovery from catastrophe—an issue that is important everywhere in *Ulysses* and is historical, political, cultural, and psychological together—is broached precisely in terms of the Irish–Jewish analogy.

An Anythingarian

The culturally split self and 'the traditional accent of the ecstasy of catastrophe' (17. 786): these are the two dominant emphases in the Irish–Jewish analogy that Joyce is most concerned to deepen. But he underlines differences as well as resemblances. In 'Calypso', Bloom swiftly recovers from a moment of 'vastation of soul' (*CW*, 80). So, too, throughout the novel, his psychological reflexes preserve him from any prolonged, melancholy immersion in catastrophe of the kind evident in the Irishmen in 'Sirens'. Furthermore, if Joyce opens up differences within the Irish–Jewish analogy by means of Bloom, he also opens it up to difference. In Bloom, he retrieves the figure of the Irish Jew from English and Protestant claims to a community of interests. He locates Bloom solidly where he evidently belongs, in the Dublin Catholic community. Bloom spends most of 16 June 1904 in its midst, and it is much more significant in his many memories even than Dublin Jewry. Not only that: in their own mild, distinctive, and sometimes ambivalent way, Bloom's politics are readily identifiable as the politics most prominent in the community in question, post-Parnellite, anti-British, sympathetic to Sinn Féin.[52] Yet, at the same time, Bloom is both a non-Jewish Jew who has been baptized both a Protestant and a Catholic, and a non-Irish Irishman. If Keogh's account is exact, he is not even a typical Jewish immigrant, since those who arrived before the 1880s—like Bloom's father—came from England, Holland, France, Germany, Poland, Russia, Galicia, Lithuania, and even Morocco, but apparently not Hungary.[53] The fact that Bloom is not kosher is pointedly drawn to our attention almost as soon as he is introduced (4. 45–6). 'Is he a jew or a gentile or a holy Roman or a swaddler or what the hell is he?' asks Ned Lambert in 'Cyclops' (12. 1631–2). Part of the answer comes in 'Circe': Joyce's Jew is an 'anythingarian' (15. 1712) or composite of many things. Joyce reaffirms and deepens the Irish–Jewish analogy; then, only to loosen it in a host of differentiations both between and within the Irish and Jewish sides of the equation. Bloom's Jewish identity is clearly central to Joyce's project. So, too, is his Irish Catholic identification. Yet Joyce also blurs and complicates both.

Interestingly, when posed the question, Why Bloom?, it was not Bloom's Jewishness that Joyce first emphasized: 'Only a foreigner', he said, 'would do. The Jews were foreigners at that time in Dublin'.[54]

What can we make of this? Why does the Irish–Jewish identification seem to be both extremely important and rather insignificant? Why are the very principles of identification and analogy themselves so pervasively imperilled by nuance and concrete instance? As both foreigner in general and Jew in particular, Bloom is an effective weapon against the ideological and discursive formations of the two imperial masters in Ireland, for he is both intimate with those formations and yet, by virtue of his Jewishness and foreignness, the source of a doubly alienated and alienating perspective on them. At the same time, as Jew and foreigner, he is also alienated from the formations in question in a different way to the community with which he has most to do (whose alienation from the Roman Catholic imperium, in any case, is at best equivocal). He is alienated from colonial formations as someone to whom they are still foreign, and thus often a source of perplexity, common-sense surprise, amusement, or simple indifference. He has neither the intimacy nor the complicity with them that is bred of a tradition of profound hostility. Constructed in this fashion, Bloom becomes an extremely subtle and flexible instrument. Joyce uses his character to steer a delicate course between a range of political positions that are finally unpalatable as wholes. In doing so, he produces a complex, ironic, composite politics of his own.

Thus in 'Lotus Eaters', Bloom joins Maud Gonne and Griffith in a pungently critical view of the British military presence in Dublin (5. 70–3). But Joyce separates his tone from theirs, granting Bloom a measured detachment and wry, playful nonchalance at odds with their invective. Bloom avoids their 'big words'. In doing so, he also avoids their unhappiness (2. 264). His awareness of the colonial character of Irish culture, of the poor 'fit' between the cultural formations of colonizer and colonized that was so much a theme of contemporary nationalism, is similarly astute but insouciant ('They can't play it here', he notes, of cricket. 'Duck for six wickets', 5. 558–60). His sense of class can be antagonistic (notably where the gentry are concerned, 5. 99–106, 122, 268–70, 304–5). But he mainly expresses his antagonisms cheerfully, unresentfully and in sexual terms ('Possess her once take the starch out of her', 5. 106). Bloom is shrewdly aware of certain aspects of the economic exploitation of Ireland, and the significance of questions of caste and power (5. 305–12). Here, again, he seems close to contemporary nationalists, politically if not rhetorically. But equally, his hilariously uncomprehending attitude to Catholicism and Catholic culture in the All Hallows sequence (5. 340–466) has an anthropological detachment from strange customs. He is indeed remote from the Church with which nationalism was so closely allied. Here if anywhere, Bloom becomes a powerful satirical tool, exposing the ideological effects of contemporary Irish Catholicism ('Stupefies them', 'Lulls all pain', 5. 350, 367–8), providing a comically down-to-earth account of its political complicities ('Wine. Makes it more aristocratic', 5.387), remarking on its cultural power and insidious efficiency ('Wonderful organization, certainly, goes like clockwork', 5. 424–5), noting its rhetorical force and persuasiveness, the power of its trappings (5. 403–5), and its rapacity ('And don't they rake in the money too?', 5.435).

'Lotus Eaters' may therefore be thought of as constructing a political position broadly sympathetic to nationalist anti-imperialism and the levelling tendencies within nationalism, but also as concerned to separate nationalism from the Church, to moderate its cultural exclusivity (5. 465, 549–50), and, perhaps above all, to endow it with a much more urbane and thoughtful tone. This in itself is quite an intricate formulation. In each of the subsequent chapters in which Bloom is a substantial presence, Joyce adds to it or makes it still more sophisticated. Thus 'Hades' is concerned, not only with a historically specific, funerary and elegiac Irish culture, but with the extent to which it has been determined and shaped by English influences. Joyce presents the Irish culture of death and the dead as partly a consequence of the ravages of the colonial vampire. He also presents it as partly a Victorian import, whilst making us recognize how far a Catholic and nationalist community historically steeped in catastrophies was disposed to be susceptible to the importation in question. Bloom is robustly indifferent to matters that Irish funerary culture tends to clothe in solemn garb. He thus becomes a paradigm for resistance to and freedom from the culture at issue ('They are not going to get me this innings', 6. 1004). In Joyce's hands, he becomes a means of destabilizing and, indeed, promoting a radically secular view of it. Similarly, in 'Lestrygonians', Bloom restates his alienated versions of questions of class (e.g. 8. 877–89), and of colonial power and forms of complicity with it (like the 'toady news', 8. 338–9). He also adds a disabused view of colonial economics and its effects (8. 1–4, 41–5). At the same time, however, he asserts a principle of relaxed flexibility in judgement—Sir Frederick Falkiner is after all a 'wellmeaning old man' (8. 1156)—in keeping with his distance from the community with which he nonetheless has most to do.

Like all the other Bloom-centred chapters, then, 'Lestrygonians' produces what is in effect a complex deliberation within a given set of political parameters. There have been various versions of Joyce's politics. Even the classic works like Manganiello's, however, have tended to describe an international modernist's interests and sympathies, with Joyce's reading chiefly in mind.[55] In fact, critics have repeatedly made Joyce's politics sound academic. There has been comparatively little reflection on how far *Ulysses* itself might be elaborating a distinctive political position relative to an Ireland on the threshold of independence.[56] This isn't surprising: the position in question is complex to say the least. Joyce develops it partly through Bloom. In the end, for Joyce, in the Dublin of 1904, as Jew and 'anythingarian', Bloom is perhaps as close as it is possible to get to a truly independent mind. He both belongs to the Dublin Catholic community and clearly does not belong to it. He can therefore open up a different perspective or line of thought, but from within the horizons of the community rather than—as has so often been assumed—outside them. He functions partly as a corrective to what Joyce takes to he certain limitations to Irish culture that are the legacy of the colonial past.

Chief amongst these is the logic of the new nationalist anti-Semitism. Joyce repeatedly turns this logic on its head. Griffith argued, for instance, that Jews were people who came to live amongst the Irish, but who never became Irish: the Jew, he claimed, 'remains among us, always and ever an alien'.[57] Bloom's position as both insider and outsider is a principal source of his sanity, openness, moderation, and psychological resilience. That, in effect, is Joyce's retort to Griffith. *The Leader* argued that Ireland could rid itself of its Jews if the Irish grew more like them: sober, thrifty, economical, shrewd and possessed of 'industrial morale'.[58] Joyce's Jew has the exemplary status of Moran's, but is not dragooned into service as the instrument of his own elimination. In the end, however, for Joyce, what is perhaps most important about Bloom's relation to the Catholic community is not alienation but possibility. He represents possibilities, possible change, even a possible future. More importantly still, since Joyce imagines Bloom as part of an actual, historical community; he clearly also presents the possibilities in question as compatible with a determinate set of historical realities, in this instance, at least. Wyse Jackson and Costello have demonstrated the many points of comparison between Bloom and Joyce's father and the similarities between their careers. Joyce subjects Bloom to much of John Stanislaus's historical experience. In doing so, he shows how far, in principle, it could have led to a different outcome, both psychologically and culturally.[59] In his very ordinariness—a complex, exquisite phenomenon that, at this historical moment, is quite beyond the scope of the traumatized culture in which it emerges—Bloom is even a utopian figure. In order to take on this significance, however, he has to be both Irish and Jewish and more than both: He has to have an identity and be irreducible to the identifications practised by those around him. In *Ulysses*, the habit of thinking determinate identities must collapse. For it is inseparable, not only from the anti-Semitism depicted in the novel, but from a set of Irish political mythologies and their history.

NOTES

1. Davison, *James Joyce, 'Ulysses' and the Construction of Jewish Identity: Culture, Biography and 'the Jew' in Modernist Europe* (Cambridge: Cambridge University Press, 1996); and Keogh, *Jews in Twentieth-Century Ireland* (Cork: Cork University Press, 1998).

2. See *James Joyce's Judaic Other* (Stanford: Stanford University Press, 1999).

3. See Marvin Magalaner, 'The Anti-Semitic Limerick Incidents in Joyce's Bloomsday', *PMLA* 68 (1953), 1119–23.

4. For further evidence of anti-Semitic disturbances and the effects of the Limerick pogrom on Irish culture until more or less the date when *Ulysses* is set, see *DE* (Sat. 4 June 1904), 5; *FJ* (Wed. 27 Apr. 1904), 6; and *L* (Sat. 30 Apr. 1904), 148–50.

5. *FJ* (Sat. 23 Jan. 1904), 6.

6. See e.g. the editorial in *FJ* (Fri. 15 Jan. 1904), 4; and *FJ* (Wed. 27 Jan. 1904), 5.

7. See *FJ* (Mon. 4 Jan. 1904), 5.

8. Editorial, *FJ* (Thurs. 14 Jan. 1904), 4.

9. *DE* (Thurs. 7 Jan. 1904), 4.

10. From Gerald Griffin, *The Wild Geese: Pen Portraits of Irish Exiles* (1938); quoted in Richard Ellmann, *James Joyce* (rev. edn., Oxford: Oxford University Press, 1981), 58.

11. See *FJ* (Sat. 6 Feb. 1904), 6.

12. *Modern Ireland 1600–1972* (London: Penguin, 1989), 453.

13. The phrase is the Revd Dr Hogan of Maynooth's. See *DE* (Fri. 24 June 1904), 5.

14. Revd John Manning, quoted in *IT* (Mon. 18 Jan. 1904), 4.

15. *IT* (Sat. 23 Jan. 1904), 9.

16. *T* (Tues. 19 Jan. 1904), 4. Cf. 7.

17. Bishop O'Dwyer of Limerick, quoted in *FJ* (Tues. 16 Feb. 1904), 6.

18. The Protestant Irish Mission to the Jews e.g. expressed its solidarity with the Limerick Jews, and hoped that they would be 'properly protected by the Government against persecution'. *IT* (Thurs. 21 Jan. 1904), 7.

19. Mr R. Lindsay Crawford, quoted in *IT* (Sat. 23 Jan. 1904), 9.

20. Quoted in *FJ* (Tues. 16 Feb. 1904), 6.

21. Quoted in *IT* (Thurs. 28 Jan. 1904), 6. Similarly, in opposing the Catholic Association, the Protestant Defence Association cast itself as representing the 'civil and religious liberty' and 'sacred principles of mental freedom' guaranteed by being British. See *IT* (23 Jan. 1904), 9. In June, the Lord-Lieutenant was urging the Irish to respect the principles of decency and tolerance, claiming the wisdom of an 'outsider'. See *DE* (Sat. 4 June 1904), 5.

22. Quoted in *FJ* (Sat. 23 Jan. 1904),6.

23. Ibid.

24. Letter from 'Galatea', *DE* (Thurs. 14 Jan. 1904), 6.

25. Quoted in *IT* (Sat. 23 Jan. 1904), 5.

26. See *DE* (Tues. 19 Jan. 1904), 4.

27. See e.g. the account of Wyndham's speech to parliament on continuing disturbances in Limerick as reported in *FJ* (Wed. 27 Apr. 1904), 6.

28. *IT* (Thurs. 28 Jan. 1904), 8.

29. See *FJ* (Sat. 23 Jan. 1904), 6. The quotation is from 1 Kings 12: 16. Use of the phrase can be found elsewhere, e.g. in Fabian literature of the period.

30. *Jews in Ireland*, 2.

31. Ibid. 19.

32. Ibid. 26.

33. However, O'Connell's hostility to Disraeli as a Conservative leader and prime minister fiercely opposed to Irish emancipation also led him to identify Disraeli's conduct on the Irish issue with his being Jewish. See Davison, *Joyce, 'Ulysses' and Jewish Identity*, 30–1.

34. Keogh, *Jews in Ireland*, 6.

35. Ibid. 7.

36. The most famous example of this is Dr S. Hermann Adler's speech in Dublin in 1891. See below.

37. Keogh, *Jews in Ireland*, 11. Cf. J. F. Moloney, *L* (Sat. 30 Apr. 1904), 148–50, esp. 149, on Jewish 'rapacity' in exploiting the Irish poor.

38. As Davitt noted, this emphasis was part of Creagh's tactics in his Limerick sermons. See Michael Davitt, 'The Jews in Limerick', letter to the Editor, *FJ* (Mon. 18 Jan. 1904), 5.

39. See Creagh's response to Davitt's letter, *FJ* (Wed. 20 Jan. 1904), 6.

40. This was part of Griffith's argument. See Davison, Joyce, *'Ulysses' and Jewish Identity*, 68–70.

41. See Keogh, *Jews in Ireland*, 19–23.

42. See Davitt's reply to Creagh in 'Jews in Limerick': 'Let me suggest a field for his reforming energies which will not require the invocation of any poisonous feeling of racial animosity or of un-Christian hate. Let him attack the English rule of Ireland which levies £11,000,000 taxes, every year, on our lives and industries, not to the good, but to the injury of our country.'

43. According to Jason Tomes, the Act was 'not intrinsically anti-Jewish'. See *Balfour and Foreign Policy: The International Thought of a Conservative Statesman* (Cambridge: Cambridge University Press, 1997), 201.

44. Ibid.

45. Quoted ibid.; cf. 203.

46. James Loughlin, *Ulster Unionism and British National Identity since 1885* (London and New York: Pinter, 1995), 31.

47. See Keogh, *Jews in Ireland*, 6, 26 and passim.

48. 'You have come here, my foreign brethren, from a country like unto Egypt of old to a land which offers you hospitable shelter. It is said that Ireland is the only country in the world which cannot be charged with persecuting the Jews.' Quoted ibid. 19.

49. 'Jews in Limerick'.

50. Bernard McGinley points our to me that it is in fact the Cork sailor D. B. Murphy who has brought the bugs, having picked them up in Bridgewater (16. 670–2). Bridgewater is a town in England.

51. See Sylvia Beach, *Shakespeare and Company* (New York: Harcourt and Brace, 1959), 170–3. Any doubts as to Joyce's feeling for Taylor's speech may be allayed by referring to John Wyse Jackson with Peter Costello, *John Stanislaus Joyce: The Voluminous Life and Genius of James Joyce's Father* (London: Fourth Estate, 1997), 396–7. Its importance for Joyce was clearly personal as well as political.

52. See e.g. 18. 383–6, 1187–8.

53. Keogh, *Jews in Ireland*, 6.

54. Jacques Mercanton, 'The Hours of James Joyce', in Willard Potts (ed.), *Portraits of the Artist in Exile: Recollections of James Joyce by Europeans* (Dublin: Wolfhound, 1979), 205–52, at 208; quoted in Ira B. Nadel, *Joyce and the Jews: Culture and Texts* (Iowa City: University of Iowa Press, 1989), 139.

55. Dominic Manganiello, *Joyce's Politics* (London: Routledge & Kegan Paul, 1980).

56. But see Enda Duffy, *The Subaltern 'Ulysses'* (Minneapolis: University of Minnesota Press, 1994), 1 and *passim*.

57. *United Irishman* (Sat. 23 Apr. 1904), 1.

58. *L* (Sat. 4 June 1904), 234–5. I am grateful to Deirdre Toomey for alerting me to this argument.

59. See Wyse Jackson with Costello, *John Stanislaus Joyce*, 184 and *passim*. The points of comparison include a list of shared friends (82); life in Ontario Terrace (98); loss of a baby son (100); connections with Goodwin (90); Drimmie's (106); Luke and Caroline Doyle (107); Alderman Hooper (133); Matt Dillon, his family, house and party (16); canvassing for ads and the crossed keys (190–3); *Tit-Bits* (213); the City Arms Hotel and work for Cuffe's (208); employment at Thom's (216); even interest in the Wonderworker (223).

Character Profile

James Joyce claimed of *Ulysses*, "I've put in so many enigmas and puzzles that it will keep the professors busy for centuries arguing over what I meant."[1] Leopold Bloom, heroic anti-hero of *Ulysses*, is perhaps the biggest puzzle of all. This complex and charismatic figure, is, among other things, described as Irish, Jewish, Hungarian, Catholic, Protestant, and a "womanly, man."

Bloom is presented through interior monologue, a type of stream of consciousness in which a character speaks his or her internal thoughts directly, without logical progression and without the author's commentary. This leads to an often-confusing but richly complex narrative, for example in this description of Bloom walking past a candy shop in Dublin:

> Pineapple rock, lemon platt, butter scotch. A sugar-sticky girl shoveling scoopfuls of creams for a christian brother. Some school great. Bad for their tummies. Lozenge and comfit manufacturer to His Majesty the King. God. Save. Our. Sitting on his throne, sucking red jujubes white. (*U* 8: 1–4)

Despite his complex interior, Bloom appears ordinary. He's 38 years old, "height 5 ft. 9 1/2 inches, full build, olive complexion" and he lives modestly at 7 Eccles St., with his wife Molly (*U* 17: 2002–3). His daughter, Milly, lives nearby in the town of Mullingar. An advertising canvasser for a newspaper, Bloom spends the day of June 16, 1904—in which all of the events in the book occur—ruminating over everything from what kind of soap he should buy Molly to how he can put a stop to injustice and prejudice.

He is a man driven by the spectre of his wife's paramour, Blazes Boylan, scheduled to visit Molly at four that afternoon. Bloom is haunted by loss: of his wife to adultery, of his father who committed suicide, and of his dead son, Rudy.

While Bloom seems commonplace in some respects, as his friend Lenehan remarks Bloom is also "a cultured allroundman ... He's not one of your common or garden.... you know ... There's a touch of the artist about old Bloom" (*U* 10:581–2). The artistic and determined Bloom calls to mind his namesake, Ulysses. Like his Homeric predecessor, Bloom overcomes obstacles, stands up to his aggressors, and returns home to his wife at the end of many perilous excursions. Whether encountering the man with whom his wife is supposed to have an affair, worrying about his daughter reaching maturity, or dodging biscuit tins thrown in his path, Bloom has his own set of hurdles to face.

We first meet Bloom in the fourth episode of *Ulysses* where Joyce introduces him with the following line, "Mr Leopold Bloom ate with relish the inner organs of beasts and fowls" (*U* 4:1–2). Food is foremost on Bloom's mind throughout June 16, 1904, and his first actions involve walking to the local butcher to pick up a kidney for breakfast and, soon after, bringing Molly some tea and toast in bed. As he journeys from home to Dublin at large, Bloom reports to *The Freeman's Journal*, the newspaper for which he sells advertising, takes a carriage ride to a funeral, eats lunch, engages in heated debates at a pub, masturbates at the beach, checks in on an old friend at a maternity hospital, and meets the other central character of *Ulysses*, Stephen Dedalus. In a paternal manner, Bloom befriends Stephen and looks after him while they stumble around the brothels of Nighttown. He invites Stephen home for a late night cup of hot cocoa and after Stephen departs, Bloom's day ends, as it began, at 7 Eccles St. with his wife Molly.

Yet this return to Molly is qualified: Bloom and Molly have not had sexual relations since the death of their infant son eleven years earlier. Bloom joins Molly in bed, his head to her feet, while Molly's thoughts turn to Bloom and their initial courtship.

While Joyce explores Bloom's psychological turmoil, he also foregrounds Bloom's varied cultural background: his father, Rudolph Virag, was a Hungarian Jewish immigrant to Ireland; his mother, Ellen, Irish. Bloom famously articulates his relation to Ireland and to Jewishness in the "Cyclops" episode, in which he identifies himself as Jewish and Irish, but also admits to being baptized a Catholic and a Protestant. Unlike the others at the pub, Bloom does not seem bothered by his seeming contradictions:

—But do you know what a nation means? says John Wyse.

—Yes, says Bloom.

—What is it? says John Wyse

—A nation? says Bloom. A nation is the same people living in the same place.

—By God, then, says Ned laughing, if that's so I'm a nation for I'm living in the same place for the past five years.

So of course everyone had the laugh at Bloom and says he, trying to muck out of it:

—Or also living in different places.

—That covers my case, says Joe.

—What is your nation if I may ask? Says the citizen.

—Ireland, says Bloom. I was born here. Ireland. (*U* 12:1419–31).

In Bloom's mind, the Jewish "race" and the Irish nation parallel each other as both have been subject to oppression: "And I belong to a race too ... that is hated and persecuted" (*U* 12:1467).

Bloom's sexuality is also defined in terms of his national and ethnic identity. Both Jews and Irish were depicted as feminine at the turn of the last century, a stereotype which calls Bloom's own masculinity into question. A medical student, Buck Mulligan, diagnoses Bloom as "bisexually abnormal" (*U* 15:1775), while a Dr. Dixon declares Bloom "a finished example of the new womanly man" (*U* 15:1798–9). While some may disparage Bloom's seeming aberrant sexuality, Molly praises his affinity with women, "yes that was why I liked him because I saw he understood or felt what a woman is" (*U* 18:1578–9). Although Bloom, on occasion, expresses a desire for more traditional masculinity—he ponders taking up exercises to develop his muscles, "Must begin again those Sandow's exercises" (*U* 5:234)—he does not seem perturbed by repeated urgings to "stand up ... like men" (*U* 12:1475).

Seen for many years as the heroic Everyman, recent critical examinations also have questioned Bloom's agressive ways. Yet Bloom's definition of love as "the opposite of hate" (*U* 12:1485) stands strong as do his misgivings about brutality: "I resent violence and intolerance in any shape or form" (*U* 16: 1099–1100). At the end of the day, Bloom is quirky, carrying a bar of soap and a potato as talismans, yet he is also an insightful, eloquent, illogical and a sometimes pedantic character. He is an artist and clown, a know-it-all and a jumbler of history and science. Bloom's complexity accommodates, indeed invites, multiple and contradictory readings.

Whether we feel protective and caring toward Bloom, or mocking and dismissive, at the end of the day, we can easily conclude, as with Happy Holohan, "Good old Bloom! There's nobody like him after all" (*U* 15:1727).

NOTE

1. Cited in Don Gifford with Robert J. Seidman, *Ulysses Annotated: Notes for James Joyce's Ulysses*, (Berkeley: University of California Press, 1988): frontispiece.

Contributors

HAROLD BLOOM is Sterling Professor of the Humanities at Yale University and Henry W. and Albert A. Berg Professor of English at the New York University Graduate School. He is the author of over 20 books, including *Shelley's Mythmaking* (1959), *The Visionary Company* (1961), *Blake's Apocalypse* (1963), *Yeats* (1970), *A Map of Misreading* (1975), *Kabbalah and Criticism* (1975), *Agon: Toward a Theory of Revisionism* (1982), *The American Religion* (1992), *The Western Canon* (1994), and *Omens of Millennium: The Gnosis of Angels, Dreams, and Resurrection* (1996). *The Anxiety of Influence* (1973) sets forth Professor Bloom's provocative theory of the literary relationships between the great writers and their predecessors. His most recent books include *Shakespeare: The Invention of the Human* (1998), a 1998 National Book Award finalist, *How to Read and Why* (2000), *Genius: A Mosaic of One Hundred Exemplary Creative Minds* (2002), and *Hamlet: Poem Unlimited* (2003). In 1999, Professor Bloom received the prestigious American Academy of Arts and Letters Gold Medal for Criticism, and in 2002 he received the Catalonia International Prize.

DAVID HAYMAN is Emeritus Professor of Comparative Literature at the University of Wisconsin, Madison. A most distinguished Joycean scholar, he is the author or editor of more than 20 books, including Ulysses: *The Mechanics of Meaning*, The Wake *in Transit*, and *James Joyce's* Ulysses: *Critical Essays*.

RICHARD ELLMAN was the definitive biographer of James Joyce and author of many books, including *Ulysses on the Liffey*. He was the Goldsmiths' Professor of English Literature at Oxford University and Woodruff Professor of English at Emory University.

HUGH KENNER is an eminent literary critic whose articles and books on Joyce include *Dublin's Joyce*, *Joyce's Voices*, and *Ulysses*. He was a Professor of English at Johns Hopkins University and the University of Georgia.

FRITZ SENN is director of the Zurich James Joyce Foundation and author of *Joyce's Dislocutions: Esssays on Reading as Translation, Inductive Scrutinies: Focus on Joyce, Nichts gegen Joyce: Joyce Versus Nothing*, and *Nicht nur Nichts gegen Joyce*.

SUZETTE A. HENKE is the Thurston B. Morton, Sr. Professor of Literary Studies at the University of Louisville. She is the author of *James Joyce and the Politics of Desire, Joyce's Moraculous Sindbook: a Study of* Ulysses, *Shattered Subjects:Trauma and Testimony in Women's Life-Writing*, and co-editor of *Women in Joyce*.

VINCENT J. CHENG is Professor of English at the University of Utah. He is the author of *Joyce, Race, and Empire*, and *Shakespeare and Joyce: A Study of* Finnegans Wake.

MARILYN REIZBAUM is Professor of English at Bowdoin College and author of *James Joyce's Judaic Other* as well as co-editor of Ulysses—*En-Gendered Perspectives: Eighteen New Essays on the Episodes*.

PETER FRANCIS MACKEY is Professor of English at the University of South Carolina and author of *Chaos Theory and James Joyce's Everyman*.

KAREN R. LAWRENCE is Professor of English and Comparative Literature and Dean of Humanities at the University of California, Irvine. A former president of the International James Joyce Foundation, her books include *The Odyssey of Style in* Ulysses, *Transcultural Joyce*, and *Penelope Voyages: Women and Travel in the British Literary Tradition*.

ZACK BOWEN is Professor of English at the University of Miami. Editor of the *James Joyce Literary Supplement*, he is the author of ten books, including *Bloom's Old Sweet Song: Essays on Joyce and Music*.

ANDREW GIBSON is Professor of Modern Literature and Theory at Royal Holloway, University of London. He is the author of several books, including *Joyce's Revenge: History, Politics and Aesthetics in* Ulysses.

Bibliography

Attridge, Derek and Marjorie Howes, eds. *Semicolonial Joyce*. Cambridge: Cambridge University Press, 2000.

Attridge, Derek and Daniel Ferrer, eds. *Post-Structuralist Joyce: Essays from the French*. Cambridge: Cambridge University Press, 1984.

Bennett, John Z. "Unposted Letter: Joyce's Leopold Bloom." *Bucknell Review* 14.1 (1996): 1–12.

Benstock, Bernard. "Leopold Bloom and the Mason Connection." *James Joyce Quarterly* 15 (1978): 259–62.

———, ed. *The Seventh of Joyce*. Bloomington: Indiana University Press, 1982.

Budgen, Frank. *James Joyce and the Making of* Ulysses. Oxford: Oxford University Press, 1972.

Byrnes, Robert. "Bloom's Sexual Tropes: Stigmata of the 'Degenerate Jew.'" *James Joyce Quarterly* 27.2 (Winter 1990): 303–323.

———. "Weiningerian Sex Comedy: Jewish Sexual Types behind Molly and Leopold Bloom." *James Joyce Quarterly* 34.3 (Spring 1997): 267–81.

Cheng, Vincent, Kimberly J. Devlin, and Margot Nororis. *Joycean Cutlures/Culturing Joyce*. Newark: University of Delaware Press, 1998.

Costello, Peter. *Leopold Bloom: A Biography*. Dublin: Gill and Macmillan, 1981.

Davison, Neil R. *James Joyce,* Ulysses, *and the Construction of Jewish Identity: Culture, Biography, and "the Jew" in Modernist Europe*. Cambridge: Cambridge University Press, 1996.

Deane, Seamus. *Celtic Revivals: Essays in Modern Irish Literature*. London: Faber and Faber, 1985.

Ellmann Richard. *James Joyce*. Oxford: Oxford University Press, 1982.

Friedman, Susan Stanford, ed. *Joyce: The Return of the Repressed*. Ithaca: Cornell University Press, 1993.

Fuger, Wilhelm. "Bloom's Other Eye." *James Joyce Quarterly* 23.2 (Winter 1986): 209–217.

Gillespie, Michael, ed. *Joyce through the Ages: A Nonlinear View*. Gainesville: University Press of Florida, 1999.

Gifford, Don. *Ulysses Annotated: Notes for James Joyce's Ulysses*, with Robert J. Seidman. Berkeley: University of California Press, 1988.

Gordon, Tweedie. "Common Sense: James Joyce and the Pragmatic L. Bloom." *James Joyce Quarterly* 26.3 (Spring 1989): 351–366.

Harrison, Lori B. "Bloodsucking Bloom: Vampirism as a Representation of Jewishness in *Ulysses*." *James Joyce Quarterly* 36.4 (Summer 1999): 781–97.

Hart, Clive and David Hayman, eds. *James Joyce's* Ulysses: *Critical Essays*. Berkeley: University of California Press, 1974.

Herr, Cheryl. *Anatomy of Culture*. Urbana: University of Illinois Press, 1986.

Jones, Ellen Carol, ed. *Joyce: Feminism/Post/Colonialism*. Amsterdam: Rodopi Press, 1998.

Kain, Richard M. "Motif as Meaning: The Case of Leopold Bloom." *Approaches to* Ulysses: *Ten Essays*: 61–101. Thomas F. Staley and Bernard Benstock, eds. University of Pittsburgh Press: 1970.

Kiberd, Declan. *Inventing Ireland*. Cambridge: Harvard University Press, 1995.

Ledden, Patrick J. "Bloom, Lawn Tennis, and the Gaelic Athletic Association." *James Joyce Quarterly* 36.3 (Spring 1999): 630–34.

Levi, Neil. "'See that Straw? That's a Straw' Anti-Semitism and Narrative Form in *Ulysses*." *Modernism/Modernity* 9.3 (2002): 375–88.

Lloyd, David. *Anomalous States: Irish Writing and the Post-Colonial Moment*. Dublin: Lilliput Press, 1993.

MacCabe, Colin. *James Joyce and Revolution of the Word*. London: Macmillan Press, 1978.

Maddox, James H. *Joyce's Ulysses and the Assault upon Character*. New Brunswick, NJ: Rutgers University Press, 1978.

Mantell, Deborah. "Leopold Bloom: Joyce's Loveless Irishman, or

Everlasting Caricature of the Serious World?" *Irish Renaissance Annual* 2 (1981): 115–138.

Mason, Michael. "Why Is Leopold Bloom a Cuckold?" *ELH* 44 (1977): 171–88.

McGee, Patrick. *Paperspace: Style as Ideology in Joyce's* Ulysses. Lincoln: University of Nebraska Press, 1988.

Mecsnober, Tekla. "James Joyce, Arthur Griffith, Trieste, and the Hungarian National Character." *James Joyce Quarterly* 38.3–4 (Spring–Summer 2001): 341–359.

Nadel, Ira. *Joyce and the Jews: Culture and Texts.* Iowa City: University of Iowa Press, 1989.

Neeper, L. Layne. "'The Very Worst Hour of the Day': Betrayal and Bloom in Joyce's *Lestrygonians*": *Eire-Ireland: A Journal of Irish Studies* 28.1 (Spring 1993): 107–20.

Nolan, Emer. *James Joyce and Nationalism.* London: Routledge, 1995.

Raleigh, John Henry. *The Chronicle of Leopold and Molly Bloom: Ulysses as Narrative.* Berkeley: University of California Press, 1977.

Reizbaum, Marilyn. *James Joyce's Judaic Other.* Stanford: Stanford University Press, 1999.

Rose, Danis. "The Source of Mr. Bloom's Wealth." *James Joyce Quarterly* 25.1 (Fall 1987): 128–132.

Ryan, Catherine. "Leopold Bloom's Fine Eats: A Good Square Meal." *James Joyce Quarterly* 25.3 (Spring 1988): 378–383.

Schutte, William M. "Leopold Bloom: A Touch of the Artist." *James Joyce Quarterly* 10 (1972): 118–31.

Schwartz, Daniel. *Reading Joyce's* Ulysses. New York: St. Martin's Press, 1987.

Sicker, Philip. "'Alone in the Hiding Twilight': Bloom's Cinematic Gaze in 'Nausicaa'." *James Joyce Quarterly* 36.4 (Summer 1999): 825–50.

Staley, Thomas, ed. *Ulysses: Fifty Years.* Bloomington: Indiana University Press, 1974.

Stanzel, F.K. "All Europe Contributed to the Making of Bloom: New Light on Leopold Bloom's Ancestors." *James Joyce Quarterly* 32.3–4 (Spring–Summer 1995): 619–30.

Steinberg, Erwin. "Reading Leopold Bloom/1904 in 1989." *James Joyce Quarterly* 26.3 (Spring 1989): 397–416.

———. "James Joyce and the Critics Notwithstanding, Leopold Bloom is Not Jewish." *Journal of Modern Literature* 9 (1981–1982): 27–49.

Tracy, Robert. "Leopold Bloom Fourfold: A Hungarian-Hebraic-Hellenic-Hibernian Hero." *Massachusetts Review* 6 (Spring Summer 1965): 523–538.

Tymoczko, Maria. *The Irish Ulysses*. Berkeley: University of California Press, 1994.

Ungar, Andras. "Among the Hapsburgs: Arthur Griffith, Stephen Dedalus, and the Myth of Bloom." *Twentieth Century Literature* 35.4 (Winter 1989): 480–501.

Unkeless, Elaine. "Leopold Bloom as a Womanly Man." *Modernist Studies* 2.1 (1976): 35–44.

Valente, Joseph. *James Joyce and the Problem of Justice: Negotiating Sexual and Colonial Difference*. Cambridge: Cambridge University Press, 1995.

Wollaeger, Mark. "Bloom's Coronation and the Subjection of the Subject." *James Joyce Quarterly* 28.4 (Summer 1991): 799–808.

Acknowledgments

"Dublin, June 16, 1904" and "Two Characters and a City-Scape," by David Hayman in Ulysses: *The Mechanics of Meaning*: 33–42, 45–51. © 1970 by University of Wisconsin Press. Reprinted by permission of the University of Wisconsin Press.

"Bloom Unbound," by Richard Ellmann. From *Ulysses on the Liffey*: 109–116. © 1984 by Faber and Faber. Reprinted by permission.

"The Hidden Hero," by Hugh Kenner. From *Ulysses*, Revised Edition: 43–54. © 1987 by Allen & Unwin, Ltd. Reprinted by permission.

"Bloom among the Orators: The Why and the Wherefore and All the Codology," by Fritz Senn. From *Joyce's Dislocutions: Essays on Reading as Translation*, edited by Jean Paul Riquelme: 144–159. © 1984. Reprinted by permission of the author.

"Uncoupling Ulysses: Joyce's New Womanly Man," by Suzette A. Henke. From *James Joyce and the Politics of Desire*: 106–125, 242–248. © 1990 by Routledge. Reprinted by permission of the Taylor and Francis Group.

"Imagining futures: nations, narratives, selves," by Vincent J. Cheng. From *Joyce, race, and empire*: 219–224. © 1995 by Cambridge University Press. Reprinted by permission of Cambridge University Press.

"Weininger and the Bloom of Jewish Self-Hatred in Joyce's *Ulysses*," by Marilyn Reizbaum. From *Jews and Gender: Responses to Otto Weininger*, edited by Nancy A. Harrowitz and Barbara Hyams: 207–213, 296–297. © 1995 by Temple University Press. Reprinted by permission.

"Contingency and Bloom's Becoming," by Peter Francis Mackey. From *Chaos Theory and James Joyce's Everyman*: 91–117. © 1999 by the University Press of Florida. Reprinted with permission of the University of Press of Florida.

"'Twenty Pockets Arent Enough for Their Lies': Pocketed Objects as Props of Bloom's Masculinity in *Ulysses*," by Karen R. Lawrence. From *Masculinities in Joyce: Postcolonial Constructions*, edited by Christine van Boheemen-Saaf and Colleen Lamos: 163–176. © 2001 by Rodopi Press. Reprinted by permission.

"Millenial Bloom," by Zack Bowen. From *James Joyce Quarterly* 39, no. 1 (Fall 2001): 93–100. © 2001 by The University of Tulsa. Reprinted by permission.

"Only a Foreigner Would Do: Leopold Bloom, Ireland, and Jews," by Andrew Gibson. From *Joyce's Revenge: History, Politics, and Aesthetics in* Ulysses: 42–59. © 2002 by Oxford University Press. Reprinted by permission.

Index